Charles Dickens As I Knew Him

The Story of the Reading Tours in Great Britain and America – A Biography of the Author

By George Dolby

Charles Dickens' Secretary and Manager

Published by Pantianos Classics

ISBN-13: 978-1-78987-336-8

First published in 1885

This reprint is derived from a revised, illustrated edition of 1912

Charles Dickens

From a photograph by Ben Gurney, taken in New York, 1867.

Contents

Preface to Present Edition (1912)

The centenary year of the birth of Dickens, although an obvious reason, is not the only justification the publishers claim for issuing a popular edition of the present volume.

Of the numberless books devoted to the novelist's life which have appeared since his death, George Dolby's "Charles Dickens as I Knew Him" stands apart from the rest in that it deals exclusively and fully with a phase of Dickens's career but lightly touched upon by others who had perforce to secure their knowledge second-hand. By virtue of the unique position he held in regard to the particular sphere of the novelist's activity to which his book is devoted, George Dolby was able to speak from a personal, intimate, and business standpoint. The result is an authoritative work full of facts, full of life and good spirits, and one which contributes much to the knowledge of Dickens's many-sided character. To the student who follows the details of his life and travels, and to the topographer seeking to establish definitely the associations of Dickens with the towns and cities of Great Britain and America, the book is an indispensable record.

George Dolby became the novelist's secretary and manager in 1886, and remained his personal friend and business adviser, so far as his Reading Tours were concerned, until Dickens's death in 1870. He arranged all the details of the tours in Great Britain in 1866-7, in America in 1867-8, and again in Great Britain in 1868-70. The narrative of this association he has given in the following vivid pages, and so extraordinary was the excitement and enthusiasm to hear the novelist read from his own books, the story at times seems almost incredible. No such *furore* had attended anything of the kind before, nor has it since. That men and women should bring out mattresses and other creature comforts to await through cold nights, as they did in America, in order to be in time to buy tickets next morning to hear those readings some days following is as remarkable as it is true. No other person than George Dolby, excepting Dickens himself, could have told the unique story of those eventful days.

One can well understand that under such conditions the ventures were commercially successful. According to the facts revealed, Dickens netted a profit of £33,000 under Dolby's management, whilst the novelist himself estimated that £12,000 resulted from his previous readings under the management of Arthur Smith.

Valuable as are the business details of the tour as set out in the following pages, the intimate and anecdotal story interwoven in the narrative makes the book as vital and interesting as any written on the personal side of the novelist's career. George Dolby died in 1900.

The text of the present edition remains as originally written, with the addition of illustrations and portraits.

O. S.

Author's Preface

My Preface shall be a very brief one, but I feel that two or three introductory words are necessary. And in the first place (and chiefly I must confess with a wish to disarm them), I will make an apology to any and all of my critics who may miss in these pages the flavour and essence of a genuine literary work. I am far from the affectation of claiming for my book that it should rank as an artistic production. All that I have done is this: I have spent some months in the effort to tell, as simply as possible, the story of the famous Reading Tours of Charles Dickens; the most brilliantly successful enterprises of their kind that were ever undertaken. Had I the pen of a ready writer, I could have told my story a hundred times better than I have done; but such as it is, it has been a labour of love to me. Dickens was my great hero — my "Chief" — in the pleasant bygone days when we were "on the road" together — by day and by night, week after week, month after month, right through the English and American tours; and his memory is heroic now that he has gone. His death closed the brightest chapter of my life, and the warmth and vividness of my recollections of that period of his career in which I was privileged to be very close to him, are the main explanation and excuse I have to offer for attempting to tell the story with which these pages are concerned. May I venture, in the second place, to hope that the personal references in this book, which I fear are not a few from first to last, will not be thought to have had any egotistical purpose? I stood to my "Chief" in the relation of manager, and it is in the managerial capacity, and in that alone, that I have introduced myself, in obedience to the necessities of the narrative.

Lastly, while I have trusted for the most part to a good memory and a copious store of notes, I have had occasion here and there, when traversing ground that has been partially covered before, to refer to three well-known works, viz., Mr. Forster's "Life of Charles Dickens," the "Letters of Charles Dickens," and "In and Out of Doors with Charles Dickens," by Mr. James T. Fields (Houghton and Co., Boston, Mass., U.S.A.), and I desire here to make a cordial acknowledgment of my indebtedness to them.

Book One - *The Two English Tours* (1866-1867)

Chapter One - My First Tour With the Chief

EARLY in the year 1866, Messrs. Chappell, of New Bond Street, London, learned that Mr. Dickens had determined to resume his Public Readings — which had been relinquished four years previously, owing to the death of his old and valued friend and manager, Mr. Arthur Smith (brother of Albert Smith of Mont Blanc celebrity); and that, could any arrangement be effected whereby he might be relieved of all business cares in connection with the Readings, Mr. Dickens was disposed to negotiate with the firm for a series of about thirty Readings, to be given in London, the provinces, and, if necessary, in Paris. Messrs. Chappell had no doubt of the success of such an enterprise. Mr. Dickens's popularity was undimmed. The previous Readings had been brilliantly successful; and when Messrs. Chappell proposed that I should accompany the Reader as their representative and manager throughout the tour, it was without the slightest hesitation that I advised them to accept any terms Mr. Dickens might impose.

The result of the negotiations was, that Mr. Dickens agreed to give thirty Readings in London, the provinces, or elsewhere, in consideration of the firm paying him the sum of £1500 for the course, or £50 a Reading; they undertaking all responsibility and trouble, and paying all expenses, personal and otherwise, in connection with the tour; thus liberating the reader from all anxiety, and leaving his mind free and untrammelled for the work he had before him — that is to say, as free as ever he allowed it to be, for, although all responsibility of the tour was removed from his shoulders, he had still the editing of "All the Year Round," and other literary duties; and he was always anxious to make sure that the results of his agreement with Messrs. Chappell were such that they could not in any way regret their acceptance of his terms.

The sum stipulated for — viz., £1500 — was to be paid as follows: £500 on the first Reading, £500 on the fifteenth, and £500 on the termination of the agreement. That Messrs. Chappell had met Mr. Dickens in a liberal manner, and that he perfectly understood the nature of his agreement, the great author's own words, written in a letter to a friend, will testify:

"As to the Readings, all I have to do is to take in my book and read at the appointed place and hour, and come out again. All the business of every kind is done by Chappells. They take John and my other man merely for my convenience. I have no more to do with any detail whatever, than you have. They transact the business at their own cost, and on their own responsibility. I

7

think they are disposed to do it in a very good spirit, because, whereas the original proposition was for thirty Readings 'in England, Ireland, Scotland, or Paris,' they wrote out their agreement in London, the provinces, or elsewhere, *as you and we may agree.*"

That Messrs. Chappell had no reason to rue their bargain was shown by the fact that on the completion of the tour the gross receipts amounted to nearly £5000, an average of £150 a Reading. Such a success had never been known in any similar enterprise; and it was all the more gratifying as Mr. Dickens had, with that consideration for the masses which ever characterized his actions, stipulated, at the commencement of the engagement, that shilling seatholders should have as good accommodation as those who were willing to pay higher sums for their evening's enjoyment; "for," said he, "I have been the champion and friend of the working man all through my career, and it would be inconsistent, if not unjust, to put any difficulty in the way of his attending my Readings."

The scheme comprised eight Readings in London (at St. James's Hall), and twenty-two in the provinces; at Liverpool five, three each at Edinburgh, Manchester, and Glasgow, with Readings at Birmingham, Aberdeen, Portsmouth, Clifton, &c., to complete the number. This plan was laid before Mr. Dickens in the early part of March, the public having become so impatient when once the cry of "Dickens is coming" was raised, that it was found necessary to hasten matters as much as possible, and issue a definite programme; but this, of course, could not be done until Mr. Dickens had signified his entire satisfaction with the arrangements.

So there was an interview at the office of "All the Year Round" which I shall always look back upon with pleasure. Though I had known Mr. Dickens for some time previously, this was the first occasion on which I came into contact with him in a business matter; and there was naturally a feeling of constraint which might have made our first interview tedious but for that geniality, that antidote to reserve, which formed one of his chief characteristics. He expressed himself thoroughly satisfied with all the plans, and told me that Mr. W. H. Wills, his friend and partner in "All the Year Round," would travel with him, not only for companionship, but to enable him the more easily to conduct the magazine during his absence from the metropolis. When I took leave of him, he shook me heartily by the hand, and with that deep earnest look in his eyes which I have so often seen, said, "I hope we shall like each other on the termination of the tour as much as we seem to do now."

Next day Mr. Dickens wrote to Messrs. Chappell that "he hoped Mr. Dolby was a man of resources, otherwise he would find considerable pressure put upon him, and the same difficulties would present themselves as had caused the abandonment of the Readings for three years." It may be as well to explain here the matter to which this letter referred, and of what those difficulties consisted. At the commencement of one of his earlier Reading tours, in October, 1861, Mr. Dickens had the misfortune to lose his much-cherished and valued friend, Mr. Arthur Smith, a most astute business manager. Before his death Mr. Smith had expressed a wish that the gentleman who had acted as his subordinate and assistant might, in consideration of his knowledge of the business, be retained to carry out the arrangements for the tour then commencing. Mr. Dickens, out of respect for his dying friend, readily responded to this wish, though it is but too apparent, from a letter written immediately after Mr. Arthur Smith's death, that his faith in his late manager's colleague was none of the strongest. "My Readings," he wrote, "are a sad subject to me now, for I am going away on the 28th, to read fifty times, and I have lost Arthur Smith — a friend whom I can never replace— who always went with me and transacted, as no other man ever can, all the business connected with them, and without whom I fear they will be dreary and weary to me." Mr. Dickens's forebodings were only too fully realized, for the new manager, though he had proved himself an admirable adjutant, was entirely unfitted for his new duties. Quite unwittingly, he caused great trouble and anxiety to Mr. Dickens, especially as the blame for his shortcomings was laid by the dissatisfied public, not on the manager's, but the reader's shoulders.

Thus, in Edinburgh, where two Readings were given, tickets, sufficient to fill the place, had been sold before the commencement of each Reading; but, as Edinburgh audiences are shy of "first nights," and the tickets were not dated, many seatholders who should have attended the Reading on the first night, held aloof until the second, swelling the crowd on that night to an alarming extent. It was at such a time that the new manager was at a loss, and a scene of indescribable confusion always followed. Hundreds poured into a hall already crowded to suffocation, amid rent garments, expostulations, threats, cries for "the manager," and "Where is Mr. Dickens?" It was a surging roaring sea that overflowed everything, even the plat form on which Mr. Dickens was to read. The attendants and men at the doors suffered much — to use Mr. Dickens's own words in telling the tale: "They were all torn to ribbons; they had not a hat and scarcely a coat amongst them," Indeed, so futile were the efforts of the attendants to control or in any way to stem the tide, that Mr. Dickens found it necessary to come forward and address those who were already in the hall, while an intimate friend, from a prominent position, endeavoured to instill reason into those who were outside. It was the recurrence of such scenes, entailing much worry and anxiety, and no inconsiderable expenditure of physical strength and energy, which often at the commencement of a Reading left Mr. Dickens almost in a state of collapse, and eventually forced him to discontinue his Readings until he could find a manager who would not expose him to the risk of such disasters.

Here I had better explain that the record of the first "Dickens Readings" of which I had undertaken the management must necessarily relate more to business detail than to my intercourse with Mr. Dickens, as at the outset I was brought but very little into his society, owing to the great stress put upon me at first by the difficulties which had overwhelmed poor Arthur Smith's colleague. Still, these details may be interesting to many, and they are entirely essential to the purpose of this work.

No time was lost in arranging the opening Reading, which was given in St. James's Hall, London, on Tuesday evening, April 10, 1866. Independently of the interest created by the reappearance of Mr. Dickens on the platform as a public reader, there was much excitement when it became generally known that he had decided upon reading "Doctor Marigold" for the first time on this occasion. This Reading, like all the others, had been most carefully prepared; and, in order to test its suitability for its purpose, a private rehearsal was given on March 18th, at Southwick Place, Hyde Park, in a furnished house which Mr. Dickens had taken for the season. This audience consisted of the members of his family, and Mr. Robert Browning, Mr. Wilkie Collins, Mr. Charles Fechter, Mr. John Forster, Mr. Arthur Chappell, Mr. Charles Kent, and myself. It is hardly necessary to say that the verdict was unanimously favourable. Everybody was astonished by the extraordinary ease and fluency with which the patter of the "Cheap Jack" was delivered, and the subtlety of the humour which pervaded the whole presentation. To those present, the surprise was no less great than the results were pleasing; indeed, it is hard to see how it could well have been otherwise, for seldom, and but too seldom in the world's history, do we find a man gifted with such extraordinary powers, and, at the same time, possessed of such a love of method, such will, such energy, and such a capacity for taking pains. An example of this is the interesting fact that, although to many of his hearers at that eventful rehearsal of "Doctor Marigold" it was the first time it had been read, Mr. Dickens had, since its appearance as a Christmas number, only three months previously, adapted it as a Reading, and had rehearsed it to himself considerably over two hundred times — and this in addition to his ordinary work.

Great as was the success of "Doctor Marigold's Prescriptions" as a Christmas number — the sale of which exceeded 250,000 copies in the first week — "Doctor Marigold," as a reading, more than realized the anticipations of even the most sanguine of Mr. Dickens's friends, whilst the public, and those who in various ways were more immediately interested in the Readings, were convinced that up to that time they had had but a very faint conception of Mr. Dickens's powers either as an adapter or an elocutionist.

Mr. Wills having been retained as "travelling companion," I was, on the occasion of the first London Reading of this series, brought but very little into contact with Mr. Dickens; indeed, beyond informing him at the appointed time that the audience were seated, and, in their eagerness to hear him, and as a mark of the esteem in which they held him, had honoured the request which had been preferred in all announcement bills and tickets, and in all advertisements, that, as "the Reading would be comprised within two hours, the public were respectfully requested to be seated ten minutes before the commencement of the Reading," I took no active part, and indeed had little or nothing to do, in the management of the "platform."

"Doctor Marigold" was followed by "Mr. Bob Sawyer's Party," which was read to an accompaniment of uproarious laughter and applause. The whole entertainment was a most gratifying success, the receipts amounting to nearly £300. So much was Mr. Dickens beloved and admired, so strongly had he taken possession of the hearts of the English people, that the astonishment of his audience at his skilful manipulation, if I may use the expression, of "Doctor Marigold," and their appreciation of his rendering of the character, found vent in rounds of applause and shouts of delight, Mr. Dickens being called over and over again to the platform to receive their vociferous congratulations.

Next day, Messrs. Chappell's establishment in New Bond Street, and the various ticket agents' offices in the City, were besieged by crowds of people, anxious to secure seats for future Readings, thus assuring, so far as London was concerned, the success of the enterprise, not only artistically as affecting Mr. Dickens, but financially as affecting Messrs. Chappell.

In the same week, our plans included three Readings at Liverpool — on Wednesday the 11th April, Friday the 13th, and the afternoon of Saturday the 14th — and one Reading at Manchester on the 12th. The journey to Liverpool, therefore, had to be made on the morning following the London Reading, and I was invited to travel in the same compartment with Mr. Dickens and his companion. I cannot at this distance of time, and in affectionate remembrance of our after intimacy, look back upon that first journey, without experiencing a certain feeling of amusement at the recollection of the furtive manner in which we took stock of one another. First we digested the news in the daily papers, an operation never of great length with any one of the three who formed our little party; more stocktaking and a cigar brought us to the time when we were due at Bletchley (forty miles' run from London). During this interim Mr. Dickens had worn an expression of anxiety and nervousness, which, after we had left Bletchley behind us, he explained was attributable to his reminiscences of the fearful railway accident in the previous year (1865) at Staplehurst, in which he had figured so prominently, and from which he had so providentially and miraculously escaped. He never, he explained, had travelled since that memorable day (the 9th of June) without experiencing a nervous dread, to counteract which in some degree he carried in his travelling bag a brandy flask, from which it was his invariable habit, one hour after leaving his starting-point, when travelling by express train, to take a draught to nerve himself against any ordeal he might have to go through during the rest of the journey.

Bletchley, then, having been passed, the flask was brought into requisition; and, cheered by further cigars, we gave up the unpleasant system of merely "eyeing" one another, and fell freely into conversation on matters connected with the ulterior object of our journeyings.

Mr. Wills, "the companion," was, however, doubtful as to the resources I had at command in the event of any unforeseen and sudden pressure being put upon us, also as to the convenience of our routes. With Mr. Dickens it was different: he had known me, and my reputation as a manager, for some years; and Mr. Wills's volley of questions — and I must certainly confess he would have made a very good cross-examining counsel — evidently had the effect of making Mr. Dickens somewhat uncomfortable and ill at ease. But he restored his serenity by launching out into anecdotes, only one of which I shall reproduce here. The late Catherine Hayes's mother did not possess any talent in a remarkable degree, except perhaps that of committing astonishing blunders. Charles Dickens, whom she used to dub *Carlo* Dickens (for the old lady had been to Italy, and deemed perhaps that it was her duty, as the mother of a singer, to drag into her conversation Italian names, which she spoke with a broad Irish accent) was somewhat of a favourite with her. One day she was at his house with her daughter, and expressed the great pleasure it gave her to be the guest of the "celebrated Carlo Dickens." Seeking to add compliment to compliment if possible, she turned to some paintings and drawings, by Stanfield, Millais, and Frith, which hung on the walls, and, after being loud in their praises, complimented Mr. Dickens on "the wonderful talent which his father-in-law possessed for making such beautiful pictures." Mr. Dickens's father-in-law was Mr. George Hogarth.

After this entertainment we had the opportunity of regaling ourselves with sandwiches (and such sandwiches they were in those days!— two layers of compressed boxwood sawdust, with a layer of shoe leather in between them, would have been equally delectable) and a glass of sherry. Then I had another turn with Mr. Wills, in his *rôle* of "cross-examining counsel" (perhaps the boxwood sawdust and leather had caused slight indigestion). Another cigar whiled away the remaining time till we were at our journey's end, where we parted, to meet again at the small concert room in St. George's Hall within an hour to arrange the proper fitting of "the screen," battens, &c. — a task Mr. Dickens always superintended personally.

As I believe it has not previously appeared in any work, either in this country or in America, I will give a description of the appurtenances of the platform. At the back was a large screen consisting of a series of woodwork frames covered with canvas; this again was covered with a maroon-coloured cloth, tightly stretched. In the centre of the stage or platform was the table, on which was a slightly raised reading-desk. On the left hand of the reader, on either side of the table, were small projecting ledges — the one on the right for the water-bottle and glass, the other for his pocket-handkerchief and gloves. Further forward, and on each side of the stage, ran two uprights; these were gas barrels, secured with copper wire "guys," securing the batten and reflector, and communicating above an below with another range of lights with reflectors, so that the reader's face and figure were fully and equally distinct to the vision of the audience, and no effects were marred either by too much light overhead or by a super-effulgence from below.

Inquiries at the local ticket offices elicited the fact that enthusiasm had reached the highest pitch with regard to Mr. Dickens's reappearance, and that the tickets were all disposed of except "the shillings," an indication that there would be a tremendous "rush" when the doors were opened. Long before the time for opening arrived the crowd outside was so enormous that a large staff of police was unequal to the occasion, and the entrance to the hall

12

(a large circular vestibule with staircases and galleries, and capable of holding some 3000 or 4000 people) was soon filled. The staircases leading to the hall were carefully guarded, and those with tickets passed in comfortably, leaving those who were anxious to purchase no alternative but to get into the "scrimmage" at the pay-box. Perfect in itself as is the smaller room at St. George's Hall, Liverpool, which Mr. Dickens always spoke of, and with justice, as the most "perfect hall in the world," it is to be regretted that the convenience and safety of the public did not suggest the provision of suitable barriers and "pay-boxes" at the entrances, such as are enforced in the case of theatres and halls built by private enterprise. On the occasion of which I am writing the scene was one of the most exciting description, and the "man of resources" had a very bad quarter of an hour. But a good staff of officials and police, and a great deal of good temper on the part of the crowd, soon put matters right; and, although it looked at one time as if those who *had* tickets could not get in, and those who had *not* tickets could not get out, we managed eventually to clear the way.

Now that the brunt of the battle was over, Mr. Wills suddenly appeared, and, without making any allowance for the confusion which the want of proper barriers at the entrances had caused, and without satisfying himself whether the audience were seated or not, induced Mr. Dickens to go on to the platform punctually at eight o'clock, a course which necessitated his standing book in hand for some minutes before he could commence reading — a *contretemps* so distasteful to Mr. Dickens, as to elicit from him the expression of his determination "never again to go on the platform until Dolby puts me there," to which resolve he rigidly adhered. Great as was the success of "Doctor Marigold" in London, it was nothing in comparison with the *furore* it created at Liverpool; the pleasure experienced from an artistic point of view being greatly enhanced, to the managerial mind, by a receipt of nearly £240, and, according to police calculation, a "turn-away" of over 3000 people, who, as every manager is aware, would freely advertise the two remaining Readings, which were announced to take place on the following Friday evening and Saturday morning (the 13th and 14th April).

It will not be surprising to any one who is conversant with Manchester to learn that the reception there was but a repetition of the London and Liverpool successes. Inquiries showed, on my arrival, that over eight hundred stalls were booked, and a proportionate number of second-seat tickets bought for the reading advertised to take place that evening — Thursday, April 12, 1866; — a circumstance which gave Mr. Dickens great satisfaction on his arrival later in the day. There was a prospect of another "rush," such as that at Liverpool, and it was realized, but with this difference, that at "the Free Trade Hall," Manchester, the "appliances" and conveniences for the safety and comfort of the public and management were as perfect in that building as they were imperfect in the St. George's Hall, Liverpool. So spontaneous was the enthusiasm of the Manchester audience that, accustomed as Mr. Dickens was to the most genial, hearty, and vociferous greetings, this affected him deeply: indeed, he was always so susceptible to a popular tribute of this kind, that it took him some moments to recover himself sufficiently either to commence or continue the reading. Every word he uttered, and every look and gesture, always told with wonderful effect in that gigantic hall. So deeply were the Manchester people impressed that, when it became known that Mr. Dickens would return to Manchester that day fortnight (the 26th April), Messrs. Forsyth's establishment in that city was besieged all the next and following days by people anxious to secure tickets for the second reading.

After the Reading on the 12th, we returned the same night to Liverpool, as amongst the hotels in the large towns in England none was such a favourite with Mr. Dickens as the "Adelphi" at Liverpool — then kept by the late Mr. James Radley (son of a worthy sire, also dead), the man who by geniality and good management obtained for the hotel a popularity which, despite the fact (a most unusual circumstance as regards hotels) that it is managed under the provisions of the Joint Stock Act, it still retains. Railway accommodation, too, being so good between the two towns, it is not to be wondered at that Mr. Dickens should prefer to return to this his favourite hotel, and, except London, his favourite city — or perhaps as it was not a "city" then, I had better say "urban retreat" — rather than spend the night in the gloomy atmosphere of Manchester.

When we arrived in Liverpool from Manchester, an excellent supper awaited us — a pleasant finish to a day of hard work and excitement. Mr. Dickens brewed a bowl of punch, an accomplishment in which he stood pre-eminent, as in all matters to which he put his hand. And here, as in all probability the recurring mention of such luxuries as these may lead to misapprehension as to Mr. Dickens's character as an epicure, I must take the opportunity of stating that, although he so frequently both wrote and talked about eating and drinking, I have seldom met with a man who partook less freely of the kindly fare placed before him. In this observation I am not singular, as the following quotation from a letter written by a common friend, Mr. James T. Fields, of Boston (U.S.), will testify: "He liked to dilate in imagination over the brewing of a bowl of punch, but I always noticed that when the punch was ready he drank less of it than any one who might be present. It was the *sentiment* of the thing, and not the thing itself, that engaged his attention." To the consideration of those who, from want of appreciation of a good man's heart, deprecate the frequent allusions in his writings to the good things of this life, I would seriously and earnestly commend this quotation.

I look back with peculiar pleasure to that supper at Liverpool, because it was there that Mr. Wills showed that he no longer thought it necessary to play the barrister. From that time until the day of his death, I am proud to say that I was honoured with Mr. Wills's confidence and friendship.

The *entente cordiale* having been established, Mr. Dickens suggested that, as we were all staying at the same hotel, I should share their sitting-room; for, said he, "It's all nonsense Wills and myself living alone together, with you in the same hotel; let us in future travel together, and make our sitting-room

14

yours, and have you living entirely with us" — a suggestion which was subsequently acted upon; and from that day we lived together on terms of affectionate companionship and intimacy.

The Readings announced for the two days following the Manchester Reading were "David Copperfield" and the "Trial from Pickwick" on Friday, April 13th, and on Saturday "morning," the 14th April, the "Story of Little Dombey," both at St. George's Hall, Liverpool, in the small concert room. It is well known with what care and elaboration Mr. Dickens prepared his books, and the same system was carried out in the preparation of his Readings. He had a singular habit, too, of regarding his own books as the productions of some one else, and would almost refer to them as such. Chief among his favourites was "David Copperfield," so that it is not a matter of surprise that, when he presented it to the public as a Reading, he should throw into it all the colour, light, and shade, of which his artistic nature was capable, until the word-painting made such a picture as has never been surpassed. That wonderful combination of pathos and whimsicality was received with visible expressions of rapt interest on the part of the audience, until the termination of the Reading with the wreck and drowning of Steerforth, when he was greeted with a burst of applause almost as wild and boisterous as the gale of wind which the reader had, but a moment before, described. The "Trial from Pickwick," which closed that evening's Readings, was, it is hardly necessary to say, received with laughter of the most magnetic and contagious kind.

The "Story of Little Dombey," from "Dombey and Son," given the following afternoon (Saturday, the 14th April), was always a painful one to Mr. Dickens, and never read by him except by particular request and under the greatest of pressure. His intuitive identification of himself with his audience was the cause, in this particular instance, of the most acute suffering; and it was with the greatest relief that he drew his hearers from the thraldom of melancholy, in which they were bound in the earlier part of the Reading, by introducing Mr. Toots and his boyish absurdities. But there was the inevitable relapse into the solemnity of the death of "little Paul;" a shadow of sorrow which would be visible on the brow of the reader for some considerable time after the recital, especially when, as on the present occasion, there was no after-piece of a character more genial and humorous, and so more in keeping with his nature.

A complete and triumphant success was the result of the two days' Readings. There were the same crushing and jostling, the same discomfort, and the same disorder, consequent upon the defective arrangements previously alluded to; but there were also the same good temper, the same hearty congratulations, the same *furore,* and the same inquiries as to his return.

The Reading of the 14th of April having been given in the afternoon, we had thus an evening to ourselves, and a consultation was held as to the best means of whiling away the hour. Mr. Dickens's tastes being inclined to theatre or circus, we repaired to the circus; for, appreciative as he was of the actor's art, he had an immense admiration for the equestrian, and never failed to visit a circus whenever the chance presented itself. The admiration he felt and the pleasure he derived from witnessing legitimate feats of horsemanship were, however, frequently marred by the indiscretions of the clown, who, as soon as it became known that Mr. Dickens was amongst the audience, would improvise some stupidly contrived pun having reference to his name or books, or would perpetrate an atrocity in the shape of a conundrum, such as, "Thuppose you was to see a 'ouse a-fire, what three authors would you be likely to mention? Give it up? Oh! well, you would say, 'Dickens Howitt Burns!'" at which the audience would stamp and roar in an ecstasy of delight. On such occasions it was amusing to watch Mr. Dickens's face. Immediately he became aware of what the mountebank in the ring purposed, he would assume an air and expression of the utmost indifference and *ennui;* and his inattention and apparent deafness to the applause with which his name was greeted were usually a reproof that the clown and public invariably accepted, and he would be left to the enjoyment of the remainder of the entertainment, secure from further annoyance.

On the following Monday, the 16th April, we journeyed northwards as far as Glasgow and Edinburgh, repeating, with the addition of the "Christmas Carol," the Readings already given during the previous week. This, the first long journey after the disappearance of that shadow of reserve which had fallen on us at the beginning, was far too short. Owing to the courtesy of the officials of the London and North Western Railway Company, I had been fortunate enough to secure a saloon carriage, and a luncheon (to be partaken of *en route*); and here, for the first time, I had the opportunity of judging of the wonderful amount of energy Mr. Dickens could exercise in endeavouring to mark his appreciation of any extra attention shown to him. Describing the journey, Mr. Dickens wrote to a friend on the 17th of April, from Glasgow, "Dolby provided the lunch, with the 'best of drinks,' and we dined in the carriage. I made him laugh all the way."

The usual calls having been made at the offices of the ticket agents, the day after the arrival in Glasgow, the same prospects of success as in Liverpool and Manchester presented themselves; and when the time came for opening the doors, the inevitable "shilling" rush was apparent. Mr. Wills, having had sufficient experience in the shilling market, begged to be excused from assisting in that department on this particular occasion, alleging as his reason that he was anxious to see the effect of an English "Cheap Jack" ("Doctor Marigold") on a Glasgow audience; and, "leaving me in my glory," he went in for the "genteel," as Mr. Dickens described it in the letter above quoted. "Wills is to do the 'genteel' to-night in the 'stalls,' and Dolby is to stem the shilling tide, *if he can.*"

What was the effect of "Doctor Marigold" on the Glasgow audience is best described in a letter written by Mr. Dickens, from Edinburgh, on the 18th of April. "We had a tremendous house again last night at Glasgow and turned away great numbers; not only that,' but they were a most brilliant and delicate audience, and took 'Marigold' with a fine sense of quickness not to be surpassed. The shillings pitched into Dolby again, and one man writes a sensible letter, in one of the papers this morning, showing to *my* satisfaction (?) that they really had through the *local agent* some cause of complaint. Nevertheless, the shilling tickets are sold for to-morrow, and it seems out of the question to take any money at the doors, the call for all parts is enormous."

The "cause of complaint" referred to arose from the fact that the local agent, yielding to the pressure put upon him, had disobeyed his instructions and sold shilling tickets in advance, thereby causing great dissatisfaction amongst those who had been standing in the streets for hours before the doors were opened.

The first Reading in Edinburgh was most successful from an artistic point of view, but the rush was not so boisterous and determined as in the other places. It is a curious fact, which is always presenting itself to the managerial mind with regard to Edinburgh, that the first performance of any kind in that city is always, financially, attended with results the least satisfactory. This was always the case with Mr. Dickens's early Readings under the management of Arthur Smith, and the same thing occurred during my own period of management; a circumstance, however, which never caused us the least anxiety, for ultimate results always proved of a most satisfactory character. Mr. Dickens was also aware of this singularity of the Edinbro' people, and slightly refers to the fact in a letter, which he wrote on the 19th of the month: "The house was more than twice better than any first night here previously. They were as usual remarkably intelligent and the Reading went brilliantly. Dolby gone to Glasgow for to-night's Reading by an early train. Wills and I follow at half-past eleven. We have laid half-crown bets with Dolby that he will be assaulted to-night at Glasgow. He has a surprising knowledge of what the receipts will be always, and wins half-crowns every night."

These innocent bets arose from the fact that Mr. Dickens (in the modesty of his nature in all matters appertaining to himself) never appreciated to the fullest extent his ability to attract large audiences, although he felt certain, in the main, of reaching a high standard of success. I always treated him with confidence as to the statistical results of each Reading; he was always surprised at the figures, and nothing gave him greater pleasure than to learn that a great financial success had been achieved, and that results were satisfactory, indeed more than satisfactory, and far in excess of anything ever anticipated by Messrs. Chappell.

On my arrival in Glasgow on the morning following the Edinburgh Reading, I found that every ticket was sold for all the available parts of the city hall, even to the shilling places; and that the agents, in the hope of saving the public from visiting the hall on a fruitless errand, and desiring to avoid a recurrence of those expressions of discontent which had been lavishly bestowed upon them on a former occasion, had, with a caution characteristic of their nationality, issued bills and advertisements to the effect that "no money would be taken at the doors." Notwithstanding the notice, however, large crowds collected, to be again disappointed.

The Readings on this occasion were the "Christmas Carol" and the "Trial from Pickwick." The former, next to "David Copperfield," was the most popular with the author. He had learnt it so well, and read it so often, *that he couldn't remember it,* and used (as he said) "to go dodging about in the wildest manner to pick up lost pieces." This only occurred, however, when he had a thoroughly sympathetic audience, with which he could so identify himself as to be powerless to do other than laugh when they laughed, and cry when they cried. The scenes in which appeared "Tiny Tim" (a special favourite with him) affected him and his audience alike, and it not unfrequently happened that he was interrupted by loud sobs from the female portion of his audience (and occasionally, too, from men) who, perhaps, had experienced the inexpressible grief of losing a child. So artistically was this reading arranged, and so rapid was the transition from grave to gay, that his hearers had scarcely time to dry their eyes after weeping before they were enjoying the fun of Scrooge's discovery of Christmas Day, and his conversation from his window with the boy in the court below.

All these points told with wonderful effect, the irresistible manner of the reader enhancing a thousand times the subtle magic with which the carol is written.

Returning to Edinburgh the following day for the last Reading of the Scotch series, we found the usual state of affairs — every ticket was sold before the time for opening the doors. "Why was Mr. Dickens' stay in the city so short?" grumbled the disappointed ones; because, with true Edinbro' idiosyncrasy, they had thrown away their chances of hearing Mr. Dickens on the previous Wednesday, the 18th, and now wished to crowd some three thousand persons into a hall that would only hold half the number, or very little more; and as they were not allowed to try the experiment of putting two people instead of one into each seat, they were thoroughly dissatisfied with everybody, except those to whom the disappointment was really attributable, *i.e.,* themselves.

A pleasant journey to London — in a saloon carriage, wherein was provided an excellent luncheon and most excellent company — was made next day; and thus terminated nearly a-third of the original scheme, with a most satisfactory profit; the receipts amounting to more than sufficient to pay Mr. Dickens the sum he stipulated for, viz., £1500, and all other expenses which had so far been incurred; thus leaving Messrs. Chappell and Co. the proceeds of the remainder of the tour (twenty-one Readings), which, after the incidental expenses, hotel, travelling, local and otherwise, had been deducted, would be net profit. Part of the original scheme was to give "David Copperfield" for the second London Reading at St. James's Hall, on Tuesday, April 24th; but the success of "Doctor Marigold," at the first Reading, was so pronounced, and the desire on the part of the public for its repetition so evident, that Messrs. Chappell, notwithstanding the fact that "David Copperfield" had been already announced, acceded to the general expressed wish. Supplemented by the ever-welcome recital of the "Trial from Pickwick," this reading excited, if possible, a greater *furore* than on the previous occasion.

The "Trial Scene" was greeted with vociferous applause, as in other places; but its effect was greatly increased here by the presence, amongst other distinguished men, of the late Lord Chief Justice Cockburn, an intimate friend of Mr. Dickens, whose readings in London he never failed to attend. To the Lord Chief Justice the reader always addressed the most salient points of the selection; and at the delightful reunions in Mr. Dickens's dressing-room after the reading, none, save the members of Mr. Dickens's own family, were so welcome as Sir Alexander Cockburn, whose judgment and opinion as a critic he most highly valued and appreciated.

The following afternoon the travelling party were once again on their journeyings, *en route* for Manchester and Liverpool, at which latter place Mr. Dickens was announced to give two Readings, and at the former, one.

On this journey a slight accident to the train led to a circumstance which gave Mr. Dickens an opportunity, for which he had long been looking, to write with the object of improving the commissariat at railway stations, which, it may be within the experience of my readers, was at that time conducted in a most unsatisfactory manner. On the arrival of the train at Rugby, it was discovered that the carriage in which we were travelling was on fire. Futile efforts were made to extinguish the flames, and it was at last found necessary to transfer the passengers to another carriage, and, with this view, to detach the burning one from the train, and replace it by another. Mr. Dickens, not being aware of this, had entered the refreshment-room with Mr. Wills to get some coffee. While I was busy superintending the transfer of the light baggage, Mr. Dickens came along the platform in a state of great excitement, and requested me to accompany him to the refreshment-room. Then, standing in the doorway, and pointing with his finger, he described the picture he particularly wished to impress on my mind. "You see, Dolby — stove to right hand— torn cocoanut matting on floor — counter across room — coffee-urn— tea-urn — plates of rusks — piles of sawdust sandwiches and shrunken-up oranges —bottles— tumblers— and glasses on counter— and, *behind* counter, *note particularly* OUR missis." To this I might have added: two figures standing in the doorway — one, myself, whom my inherent modesty will not permit me to describe — the other, a man respectably attired in the usual lower garments, well cut and well made; over which a pea-jacket or "reefer," Count D'Orsay cloak, or "wrap-rascal," while a hat, soft felt of the "wide-awake" species, "broad in the brim," and worn jauntily on one side, gave a sort of roving appearance, or "modernized gentlemanly pirate" look, to the wearer, who was tall, upright, and sinewy; his face, adorned with a wiry moustache and grizzly beard, struck one at once; deep lined and bronzed, it was a philosopher's; the eyes, whose depths no man could fathom, were large and eloquent, and side by side lurked the iron will of a demon and the tender pity of an angel. His face had all the romance of the ancient

Norseman, while his whole mien reminded one of nothing so much as a Viking.

When the train was fairly off again, Mr. Dickens proceeded to explain. Entering the refreshment-room, he and Mr. Wills had each asked for a cup of coffee, which was supplied to them. While Wills was feeling in his pocket for some small change wherewith to pay, Mr. Dickens reached across the counter for the sugar and milk, when both articles were suddenly snatched away from him and placed beneath the counter, while his ears were greeted with the remark, made in shrill and shrewish tones. "You sha'n't have any milk and sugar 'till you two fellows have paid for your coffee."

This speech was delivered by the woman whom he had pointed out to me as "our Missis," and it gave infinite amusement to a page in buttons, who, with that demoniacal spirit which seems to seize some boys at the idea of somebody else "catching it," was so overjoyed that he burst out into an uncontrollable fit of laughter. The discomfited travellers left their coffee on the counter, after an apology for making so free with the sugar-basin. But it was an evil day for that "buttons," for he figured as "The Boy at Mugby" in the next Christmas number of "All the Year Round;" a number which, produced in the same year, 1866, under the title of "Mugby Junction," and incorporating the stories of "Barbox Bros." and "Barbox Bros, and Co.," attained a circulation, in the first week of publication, of over *two hundred and fifty thousand* copies.

The same successful results, as on the previous visit to Manchester and Liverpool, attended the Readings on the 26th, 27th, and 28th of April; "Doctor Marigold" and "David Copperfield" being the special favourites.

Fourteen of the original thirty Readings had now been given, and Mr. Dickens proceeded to fulfil an engagement to return to Scotland. Considerable pressure having been put upon myself in order to induce me to arrange for a Reading at Aberdeen, that city was included in the scheme. In addition to these "Scotch" Readings, we were obliged to arrange also to visit Birmingham and Clifton. An incident, wherein the Birmingham public had the advantage, may be mentioned to show with what integrity and faithfulness Mr. Dickens carried out everything he undertook. The Readings announced were "Doctor Marigold" and the "Trial from Pickwick." From some unaccountable cause, in going on for the second Reading, Mr. Dickens took the wrong book to the platform with him, and before I had time to stop him he was well on with the story of Nicholas Nickleby at Mr. Squeers's school. There was nothing for it but to let the Reading proceed, as proceed it did, to the end, with perfect success. The immense audience, numbering 2100 people, remained seated, and the mistake that had been made was pointed out to Mr. Dickens by Mr. Wills; upon which, with characteristic generosity, he at once returned to the platform, and, in one of his appropriate and good-humoured speeches, explained the accident to the audience, and put it to the vote, by a show of hands, whether they would like, after listening to him for two hours, to hear him for another half-hour in the "Trial from Pickwick." To use his own words whenever he told the story against himself, "they *did* like," as the ringing cheer of approval with which the little speech was received amply testified. So, after two hours' hard work, he buckled to once more, and amidst uproarious merriment read the famous "Trial."

W. H. Wills
From a photograph by Cundall, Downes & Co.

After the London Reading on the 14th of May, we started for Aberdeen on the following morning. The journey, being an unusually long one, occupying about eighteen hours, extra supplies were deemed necessary in the commissariat department, with a view to rendering the party independent of the vagaries of the refreshment-rooms *en route*, Mr. Dickens undertook to provide the "artful sandwich" and the iced gin punch by way of a "tiffin," whilst I arranged to provide the more substantial part of the repast for ourselves and the men, *i.e.,* Mr. Dickens' servant and the gasman.

The early summer weather being exceptionally fine, everything promised what our American friends would call "a good time." The first thing to be done, when we had fairly started on our journey, in the comfortable saloon carriage in which we spent all our hours of Scotch travel, was to "put the house in order," at which everybody worked hard. The baskets had to be unpacked, and the plates, linen, knives, forks, spoons, glasses, &c., were carefully stowed away in the "pantry; "a larder was improvised and the "substantial comforts "placed within it. The wines were taken from the travelling basket, and placed with the gin punch, in ice, in the wash-hand-stand, so that the whole presented the appearance of a well-ordered house rather than of a railway carriage which was being dragged along at the rate of fifty miles an hour by the "Flying Scotchman."

For the benefit of epicures a description of the "artful sandwich" (as Mr. Dickens was wont to call it) may not be out of place. A French roll, cut in slices and well buttered; on the buttered side place chopped parsley; and lastly, a hard-boiled egg, cut in slices, with the addition of either anchovy paste, or, better still, the anchovy fish itself. A pleasant game of three-handed cribbage having been enjoyed, with a *modicum* of gin punch and some of the "artfuls," we found ourselves at York; and then thoughts were concentrated on the repast of the day. With some salmon mayonnaise, a plain lettuce salad, some pressed beef, cold fowls and tongue, and a cold cherry tart, with a little *fromage de Rochefort* to finish, together with some coffee, made by the aid of a spirit-lamp, we contrived to pass the time very pleasantly until within a short distance of Newcastle-on-Tyne.

The conversation turned upon the subject of dancing, and Mr. Dickens being an adept in the terpsichorean art, and, above all, in the performance of a "sailor's hornpipe," it was agreed that he should execute this national dance. Here, however, an unforeseen difficulty presented itself, for — though I had used every endeavour to make my arrangements for the journey as complete as possible — such a thing as an orchestra had never suggested itself as indispensable to travel. But it was settled that Mr. Wills and myself should form the orchestra; so we supplied a whistling accompaniment while the dancer footed it merrily, in spite of the frequent collapses of the orchestra in explosive laughter at the absurdity of the situation and the pretended indignation of the dancer at the indifference of the music. The sudden "breakdown" of the engine through the bursting of a pipe brought "the entertainment" to a close, and we had a walk in the fields and woods a little north of Morpeth for nearly half an hour, until another locomotive could be found somewhere to take the train on to Berwick. Ever memorable to me will be these my journeyings and their agreeable surroundings, and I trust they will enable me to give the reader some idea of a phase in Mr. Dickens's nature, which was apparent only to a limited circle of friends with whom he felt himself quite at his ease, and to entertain whom, in that genial way of which he seemed to be sole possessor, he would take any amount of pains and trouble. In all his actions the dominant motive was a consideration for others.

As evening closed in, the party amused themselves with more games of cribbage and some "dummy" whist, and after supping upon the remains of the banquet, and partaking of a glass of grog, we "turned in" for a comfortable sleep on the sofas until we arrived at Aberdeen and found comfortable quarters at the Royal Hotel, a house then kept by the late Davy Robertson, the most genial of Scottish landlords, and patronized by the Royal Family, when journeying from London to Balmoral, before the railway system was completed as far as Ballater.

The Reading itself, though a success from a monetary point of view, was perhaps the least enthusiastically received of any given, before or since; a fact which may perhaps be accounted for by the remark of the local agent when I questioned him about the probability of success: "Weel, Misther Doalby, I'm no prapared t' state positively what yewr actiel receats'll be, *for ye see, sir, amangst ma ain freends there are vairy few wha ha' tver haird o' Chairles Dickens."* This man held a good social and commercial position, and was connected with the best musical societies in Aberdeen! Thinking that musical artists were perhaps more to his taste, I sounded his knowledge of the leading singers; by this means I discovered that those coming from Edinburgh and Glasgow were the most popular, while the name of Sims Reeves (so far the greatest, and deservedly the most popular, of English tenors) was even less known than that of Charles Dickens.

On the following day. May 17th, there being no Reading, and nothing to do but to travel to Glasgow, it was determined to break the journey at Perth, with the intention of taking, on the banks of the Tay, one of those long walks in which Mr. Dickens so much delighted. It was a lovely day, and we enjoyed the walk thoroughly; also the early dinner in the coffee room of the George Hotel; from the windows of which there is a view of the quaint old bridge over the river, which is one of the most picturesque in my memory.

On arriving in Glasgow Mr. Dickens was attacked by a severe cold, and it was with difficulty that he could get through the Reading; indeed, but for the fact that all the tickets had been sold, and that great inconvenience would result to so large a concourse of people in the event of his not giving his Reading, he would have postponed it. In the hope that a little fresh air and a change from the depressing effects of the Glasgow atmosphere would do him good, a trip in a private steamer was taken down the Clyde. This had the desired effect; for in the evening he appeared on the platform in the best of spirits, and read with all his wonted vigour of freshness.

After the Edinburgh Reading my first provincial tour with Mr. Dickens ended at Portsmouth.

In the hope that the sea breezes might have the effect of relieving Mr. Dickens of the cold from which he was still suffering, we decided to visit Southsea before the Portsmouth Reading. And here two amusing incidents occurred.

On the morning after our arrival we set out for a walk, and turning the corner of a street suddenly, found ourselves in Landport Terrace. The name of the street catching Mr. Dickens's eye, he suddenly exclaimed, "By Jove! here is the place where I was born;" and, acting on his suggestion, we walked up and down the terrace for some time, speculating as to which of the houses had the right to call itself his cradle. Beyond a recollection that there was a small front garden to the house he had no idea of the place — for he was only two years old when his father was removed to London from Portsmouth. As the houses were nearly all alike, and each had a small front garden, we were not much helped in our quest by Mr. Dickens's recollections, and great was the laughter at his humorous conjectures. He must have lived in one house because "it looked so like his father;" another one must have been his home because it looked like the birthplace of a man who had deserted it; a third was very like the cradle of a puny, weak youngster such as he had been; and so on, through the row. According to his own account, Southsea had not contributed much to his physical strength, neither indeed had Chatham; for, he used to say, he always was a puny, weak youngster, and never used to join in games with the same zest that other boys seemed to have. He never was remarkable, according to his own account, during his younger days, for anything but violent spasmodic attacks, which used to utterly prostrate him, and for indomitable energy in reading: — cricket, "chevy," top, marbles, "peg in the ring," "tor," "three holes," or any of the thousand and one boys' games, had no charm for him, save such as lay in watching others play. But as none of the houses in Landport Terrace could cry out and say, as he recounted these facts, "That boy was born here!" the mystery remained unsolved, and we passed on.

The other incident occurred in the course of the same walk. It is well known what interest Mr. Dickens took in all matters connected with prison life; and Mr. Wills having mentioned that he was intimately acquainted with the governor of a military prison somewhere in Gosport (the name of which, also the name of the governor, he had forgotten), a search was made, in the hope of refreshing Wills's memory. After walking some distance through clouds of dust driven by a cold easterly wind (by no means unusual in England in the month of May), and meeting no one on the road, either of a civil, naval, or military character, able to give any information about the prison, it was suggested that this institution existed only in Wills's imagination; a suspicion which broadened into a fact when inquiries were made of the landlord of a most comfortable-looking hostelry on the roadside.

Returning to Southsea by another road, we suddenly found ourselves in a sort of elongated "square," that should be called "oblong," open at each end, such as is to be met with in Dutch towns; the houses on each side resembled a scene "set" for the comic business of a pantomime; they were of red brick, with clean windows and white window frames, while green *jalousie* blinds of the most dazzling description added a little to the "tone" of the place. Here the temptation to Mr. Dickens to indulge his predilections for imitating the

24

frolics of a Clown — of the Grimaldi, Flexmore, and Tom Matthews type — presented itself. The street being entirely free from people, Mr. Dickens mounted three steps leading to one of the houses, which had an enormous brass plate on its green door; and, having given three raps on the doorpost, was proceeding to lie down on the upper step, clown fashion, when the door suddenly opened and a stout woman appeared, to the intense amusement of the "pantaloons" (myself) and Wills, who immediately beat a retreat in the style known in pantomime as a "rally," followed by Mr. Dickens with an imaginary policeman after him. The wind, which was very high at the time, added to the frolic, driving Mr. Dickens's hat before it, in the direction of the river, causing us to forget the situation and eagerly chase the hat to catch it ere the frolicsome blast drove it into the water. Then, and then only, we turned to take a parting look at the scene of action, when, to our dismay, we saw every doorstep and doorway occupied by the amused tenants of the houses. There was another stampede, which was stopped by an open drain, from which emanated an odour of anything but a pleasant character, suddenly making the party pale as ghosts, and necessitating the administration, medicinally, of course, of a strong dose of brandy-and-water at the nearest hotel.

Three more Readings in London followed. On Tuesday, May 29th, "Doctor Marigold" and "Nicholas Nickleby at Mr. Squeers's School;" on Tuesday, June 5th, "David Copperfield" and "Boots at the Holly Tree Inn;" and on Tuesday, June 12th, "Doctor Marigold" (by general desire) and the "Trial from Pickwick." Thus the first engagement with Messrs. Chappell was completed to the satisfaction of every one concerned. Writing shortly before the close of the tour, Mr. Dickens said, "Everything is done for me with the utmost liberality and consideration; every want I can have on these journeys is anticipated, and not the faintest spark of the tradesman spirit ever peeps out."

It was, and is, a matter of pride with me that my efforts — supported by the liberality of the Messrs. Chappell — to make the tour a successful and, at the same time, a pleasing one to Mr. Dickens, should have been so appreciated by him; an appreciation which he showed, not only by his confidence, but by presenting me with a complete set of the Illustrated Library Edition of his works, and a letter which I cannot read, even at this distance of time, without a keen pang for the loss of so kind and true a friend, and for the bereavement which the world suffered by the death of one of the greatest of its social benefactors.

Chapter Two - A Glimpse of Life at "Gad's."

THE success of the first tour having proved to Mr. Dickens that the difficulties which had compelled him to give up his Readings for so long a time had been overcome, it was but natural that he should be desirous of continuing an enterprise which, in addition to the pleasure it afforded him, was a means of adding largely to his income; and that, when Messrs. Chappell made a proposal to him for a second tour, under their management, it should be favourably considered, especially as Messrs. Chappell gave him to understand that, taking into consideration the facts of the great success of the first tour (at a season of the year not the best for indoor entertainments), they considered they would only be acting fairly to Mr. Dickens in augmenting the terms for the second tour, which they suggested should commence at the beginning of the coming year (1867), and which they proposed should extend to "fifty Readings in Great Britain and Ireland" (and in Paris, as in the first engagement, *if necessary*).

Mr. Dickens's first idea was to ask Messrs. Chappell seventy pounds each Reading, with all expenses paid as before; but, at a conference which I had with him whilst on a visit to Gad's Hill, in the month of August, 1866— wherein I held the dual position of agent, or manager, to Messrs. Chappell, and friend and adviser, in this respect, to Mr. Dickens — he decided on accepting an engagement with those gentlemen to give forty-two Readings for the round sum of £2,500; and afterwards, writing to a friend who acted in all cases as his business adviser, he thus expressed his views: "It would be unreasonable to ask anything now on the ground of the extent of the late success, but I am bound to look to myself for the future. The Chappells are speculators, though of the worthiest, and most honourable kind. They make some bad speculations, and have made a very good one in this case, and will set this against those. I told them when we agreed: 'I offer these thirty Readings to you at fifty pounds a night because I know perfectly well beforehand that no one in your business has the least idea of their real worth, and I wish to prove it.'"

The result of the negotiations was thus described by Mr. Dickens: "Chappell instantly accepts my proposal for forty nights at sixty pounds a night, and every conceivable and inconceivable expense paid. To make an even sum I have made it forty-two nights for £2,500; so I shall now try to discover a Christmas number, and shall, please heaven, be quit of the whole series of Readings, so as to get to work on a new story for the new series of 'All the Year Round,' early in the spring. The Readings begin probably with the New Year."

This arrangement being completed, as much of the interim as possible between the first and second tours was pleasantly passed in the society of Mr. Dickens. A personal sorrow which fell on myself at this time was greatly alleviated by frequent visits to "Gad's," and by a chat every Thursday at the office of "All the Year Round," in Wellington Street, Strand — Thursday being the day devoted by Mr. Dickens to the "making up" of the paper — an engagement that was never broken when both were in town, unless some unavoidable circumstance occurred to prevent its observance.

The domestic staff at the office of the "A. Y. R.," as he called it, was composed, at the time of which I am speaking, of a man-servant (the one who travelled with Mr. Dickens) and an old and valued female servant who was an excellent cook. The luncheon at one o'clock was of the simplest character, but its simplicity was made really luxurious by the geniality of the host. He seemed to invest everything with an odour of gratefulness; everything he placed before you seemed to be imbued with a virtue that nothing else in the world possessed; the most ordinary things in life became special in his presence — he gave you a cigar, which you or I might have smoked the counterpart of many a time, still there never was such a cigar as the one he had just presented to you. A little brandy never rolled down man's throat before in the way in which *that* drop of liquor went down yours. You knew that you were being entertained by a *connoisseur* and a man of taste, and everything was doubly grateful; and yet, notwithstanding that he gave such choiceness to everything, he partook but sparingly himself, and seemed to participate in other people's enjoyment of what was laid before them, rather than to have any pleasure in the good things himself.

The "office" having been spoken of, a few words about Gad's Hill may not be out of place; and a reference to the way in which it became the property of its distinguished owner may not be uninteresting.

Gad's Hill, as everybody knows, is situated about half way between Gravesend and Rochester, on the high-road to Dover from London; which high-road divided the ground appertaining to the property into two parts — one of which contained the house, lawns, pleasure grounds, kitchen gardens, and walled-in croquet ground, stable-yard, stabling, &c.; and the other consisted of a well-wooded piece of ground, forming a sort of wilderness, in which stood two magnificent cedars. There were also picturesque banks, on which grew ivy, and, in the summer, nasturtiums, mignonette, and other flowers, affording a combination of colour as unusual as it was pleasing to the eye.

The house itself was approached through massive oak gates, from either corner of the property, by a semi-circular carriage drive, and was a two-storeyed, plain, red-brick building, looking rather more ancient than it really was, with a belfry in the roof and a quaint-looking porch, approached by stone steps in front. At each side of the porch was a bay window, that to the left lighting the drawing-room, and that to the right the library — a room now more than ordinarily celebrated by the publication in the "Graphic," at the time of Mr. Dickens's death, of the picture of "The Vacant Chair."

The entrance hall — which was spacious and square, having a door opposite to the principal entrance, from which a staircase led to the back lawn — immediately impressed one with the idea of an amount of comfort, regularity, and order not usually met with in other houses; while it also suggested a hospitality of the most genial character to come — a hospitality such as one might have been led to expect by the kindest of receptions from the host himself at the railway station of Higham, two and a half miles distant from the house. A drive through the pleasantest of the Kentish country, either on an "outside" Irish jaunting car; or, in fine weather, in a basket carriage, with the nattiest of ponies, driven by Mr. Dickens; or, in wet weather, with a brougham drawn by the most knowing and best trained of cobs with a "hog-main;" always escorted by three or four enormous dogs of the Mount St. Bernard, mastiff, or Newfoundland species, brought the visitor to the house.

Gad's Hill Place, as the house was called, was the fancy of Mr. Dickens's boyish days; for in his youth he had always had a longing to become possessor of the place, which longing was satisfied in a curious way.

In 1856, Mr. Wills happened one day to be seated at table next to a lady slightly known to Mr. Dickens, who turned out to be the owner of the property. In the course of conversation with Mr. Wills this lady happened incidentally to mention that she was desirous of parting with the place, a fact which Mr. Wills took the earliest opportunity of communicating to Mr. Dickens, who gave instructions for negotiations to be entered into for its purchase and transfer, which Mr. Dickens regarded more in the light of an investment than anything else — as he had a house in London at the time, viz., Tavistock House, which he did not leave until 1860.

Having, however, disposed of Tavistock House, he determined on making "Gad's" his home, and set to work to effect such alterations as would be necessary to convert it into a fitting residence for himself and family. Since it had been built, somewhere about the year 1780, it had changed hands several times, but without being much improved.

In fact, from the time Mr. Dickens abandoned the idea of regarding the property merely as an investment, and decided to make the place his home, workpeople of one kind or another were always employed in converting "Gad's" into the most perfect and comfortable of houses to those privileged friends who were fortunate enough to be visitors there.

Between the study and billiard-room doors, the walls were decorated with two notable paintings by Clarkson Stanfield, one of which represented the Eddystone Lighthouse, and had been used as an act drop in some private theatricals at Tavistock House, in 1855. Although it took the great painter less than a couple of days to execute, and that at a time when he was very ill, this picture fetched 1,000 guineas at the sale at Gad's Hill, after the 9th of June, 1870. The other picture was a scene used in the "Frozen Deep," also played at Tavistock House, and subsequently at the Gallery of Illustration in 1857, before Her Majesty the Queen, H.R.H. the Prince Consort, and the Court, for the "Jerrold Fund." In the hall, a conspicuous object was a letter-box, with a capacious mouth capable of receiving books, official letters, and parcels of manuscript, with the times of departure of the mail painted on it in large figures. At the further end of the entrance hall, a flight of steps led to the back lawn, which was divided from a field at the back by a stone wall, resembling a terrace with balustrades, and massive iron gates, which gave ingress to the field over a "haw-haw."

A peculiarity of the household was the fact that, except at table, no servant was ever seen about. This was because the requirements of life were always ready to hand, especially in the bed-rooms. Each of these rooms contained the most comfortable of beds, a sofa, and easy-chair, caned-bottom chairs — in which Mr. Dickens had a great belief, always preferring to use one himself— a large-sized writing-table, profusely supplied with paper and envelopes of every conceivable size and description, and an almost daily change of new quill pens. There was a miniature library of books in each room, a comfortable fire in winter, with a shining copper kettle in each fireplace; and on a side-table, cups, saucers, tea-caddy, teapot, sugar and milk, so that this refreshing beverage was always attainable, without even the trouble of asking for it.

There was no specified time for the guests to be at breakfast, that meal being on the table from nine to ten, or half-past; and unless some early excursion to a place of note in the neighbourhood had been arranged, the visitors were left to do as they pleased in the morning; Mr. Dickens, as a rule, taking a turn or two round the domain to see that everything was in order outside as well as inside the house, visiting, each in its turn, the gardens, stables, kennels, and afterwards devoting himself to his literary duties and correspondence.

Luncheon was served at half-past one, when all were supposed to have got through their letters, reading, writing, or lounging, or whatever occupation might have engrossed their morning leisure; and then the pleasure of the day began, or was arranged systematically — for Mr. Dickens was always systematic — over that most pleasant of repasts, generally resulting in a walk through one of the beautiful woods which abound in that part of the country, such as Cobham Park — with its noble avenues, its rich green grassy slopes, its noble oaks and elms, beneath which the deer graze in peaceful security, and its magnificent old hall — the residence of Lord Darnley, who with characteristic generosity had presented Mr. Dickens with a private key to all the gates in the Park, so that, whether walking, driving, or riding, there was no "let or hindrance," so far as he and his friends were concerned, to their thorough enjoyment of the beauties of the place. For those for whom the place had a fascination, a visit to the "Leather Bottle," the retreat of the disappointed Tracy Tupman, to Rochester Castle, or some other distant place, or a game at croquet or bowls on the lawn, passed the hours agreeably till dinner-time, when, to use a theatrical phrase, everybody was supposed "to be on;" and, whether the house were full of guests, or whether only one or two were staying there, there was never any difference made in the arrangements, a fact which was apparent in the ease and order with which everything was done. The dinners were like everything else in the house — superlatively good, with a *menu* calculated to baffle the criticism of the most epicurean, and the conversation, under the generalship of such a host, never flagging for a moment.

Then came an hour or two in the drawing-room, where Miss Dickens and Miss Georgina Hogarth held their genial court — it was all geniality at "Gad's." After this the gentlemen adjourned to the billiard-room, where, before going to bed, some little time was spent in the enjoyment of some excellent cigars and a walk round the table to the "click" of the balls, either in a game at "pool" or a "contest" at billiards, Mr. Dickens being fond of contests, for, he used to say, "it brings out the mettle." Then, so far as the host was concerned, the day was done, for it was his invariable habit to retire to bed at midnight — but without imposing any condition upon his guests, that they should follow his example — the most intimate of his male friends present, if none of his sons were there, being delegated "host" in his absence, with strict injunctions to "see the gas out all right," and to take great care of the keys of the sideboard until morning. The billiard-room being far away from the residential part of the house, and with no sleeping rooms near it, except the "bachelors' rooms," it not unfrequently happened, especially in summer-time, that the gas was "seen out" by the brilliance of the morning sun, which made the carrying of a night candlestick to the bed-room a matter of form. Under these circumstances it was amusing, and at times a trifle disconcerting, on entering the breakfast-room in the morning, to watch the merry twinkle in the host's eyes as he expressed a hope that "you had slept well," and remained in apparent ignorance of the fact that the guest so addressed had not been in bed. It is not surprising that such time as I had at disposal for runs down to "Gad's" was happily spent there; and that those visits tended to render our friendship stronger and firmer, and promised well for a pleasant time during the business campaign in the coming winter.

Over a dinner at the "Blue Posts," in Cork Street — a favourite establishment with Mr. Dickens — the plans and prospects for the forthcoming tour were fully discussed. The idea of giving Readings in Paris was abandoned, Mr. Dickens being of opinion that it would be useless to go to Paris for less than four Readings, which could not be given in a shorter space of time than two weeks, as there was so much to see and to do in that city. It was therefore decided to make Paris a special field for future operations, when he should have more time to spare.

Thus matters went on pleasantly till the Christmas of 1866. "Barbox Brothers" and the "Boy at Mugby" having been "condensed" (to use the author's own word) into reading form, and "Gad's" being full of guests, and more than full — for not only was every available room in the house occupied, but extra rooms were engaged at the Falstaff Inn, which stood opposite the entrance-gates, for those who could not be quartered in the house — advantage was taken of these circumstances to give a private Reading, or *trial,* of the works so abridged. The members of Parliament in the district, naval and military officers from Chatham, and neighbours were invited; and a grand entertainment, consisting of a dinner and a Reading afterwards, was provided. After dinner, the reading-desk, which had been specially sent down from London, was placed in the drawing-room, and a mimic Reading took place, resulting in a general verdict that "Barbox" and "The Boy" would, as Readings, rival "Doctor Marigold" — a prophecy regarded with considerable doubt and misgivings by the author and certain of the more practical judges then present, who, as matters afterwards turned out, were justified in their scepticism. After the Reading there were some games. Mr. Dickens prided himself on his skill in guessing a subject fixed upon during his absence from the room. His success in penetrating people's thoughts was so marked that it would by some have been termed "spiritualistic." For spiritualism Mr. Dickens had a profound contempt.

Many times in taking part in this game with Mr. Dickens I have been astounded at the unerring certainty with which he discovered the subject, however puzzling it might be. I remember he always mentioned with great satisfaction his triumph over a "poser" invented, I believe, by Miss Georgina Hogarth, viz., "the boot on the off-leg of a postillion." In a double way was he skilful at the game, for not only was he a very searching expositor of people's thoughts, but in the invention of subjects wherewith to puzzle others he was equally clever.

A description of Gad's Hill, and the things thereat, would be more than imperfect without a reference to the dogs, which played a very important part in the life there; not only on account of the love their master had for them individually, but on account also of his appreciation of their usefulness in protecting his property. No country road, perhaps, in England is so much traversed by tramps and beggars as the high-road between Gravesend and Rochester, especially in the hop season, when London seems to pour out every available kind of pauper — male, female, and child — for the hop-picking; although, be it said, amongst this class even, there were some to whom a deaf ear was never turned when they made their necessities known to the owner of "Gad's" or his amiable family. Amongst the beggars were many suffering from consumption, who would walk miles and endure unheard-of sufferings to find employment in a hop-garden, having a superstition that the dust of the newly-picked hop, flying into the throat of the picker, was a cure for this most malignant of diseases. Tramping long distances, without shoes in many cases, and invariably with little or no food, the men carried heavy bundles containing rags, more ragged perhaps than those on the backs of their owners, a tin kettle, and a pan or two for cooking purposes (whenever they could get anything to cook); the women were jaded and worn with the fatigue of carrying a baby, or two sometimes, while all too often had the shiver which comes of sleeping under wet hedges and in wet grass, and which points only too surely to the one cure, if the end of a disease can be called a cure — the final one — death.

Mr. Dickens's kindness of heart and his love of children (no matter of what class) always enlisted his sympathies with these people; and, profligate though they might have been, he always had a kind and encouraging word to say to them, and something to give by way of endorsing his principles in a practical way; his wonderful judgment of character doubtless assisting him in this respect, and, if nothing else, his parting greeting of "God bless you," and the earnest way in which it was said, seemed to give the poor creatures a sense that there were yet kind hearts in the world, and that they poor sufferers were not *so* "low down" but that true sympathies were to be met with, even in the most unexpected quarters and under the most adverse circumstances.

It was not only in the hop season though that the pedestrian element was of a "vagarious character." There seemed all the year round to be a perpetual tramping along that road, occasionally relieved by the march-past of a regiment of soldiers, either going to Gravesend for rifle practice or returning from it, or of a battery or two of artillery changing quarters between Woolwich and Chatham. Sometimes there came a load of Americans, who had snatched sufficient time from their London pleasures to run down to Gravesend, and, having chartered a cab, pulled up on the roadside to take a look at the place "where Dickens lived." Such of these as were enterprising enough — and there are very few of our "American cousins" who have not this qualification — to send in their cards (prompted as a rule to do so by the cabman, who, by the by, "just wanted to wash his horse's mouth out" at the "Falstaff" opposite), asking permission to walk round the grounds and through the house, invariably met with a hearty response to their request; and, while apologizing, as they generally did, for the seeming intrusion, were made to feel that their visit was a source of pleasure to Mr. Dickens and his family; and, if he happened to be about, the visit was not the less appreciated for a few friendly words from him, in grateful remembrance of the many dear friends he had in America.

The tramping and vagrant element made the dogs a necessity; not that they were (with one exception) ferocious, unless "set on," which, however, was never necessary, for it was sufficient for a tramp to cast his eye over the stable-yard to be convinced of the prudence of not pursuing his inquiries any farther. Four or five big dogs of the mastiff or Newfoundland breed, attached to chains sufficiently long to cover any portion of the yard, acted as a deterrent to the inquisitive mind of any stranger of the beggar class, for the animals hated rags, as do most dogs.

These dogs were perfectly trained, and had the instinct never to forget a visitor to whom they were properly introduced, and who was accordingly allowed to go in and out of the yard as though the dogs had known him or her all their lives. So it was as much a duty on the part of the host to introduce his guests to the dogs as it was to introduce a stranger to his family and the other guests staying in the house. Thus the hospitality of "Gad's" included the stableyard; and it was a curious thing to notice the retentiveness of memory on the part of the dogs, save the ferocious exception "Sultan," who was always kept muzzled.

When I first visited Gad's Hill "Linda" was the favourite, vice "Turk," who had been killed by a railway accident. She was the puppy of a great Mount St. Bernard brought to England by the late Albert Smith, and one of the dogs exhibited by that most excellent of "showmen" in his entertainment "Mont Blanc," at the Egyptian Hall, Piccadilly, and since immortalized by the late John Leech, in one of his admirable "Pencillings from Punch." The mother of "Linda" and her companion are now, if not dead, receiving royal hospitality at the hands of Her Majesty the Queen, at Windsor Castle. As an instance of the sagacity of these two dogs, Mr. Dickens, some three or four years before

32

his death, used to relate how, when walking one day between Slough and Windsor, he met a royal groom on horseback accompanied by the dogs. The dogs recognized Mr. Dickens, and it was with difficulty that the groom could get them to leave him.

But "Sultan," the Irish mastiff, was a most ferocious beast, and the only person who had any control or power over him was his master. This fellow was always kept muzzled, but on one occasion he broke his strong chain, rushed into the road at a moment when a regiment of soldiers were passing on their way to Gravesend, and made such havoc in the ranks by upsetting several of the men, that he escaped immediate annihilation only through the intervention of the officer in command, who, being in the habit of visiting at "Gad's," and knowing the dog, had him arrested and taken to his own yard in charge of an orderly guard.

Having killed a favourite kitten, and, it is supposed, eaten it, for the kitten's remains were never found, and very nearly swallowed "Mrs. Bouncer," Miss Dickens's white Pomeranian dog, "Sultan" made a dash, one day, at a little girl, inflicting slight injury (the dog being muzzled), but giving the child a great fright. This last rash act sealed his doom, and, sorry as was his master to part with so handsome a beast, still law and order had to be maintained, and popular prejudice against ferocious dogs had to be supported. There was, therefore, nothing for it but to order the dog off for immediate execution; the story of which tragedy was one which Dickens used to tell with a comical seriousness that made the listener feel sorry both for the dog and his master.

The order for execution having been given, but with strict injunctions that the public were to be excluded, and no one in the house to know when it was to take place, a procession was formed, consisting of some six or seven men and boys from the stables and garden, a wheelbarrow, and a gun. The dog evidently thought, in the bloodthirstiness of his nature, on being let loose to join in the procession, that they were going to kill some one or something *else;* and it was only when he had gone about half-way across the large field at the back of the house, that his eye rested on the wheelbarrow with a gun in it. It seemed to strike him there was something wrong, and he at once became depressed, looked steadfastly at the gardener, and walked to his place of execution with his head down.

Arrived at the corner of the field farthest from the house, one of the boys threw a large stone to induce the dog to go after it, or to lead him to believe there was something in the hedge where it struck. When "Sultan's" attention was thus diverted, two barrels were discharged into his heart, and he died without a struggle or a cry, deeply regretted by his loving master, who, be it said, was the only friend he had. He was buried in the field where he fell, and, despite the extraordinary precautions taken by the executioners not to disturb the family, the fatal shot was understood by them all, and a gloom rested on the house the whole of that day.

Of another dog, "Bumble," there are many stories. Although well trained and obedient in every respect, he had a bad habit on returning from a long walk of eluding, if he could, his master's attention, and, when about two miles from home, would race there as fast as he could; whether to get his own dinner, and that of the other dogs as well, never could be ascertained.

This freak had cost him many beatings from his master, and all to no purpose; when, one day, after castigating him more severely than usual, it occurred to Mr. Dickens, that he would give him a strong dose of castor oil. The next day the dog was very ill, and could not take his meals, but he never again ran away. Whenever he came to a place which reminded him of his past iniquity, he invariably ran to his master's heels, and nothing could induce him to leave them until he found himself in his own yard.

In time "Bumble" became a parent, and one of his sons, christened by Mr. Dickens "Chops," was presented to me. He gave me ample scope for studying the heredity of genius.

Chapter Three - On Tour in Scotland and Ireland

MR. DICKENS was a great lover of cricket, and in the summer of 1866, he would often hurry back to Gad's Hill after a visit to town, in order to be present at a cricket match in the field at the back of his house — between his own Higham Club and some other club in the neighbourhood.

This field was placed at the disposal of the Higham Club, the only condition being that a single case of drunkenness, or the use of bad language on the part of the members of the club, cancelled the privilege of using it; and although there was a drinking booth on the ground, kept by the landlord of the Falstaff Inn, and notwithstanding that on match days, all kinds of people would be assembled there, including soldiers, sailors, and operatives from Chatham Dockyard, no case of disorderly conduct ever occurred in that field.

The summer over, our thoughts began to be seriously occupied with the renewal of the Readings. I have already described the experimental reading of "Barbox Brothers" and the "Boy at Mugby." Mr. Dickens "got it up" (as he would say) with his usual elaborate pains; and, as if the work of this were not sufficient, with his other labours, he worked incessantly with Fechter in the production of a sensational drama at the Lyceum, entitled the "Long Strike" by Dion Boucicault; which, however, did not prove such a success as the time and energy bestowed upon it should have justified.

The first public Reading of "Barbox Brothers" took place in St. James's Hall, on Tuesday, January 15th, and justified the misgivings felt at the rehearsal. It was received cordially by the audience, but it was apparent that it would never take rank with the other works of its kind; and but for the extraordinary power possessed by the author in the rendering of his own works, and the curiosity which always attached to anything new from Mr. Dickens, it is doubtful whether the expression of opinion would not have been less favourable than it was.

He himself was conscious of this, and but for the fact that the Reading was already announced for some of the towns in the early part of the tour, it is probable that "Barbox" and "The Boy" would have been shelved, then and there.

Liverpool endorsed the opinion of London, as did also Birmingham; and after one more trial in London, and another in Leeds, the work was condemned for Reading purposes, and has never been heard since.

We were now once more on our travels, and this time without Mr. Wills, whose time could be more profitably employed in conducting the affairs at the office, in Mr. Dickens's absence, than in travelling about the country for mere companionship.

In the intimacy which had sprung up between Mr, Dickens and myself, it was not always convenient, either in addressing him personally, in correspondence, or in speaking of him to our friends, to refer to him as "Mr." Dickens, and as my respect for him prevented my calling him "Charles" or "Dickens," and as he disliked being addressed as "Sir," except by strangers, I was at times in difficulties.

A trifling circumstance came to my rescue in the early part of our second tour. It was at Chester, on January 22, 1867, a day memorable to many in all parts of England, as one of the most severe during the winter of that year.

We had left Liverpool early in the day for a Reading in Chester, that evening, in a blinding snow-storm and a furious easterly gale; so bad was it that the Mersey was lashed up into a tremendous sea, the waves dashing over the boat. Arrived at Chester, we went to the Queen's Hotel, and here I left Mr. Dickens in what had the appearance of a most comfortable sitting-room, with a blazing fire, whilst I went into the city to attend to matters of business in connection with the evening's Reading.

I had been absent about two hours, and on my return found him sitting on the hearthrug in front of the fire with my Turkish fez on his head, and a large coloured muffler round his neck, to protect him from a strong draught between the door and a double French window. As neither door nor window could be properly shut, the cold air had pretty much its own sportive way.

I was amused to see him in this position, but when I asked him how he felt, he replied gruffly, "Like something good to eat being kept cool in a larder. What do *you* think I look like?" he asked. "Like an old chief," I replied, "but without his pipe." The idea of his looking like a chief seemed to please him, and from that time I always addressed him by this name, which was generally adopted by his associates, and proclaimed as his title in the office of "All the Year Round."

In such fearful weather as we were then experiencing, it is not surprising that even so potent a name as Charles Dickens should have failed to draw a large house in a country place, and the receipts on this occasion may be mentioned as the worst I ever knew during these tours.

The snow on the ground was frozen, and, to make matters worse, a heavy rain-storm had set in, the rain freezing the moment it touched the ground. Such a thing as a cab, or a vehicle of any kind, it was impossible to get, so that we had to walk to the hall as best we could, for the streets were like glass. Walking as cautiously as we did, it was impossible to keep from slipping occasionally, and in one of my efforts to save myself, I gave Mr. Dickens a back-hander below the chest. Although the blow was rather a serious one, his sense of the comic came to my relief. "The next time you want to chuck me under the chin, Dolby, have the kindness to do it a little higher, if you please."

Two evenings after this, we were at the Town Hall, Birmingham, when "Barbox" and "The Boy" had another chance, and where a catastrophe very nearly occurred, which in its effects might have been almost worse than the disappointing reception of this particular Reading. The reflector of the gas batten above Mr. Dickens's head was suspended from the supports by strong copper wire. By some mischance (probably owing to our having with us on this occasion a gas-man strange to the work, in place of our own man, invalided for the time) the copper wire was brought immediately over one of the gas jets of the batten, which caused it to get red-hot. This had passed unnoticed by every one, until close upon the conclusion of the Reading. As was my wont, I went to the side of the screen to receive Mr. Dickens at the end of his task, and happening to cast my eye along the batten discovered the red-hot wire. Pointing to the place of danger, I whispered, "How long shall you be?" He saw the state of affairs in an instant, and without in the least pausing in his reading, or displaying the slightest uneasiness, held up two fingers to me, by which I knew he meant either two minutes or two seconds. It turned out to be the latter, for in the most inconceivable manner he altered much of the reading to suit the occasion, and brought it to a speedy termination. To turn the gas off after he had left the platform was the work of a moment, and thus prevented a heavy sheet of iron falling amongst the audience, and doing incalculable damage. Mr. Dickens had seen the danger much sooner than I had, for he told me that he had been watching the heating process from the middle of the Reading, and had calculated in his mind how long the wire would last!

It was on February 14th, after a Reading at St. James's Hall, that we started for Scotland, breaking our journey at Liverpool and Manchester, for three Readings.

After this journey, Mr. Dickens complained very much of the effects of travelling by express trains, and he kept constantly referring to the Staplehurst accident, which was ever present in his mind. It was decided between us that, so far as practicable, we would in future travel by slow trains. This plan seemed to dispel his nervousness to a great extent; but it had to be given up, as the delay and the monotony of these journeys were almost worse than the shaking of the expresses.

Travelling to Glasgow by night, after a Reading in Manchester on Saturday, February 16th, we arrived there early on Sunday morning for a day's rest;

and having two days to spare in the following week, we decided on spending them at the Bridge of Allan rather than in the gloomy atmosphere of Glasgow.

Being fortunate in our weather, we passed a most enjoyable time, especially in the long walks so dear to Mr. Dickens.

In one of these rambles we made our way into Stirling, and thoroughly explored the Castle, finishing up the afternoon with an inspection of the gaol.

At the inhospitable-looking door a warder answered our knock, and Mr. Dickens sent in his card to the governor, who, with true politeness, came to the gate to receive us. Mr. Dickens explained that, though he had seen much of gaols, he had never been inside a Scottish gaol. There was no difficulty whatever about the matter, and the governor, with a couple of warders, conducted us personally through the establishment, opening all the cell doors and allowing us to converse with their tenants.

Here and there Mr. Dickens said kind and comforting words to the prisoners, which seemed to be a relief to them in their miserable position.

We were about to enter one cell to say a few words to a boy confined in it, but finding him reading a Bible, with a gentleman in clerical attire, we retired, thinking that perhaps the boy was receiving spiritual consolation from the chaplain. When the door was locked, I observed an amused expression on the governor's face, and inquired of him the nature of the boy's offence.

He was a London boy, who had been imported into Scotland by a gang of native burglars — London boys being more expert in the "trade" than Scottish lads. The boy had not much hard labour in the exercise of his calling, for, like Oliver Twist, he was passed through a window to make an inspection of the interior of the house, and open a door, either back or front, to enable the burglars to enter without interference. Unluckily for this particular boy, he did not understand the construction of Scotch houses, and during his first job got "lagged," whilst his friends contrived to escape.

It was not at the boy, though, that the kind-hearted governor was laughing, but at Mr. Dickens and myself, and at our respectful demeanour to the boy's spiritual adviser, who was none other than a celebrated bank forger — a lithographer by trade — who had successfully forged bank-notes to a large amount, and had got off to America with the spoil. In New York he had represented himself as a clergyman, and had been appointed with a large stipend to one of the leading churches in America, where he did duty for some time. Supposing that he and his crime had been forgotten, he returned to Glasgow to arrange some private affairs, and, in an unfortunate moment (for him), was recognized, arrested, and condemned to penal servitude.

The criminal side of the gaol being disposed of, we were conducted to the "debtors'" side, and here incarceration had quite another aspect. Here were some fifteen or twenty persons in a large room, with a comfortable blazing fire. Some were playing draughts and dominoes, others reading newspapers or books, and all seemed to enjoy themselves, and regard us as intruders on their happiness.

One of the debtors recognized Mr. Dickens, who was very soon surrounded by this queer company. Some pointed out to him the folly and iniquity of confining them in prison until their debts were paid; but most of them expressed themselves highly pleased with their lot, and declared that so long as their creditors chose to pay for their maintenance, they were quite content to stay where they were; for, except that they were deprived of the privilege of smoking, they were far happier, had better beds on which to sleep, and could get better food at a cheaper rate (out of their allowance) than many of them were in the habit of getting outside.

The regret of our friends at parting with us appeared to be great, one of them pleasantly observing, "When I saw you gentlemen come in, I was in hopes we were going to have you as fellow-lodgers for a time at the 'Stirling Castle Hotel.'"

Our trip to the Bridge of Allan was productive of the greatest benefit to Mr. Dickens's health, and he went back to his work on the platform with the old *verve.*

The business was admirable, and the nightly reception by large and demonstrative audiences very cheering to Mr. Dickens; but, although sorry to turn our backs on Scotland, we were glad, under the circumstances, to be once more journeying towards the south, where the climate was less severe.

Our last Reading in Scotland, for the time being, was in Edinburgh, on Saturday afternoon, February 23rd; and having to travel to London by the Limited Mail the same evening, we had no time for dinner. We therefore arranged to take it "on the road." When Hearing Preston, Mr. Dickens was entertaining me wi.th a song and dance (the drinking song from "Der Freischutz"), with glass in hand, when the concussion of air, caused by the passing of an express train from the opposite direction, whisked a sealskin cap off his head, and away it flew into the darkness out of the opposite window. Finding himself bareheaded, he immediately suspected me of a practical joke; but seeing me seated demurely in the opposite corner of the carriage, his surprise was all the greater. The cap being a valuable one, its loss was greatly deplored, and it was almost in vain that I promised the cap should be restored in the following week at Liverpool. Although the night was as dark as pitch, I could tell by the running time of the train pretty nearly the place where the cap had gone astray; so on arrival at Preston I communicated with the station-master, indicating to him the precise moment when the cap disappeared, and offering a reward to any platelayer or workman on the line who should find it, and return it on a certain day. A few days after our arrival in Liverpool there came a parcel addressed to Mr. Dickens, containing the missing headgear, much to his delight; but he did not resume the interrupted song.

Our travelling life had become so much a matter of system with us, that the routine of it became almost monotonous. Day after day we were doing the same things at the same time — packing our portmanteaus, travelling to a fresh town, unpacking the portmanteaus again, attending to preliminary matters of business in connection with the Readings, dining, and, after a rest for an hour or two, making for the hall, where the public sat expectant. But the monotony was a good deal relieved by the return of Mr. Wills to the scene of action.

After a call at Bradford and Newcastle-on-Tyne, we were bound for a ten days' trip to Ireland; and Mr. Wills, wanting a change, and having some business of his own to look after in Ireland, enlivened us with his company. As if in honour of the event, we had the additional excitement of visiting Dublin at a time when that city was in a state of semi-siege owing to an anticipated Fenian rising on St. Patrick's Day; and had it not been that the inconvenience and loss would have been greater in the postponement of our visit there than in carrying out our original designs, the trip would have been abandoned entirely, as Mr. Dickens was desirous it should be.

Having overcome his scruples in this respect, we started off for Dublin by the night mail on Wednesday evening, March 13th, again in the most tempestuous of weather. Running along the Chester and Holyhead Railway, in the neighbourhood of Bangor, our train was blocked up by a snow-drift, making our position not only dangerous, but uncomfortable in the extreme. We had to sit patiently in our carriage until such time as a gang of workmen could clear the road, and dig our engine out of the snow, a performance that took some four hours; Arriving at Holyhead we were not in the humour to take the steamer which was in waiting; for being nearly frozen to death, we allowed the furious gale from the east to overcome our valour, and make us stay at Holyhead until the middle of next day. As it turned out, this was the best thing we could have done; for, when we did start, we slipped across with no other inconvenience than having to encounter a heavy, rolling sea.

On arriving at Kingstown, we had a taste of the anticipated rising in Dublin, in the stoppage of some of our baggage on the quay there. The police, seeing some unusual-looking cases amongst the ordinary luggage of passengers, could not imagine that the box containing our gas-piping could be anything but fire-arms for the use of the Fenians, and insisted, in spite of our protests, on having it searched before they allowed the box to be put in the train. When nothing but the innocent gas-piping was discovered, the breathless bystanders seemed quite disappointed.

When we got to Dublin, we could see that there were good grounds for alarm; the whole city being alive with constabulary and soldiery, and a visit to our local ticket agent on the following morning convinced me that for our first Reading certainly our house would not be very good; but as St. Patrick's Day would intervene between the first and second Reading, it was fair to suppose that unless some serious disturbance took place on that day, matters would speedily right themselves, and that Mr. Dickens's reception would be as cordial as it always was in Dublin.

On the eve of St. Patrick's Day, a dinner party was given in Mr. Dickens's honour by an old and intimate friend, to which were invited all the luminaries of the city, and amongst them many of the official dignitaries and several of the highest military authorities, amongst whom was a distinguished colonel of Guards, who up to that time had made the Fenian organization his special study, being reputed to know more about it than any one in the service. During the dinner orderlies were continually arriving at our host's house with despatches, giving such details as could be collected of the probable "rising" that night, and it was clear that had any such movement taken place, the authorities would have proved fully equal to the occasion.

As a precautionary measure, the public-houses were ordered to be closed from Saturday evening, March 16th (St. Patrick's Eve), till the following Tuesday morning. The public buildings had strong forces within their walls, and the troops were all confined to barracks. Notwithstanding all this, the city life went on as if no danger were anticipated, and hospitality played — as it always does in Dublin — a leading part in the affairs of life.

At dinner, Mr. Dickens expressed a wish to make an inspection of the city, and as some of the guests at our friend's house had to do the same thing officially, his desire was very easily gratified. Returning to our hotel for a change of costume, we sallied forth in the dead of the night on outside cars, and under police care, to make a tour of the city; and so effectual were the precautions taken by the Government, that in a drive from midnight until about two o'clock in the morning, we did not see more than about half a dozen persons in the streets, with the exception of the ordinary policemen on their beats. Several arrests of suspected persons had been made in the night, and some of these became our fellow-travellers in the Irish mail on our return to England.

Contrary to our fears, the political disturbances had done no harm to Mr. Dickens's reputation in his capacity as a reader, for our audiences were quite up to the average of our visits to Ireland in quiet times; and what at the outset looked most embarrassing, turned out a really enjoyable time, which was rendered not the less pleasant by a demonstrative reception in Belfast, where no trace of Fenianism could be discovered.

As the mail boat leaves Kingstown for England at an inconveniently early hour in the morning, we decided on sleeping on board the steamer, on the night after the last Dublin Reading, and, accordingly, we drove down to Kingstown for this purpose.

The intention was good, but the execution was a failure, for at about two o'clock in the morning we were awakened by the tramping of soldiers on the deck overhead, and as the sound was a disconcerting one in such a place and at such a time, we went up to see what was the matter. There we found a strong escort of marines in charge of some of the arrested Fenians of the previous week, on their way to England for safer custody.

These persons having been carefully stowed away in the lower part of the vessel, the marines and the police were free to roam about the ship at their will, and they created such a disturbance as to prevent anything like sleeping in comfort; so Mr. Dickens and myself spent the three or four hours before daybreak in the saloon, playing cribbage, after which we started off for a walk round the harbour until the time for the sailing of the mail boat.

Arrived at Holyhead, all the passengers were detained on the steamer until the Fenians were disposed of in the train, and at every stopping-place on the road from Holyhead to London there were strong escorts of police.

At Euston Square we were all locked in our carriages until the cavalcade of mounted police with the vans containing the prisoners had left the station, and then we were allowed to go our several ways, and glad we were to do so after ten days full of adventure, and many fears and anxieties as to the result of our visit to Ireland in troublesome times.

The Irish business being over, our long journeys ceased with it, leaving only such places as Cambridge, Norwich, Bath, Bristol, Gloucester, Cheltenham, Swansea, Hereford, Wakefield, Preston, and Blackburn to be visited.

The two last towns being only about twelve miles distant, we decided on performing this journey on foot, sending the men on alone with our effects.

There was nothing particular on the road to interest us, the route lying almost entirely amongst factories and mills; and it was with no ordinary degree of pleasure, when about seven miles on our way, that we discovered, high up on elevated ground to our left, the picturesque ruins of an old mansion, fast falling into decay, but standing out weird and melancholy on the summit of the precipice on which it was erected. Such a building had always a fascination for Mr. Dickens; and inquiring of a native the name of the place, we ascertained that it was called Hoghton Tower.

Having some knowledge of the history of the place, Mr. Dickens decided on making an inspection, if permission could be obtained. There was no trouble about this, for the habitable part of the place was in the occupation of a farmer, who readily assented to our request. We were allowed to roam about the curious old ruin at our leisure, much to the gratification of Mr. Dickens, who at that time was occupying himself with the construction of a new story which he had undertaken to write for America. This spot at once suggested to him the idea of making Hoghton Tower the scene of the tale, then imperfectly fixed in his mind; and it is here that the story entitled "George Silverman's Explanation" found its local habitation.

The story took him but a very few days to complete, and, when finished, did not exceed in quantity an ordinary number of "All the Year Round."

It was originally intended that it should appear in a New York periodical, and the price agreed upon was one thousand pounds, the largest amount ever paid for a story of similar length.

The fate of "George Silverman's Explanation" was peculiar. In England it appeared in "All the Year Round" in the early part of 1868; but its adventures in America I shall have to describe in a subsequent chapter.

One of the Lancashire towns had the honour of affording Mr. Dickens an unexpected entertainment. In choosing places for the Readings, it was my duty to write to the town a month or two in advance, to ascertain if the hall, concert or assembly room, was at liberty for the particular evening on which we required it.

To the town clerk of the community in question, I wrote as usual, requesting the use of the Town Hall for a Reading by Charles Dickens from his own works. I was not a little surprised to receive an official letter from that functionary, informing me that "before the use of the Town Hall could be granted, it would be necessary to supply him with full particulars of the *nature* of Mr. Dickens's *entertainment.*"

The request was so unusual, and betrayed such extraordinary ignorance in an exalted official, that I did not feel equal to the task of satisfying this remarkable town clerk's scruples, so I referred the matter to Mr. Dickens for precise information on the subject.

He enjoyed the joke immensely, and greatly relished the idea that the Town Hall might be polluted by the appearance of a fat woman, or a dwarf, or some other monstrosity. However, a serious assurance had to be given to the conscientious clerk, so Mr. Dickens dictated to me the following note —

"In acknowledging the receipt of your letter I have to inform you that the subject matter of Mr. Dickens's Readings is to be found in a long row of books published by Messrs. Chapman and Hall, in Piccadilly, London."

Charles Dickens Giving a Reading
From a contemporary print.

This reply was deemed satisfactory, and the use of the Town Hall being granted on the usual terms and conditions, the Reading came off with a result far from gratifying. Indeed, it was almost a pity that the town clerk's strange inquiry was not accepted at once as a criterion of the taste and intelligence of his fellow-townsmen. The hall was not full, and the audience wholly failed to understand the eccentric patter of "Doctor Marigold," preferring perhaps the talk of a real Cheap Jack, who had pitched his cart immediately in front of the Town Hall, and who from behind his glare of lamps was "convulsing" (to use Doctor Marigold's own word) a delighted mob.

The "Trial from Pickwick," which was the second reading, was more successful, but that dull audience made such an impression on us that the town was always referred to afterwards, with ironical flattery, as the most cultivated of its class in the United Kingdom. Everywhere else in Lancashire, Mr. Dickens was always enthusiastically received.

At the Free Trade Hall in Manchester, Mr. Dickens always entered on his work with thorough enjoyment; and whether he was telling the story of "David Copperfield" and the "Christmas Carol," or revelling in the boisterous incidents connected with Squeers and John Brodie, or reciting the sombre story of "Little Dombey," to say nothing of the patter of "Marigold," and the humour of the "Trial from Pickwick" and "Mr. Bob Sawyer's Party," he felt that he had his public — never less than two thousand persons at a time — completely under control, so that the Reading was never in any sense a labour. The same may be said of Liverpool, Birmingham, Leeds, Edinburgh, Glasgow, and Dublin, and in fact all the large towns in England; so that an audience such as that which was inspired by the never-to-be-forgotten town clerk was an inexhaustible wonder.

An enterprise involving so much expense made it expedient to visit such places as were likely to yield a good return, and personal comfort had sometimes to be sacrificed. But if circumstances took us into a miserable town with a bad hotel, Mr. Dickens invariably put the best construction on the discomforts he had to put up with, and in the most trying situations was always more cheerful and good-humoured than any public man with whom I have ever been associated. There was no difficulty which could not be overcome by patience and good temper, of which he had a large stock.

An uncomfortable-looking sitting-room or bed-room in an hotel had to be made more comfortable by a re-arrangement of the furniture, and this was done without the assistance of the hotel servants. A badly-prepared dinner or a bad bottle of wine was something that had to be endured in the first case, and carefully neglected in the latter. A hall that seemed bad for sound had (on being tested in the early part of the day of reading) to be "cured" by means the secret of which he alone seemed to know. His spirit of cheerfulness was contagious, and every one about him worked with a will that made everything run so smoothly that persons unaccustomed to our mode of life wondered how so much could be done with so little apparent labour.

Nearly every week we were in London for a Reading in St. James's Hall, and on the following morning we were on our way to some provincial town. The visits to London were not visits of pleasure by any means. There was a mass of correspondence to be attended to, besides the work of "All the Year

Round;" and in the closing weeks of the tour, the idea of visiting America was beginning to engross the attention of Mr. Dickens, who constantly received letters and offers of engagement, which were the chief topic of our discussions.

The financial results of the English Readings were so satisfactory, that Mr. Dickens was disposed to devote his energies entirely to reading in the autumn and winter months; but whether this time was to be spent in England or America was the grave question at issue. As so much money was easily obtainable in England, the first objection was an obvious one — Why go through the wear and tear merely to pluck fruit that grows on every bough at home?

The scheme was not one that could be disposed of hastily, but as it had taken firm hold on Mr. Dickens's mind it had to be discussed in all its points. The subject had been occupying his attention for the past eight years, and he deemed it advisable to settle the question one way or another; and, if after mature deliberation the visit to America was found to be impracticable for this present year, to dismiss the matter from his mind for ever.

As many rumours had got afloat, more especially on the other side of the Atlantic, to the effect that Mr. Dickens was really going to America this year, he wrote to his friend, Mr. James T. Fields, of Boston, early in June as follows: — "I am trying hard so to free myself as to be able to come over to read this next winter! Whether I may succeed in this endeavour or no I cannot yet say, but I am trying hard. So in the meantime don't contradict the rumour. In the course of a few mails I hope to be able to give you positive and definite information on the subject."

On the 13th of the same month he wrote to Mr. Fields:—

"I have this morning resolved to send out to Boston in the first week in August, Mr. Dolby, the secretary and manager of my Readings. He is profoundly versed in the business of these delightful intellectual feasts (?), and will come straight to Ticknor and Fields, and will hold solemn council with them, and will then go to New York, Philadelphia, Hartford, Washington, &c., and see the rooms for himself and make his estimates. He will then telegraph to me, 'I see my way to such and such results; shall I go on?' If I reply, 'Yes,' I shall stand committed to begin reading in America with the month of December. If I reply 'No,' it will be because I do not clearly see the game to be worth so large a candle. In either case he will come back to me...

"We mean to keep all this strictly secret, as I beg of you to do, until I finally decide for or against. I am beleaguered by every kind of speculator in such things on your side of the water; and it is very likely they would take the rooms over our heads — to charge us heavily for them — or would set on foot unheard-of devices for buying up the tickets, &c., if the probabilities oozed out. This is exactly how the case stands now, and I confide it to you within a couple of hours after having so far resolved. Dolby quite understands that *he* is to confide in you similarly, without a particle of reserve."

I give these quotations to show the practical character the enterprise had now assumed, and with what prudence and care it was proposed to negotiate in America. The same care was taken in England in sounding the feelings of such friends and counsellors as Forster and Wills, who took widely different views of the project. But on the question of my going to judge for myself they were unanimous.

Book Two - *The American Tour* (1867-1868).

Chapter Four

DURING the period described in the foregoing pages, besides looking after the interests of Messrs. Chappell so far as Mr. Dickens's Readings were concerned, I was occupied in several other matters in connection with catering for the amusement of the public, and was consequently brought into daily intercourse, not only with all the great artists — literary, musical, and dramatic — but with most of the responsible managers and leading speculators from all parts of the world. It is not surprising then, under these circumstances, that I should meet with proposals respecting Mr. Dickens's Readings; but more especially pressing were the invitations from the American managers, who, being fully aware of the success of the English Readings, were most anxious to "run" Mr. Dickens in the States.

These proposals were from time to time mentioned to Mr. Dickens as a matter of form. They were, however, not entertained in the slightest degree, until the pressure became so great, that discussing the subject seriously with Mr. Dickens in a conversation held during one of our journeys towards the end of the last tour, I discovered that he might be disposed to rescind his decision "never again to visit America," provided I would take the matter in hand, and upon further inquiry and consideration could report that there were any reasonable prospects of success.

I may be allowed to recapitulate here the circumstances, to some extent already made public, which had awakened the American expectation that Mr. Dickens would revisit the States. Mr. Dickens had, in 1857, given Readings of the "Christmas Carol," at St. James's Hall, London, and in the Free Trade Hall, Manchester, for the benefit of the "Jerrold Fund." The fame of these Readings spread everywhere, and was so great that Mr. Fields, of Boston, although he had never heard him read, sent an agent to England to negotiate with Mr. Dickens for a series of Readings in America, Mr. Fields being anxious that his countrymen should participate in an enjoyment of which report spoke so favourably. Mr. Fields's deputy was cordially received by Mr. Dickens; but after much consideration the scheme was deemed impracticable and abandoned, at all events for the time being. Notwithstanding this, however, proposals were constantly coming from America, so that, through the persistency with which our friends on the other side "kept it up," as the boys say, the subject was ever present in Mr. Dickens's mind. Then came pressing letters from Mr. Grau, of New York, whose successes with Madame Ristori and other great artists in America, had rendered him not only a rich, but a responsible man. He declared that if Mr. Dickens would but give him "one word of encouragement," he would make a voyage to England for the special purpose of making arrangements on most liberal terms for a series of Readings in the principal cities of America; and further, that he would deposit in the hands of Messrs. Coutts and Co., Mr. Dickens's bankers, satisfactory bonds for the faithful execution of any agreement he and Mr. Dickens might enter into. Further, Fields returned to the charge, and on behalf of himself and several gentlemen of private means in Boston offered to guarantee £10,000, and bank the money in England. But the greatest pressure of all came from his desire to do his duty in promoting the interests of an already expensive family, and his wish to leave them after his death as free as possible from monetary cares — could self-sacrifice have done it, he would have left them free from every kind of care. So one July morning, during a walk with myself across Hyde Park, from the Great Western Station at Paddington, to the office, he resolved, that if I would make a voyage to America at once, to examine the field of operations, he would consider the matter practically.

At that time, however, I was so busily engaged in making arrangements for the reception in England of the Belgian volunteers, that it was a matter of impossibility for me to start at once. It was by no means a small or easy task upon which I was then engaged. Two thousand of these "brave warriors" had accepted the invitation which had been extended to them, while the committee entrusted with the charge of entertaining them had overlooked the fact that this increase of the British family would have to be provided with board and lodging. Banquets, balls, garden parties, reviews, parades, had all been provided for; but up to the last moment no thought had been given to the more immediate wants and necessities of life or comfort, in the shape of bed and breakfast. The use of the Wellington Barracks, in St. James's Park (then not occupied by the Guards), had been granted by the War Office. Lodging would thus have been fully provided for all the men — or such of them as had no personal friends in London to whom they could go — but for the fact, that within the barracks there was not an article of furniture left (except a few iron bedsteads), and no cooking appliances save the stoves and grates. The War Office, however, endeavoured partially to meet this difficulty by offering the committee as much bed-ticking, ready made up for stuffing, as they might require. This idea of "stuffing" beds so overcame the committee — two thousand to provide for and nothing but "ticks"! each to be "stuffed," singly and separately; no blankets, no bolsters, and no sheets, to say nothing of victuals! — that they declined the generous offer; and looking round for a man upon whom they could throw the whole responsibility of housing and breakfasting the invited, they selected me only three days before the guests were due. So far as actual arrangements were concerned, however, a couple of days sufficed for my purpose, after which I was despatched to Antwerp. With me I had a staff of clerks travelling in saloon carriages on each side of the Channel, to make out billets *en route* and distribute them to the men on their arrival in the troopship *Serapis,* which had been placed at the disposal of the committee by the Admiralty, at Gravesend. Before leaving Antwerp an unforeseen difficulty arose. The Belgian Commander-in-Chief, Colonel Gregoire, and his staff were mislaid. He had been seen in Antwerp early on the morning of departure galloping hither and thither, backwards and forwards, apparently without any fixed intent; but when the moment for embarkation arrived, the staff, commander and all, were missing; and as an army becomes a disorderly mob without a commander, so the noble Belgians behaved themselves in the most ruffianly manner on board the *Serapis.* The Admiralty had provided a plentiful supply of excellent provisions, yet it might have been supposed that we wanted to starve these warriors, who acted more like savages than trained and disciplined men. When the dinner hour was announced a general stampede took place, and in less than five minutes not a vestige of food was to be found on the tables. Men were seen seated on the floor gnawing at legs of mutton, roast or boiled; ducks and fowls were devoured without knife or fork touching them; "sea-pies" were clawed and mawled to pieces, and the fragments were thrown out of the port-holes— dishes, spoons, knives, forks, and all. The whole scene was like a bear-pit, and it was a matter of regret to every one, except the volunteers themselves, that the sea was too calm to punish the stomachs of the *voyageurs.* Nor was the scene less disgraceful as night closed in. The blankets which the Admiralty with a great deal of forethought had served in abundance were, on being distributed, almost torn to pieces by the men, who by this time had begun to feel the effects of the English beer which had been but too generously supplied to them; and so, as midnight approached, they sank down one by one, and lay, like heroes, "where they fell," breaking the stillness of the night with the grunts and mutterings of nightmare. Wrapped in their blankets, with their faces made ghastly by the light of a pale summer moon, they looked like corpses, each wrapped in its own winding sheet.

When we arrived at Gravesend, at the invitation of the commander, Captain Soady, I remained on the ship to luncheon; but such had been the orgies of the distinguished foreigners, that it was with difficulty that sufficient food could be collected to make a meal for the captain and his officers and guests.

At Gravesend the visitors were received by the committee, and the Lord Mayor and Corporation of London, and a complete flotilla of penny steamboats. Here, despite the precautions to ensure order, the committee and corporation got mixed, and the wrong volunteers got into the wrong steamer — those who were billeted in the neighbourhood of Westminster Bridge being landed at London Bridge, and those who ought to have been landed at Blackfriars, in the neighbourhood of De Keyser's Hotel, were taken on to Battersea and Cremorne; the result being scenes of indescribable confusion, and an amount of bewilderment to the foreigners such as they will never forget.

These incidents, which have little or nothing to do with the subject matter of this book, would not have been mentioned here but for the purpose of showing under what pressure I was labouring in one quarter alone at the time Mr. Dickens desired me to depart, and how impossible it was for me to leave England immediately to "prospect" for the tour in America.

Arrangements were however made for my departure for Boston on the 3rd of August, in the Cunard steamer *Java,* then under the command of Captain Moodie, one of my dearest and most valued friends, who died, at his house in Birkenhead, in the summer of 1881, regretted, beloved, and respected by all who knew him.

It may be as well to state that my instructions were simply to judge for myself as to the adaptability of the halls in the States for reading purposes, and, if possible, to ascertain, from observations on the spot, to what extent the Readings were likely to be a success. There was no anxiety whatever about public feeling in America, and the "American Notes" and "Martin Chuzzlewit" had no more to do with Mr. Dickens's calculations than if they had never been written. The visit to America, or a decision to remain in England for another tour, which had been already planned, depended solely upon the report I might make. For as the Presidential Election would take place in the autumn of the following year, it was deemed advisable that if the enterprise were to be undertaken, it should be in the coming winter, or not at all; but so much had been said and written to Mr. Dickens on the subject. that he had determined on settling the question of his going or not for himself, and the only way to settle it, to *his* mind, was to adopt the course he pursued; resolving, as he did so, that, in the event of the report being satisfactory, he would not accept any of the tempting offers then before him, but go on his own account, thus leaving himself unfettered and untrammelled by any consideration other than his own convenience.

Up to this time I had never visited America, and, although glad of the opportunity of so doing, especially under such conditions, the responsibility of the position was so great, that, what otherwise might have been regarded as a pleasure trip, became a matter of great anxiety. This anxiety was, however, to a certain extent, dispelled by the kindness of the passengers in the *Java.*

Mr. Dickens, always thoughtful and considerate, determined to accompany me as far as Liverpool, and so great was his anxiety for my personal comfort and safety, and his curiosity as to the class of vessels then crossing the Atlantic, that he had, immediately we arrived in Liverpool the day before sailing, an irresistible desire to see the *Java.* This being impracticable at the time, as the vessel was lying in the Sloyne, some two miles above Liverpool, an excursion was made to the Canada Dock, on the chance of there being some "Cunarders" lying there; and, although he was very ill at the time, suffering from erysipelas in the foot, he insisted on carrying out his idea in order to satisfy his mind that everything was likely to be all right. He had crossed the Atlantic in the Cunard sailing vessel *Britannia,* then commanded by Captain Hewett, twenty-five years previously, and he might have been a little curious to see how far the company had improved their vessels, and what effect a screw steamer would have on him if he decided on crossing.

The following morning he accompanied me on board the steamer, and the interest he took in all the details of the departure was most amusing. He examined everything, even to the little bunk in the state-room, as if it had been a bed at Gad's Hill, to see that it was comfortable.

It was the season of the year when Americans return home after their European tours, and the *Java* had a full complement of passengers. As the greater portion of them were Bostonians, Mr. Dickens was speedily recognized; and his lameness, which caused him to walk with a stick, having attracted attention, many were the offers, during the short trip to the Sloyne on the tug, of a deck chair, or a seat relinquished by ladies, for his convenience. There was a hope amongst the passengers that Mr. Dickens would cross the Atlantic with them, and great was the disappointment when it was found such was not to be the case, for the Boston people dearly loved him, and seemed to regard him as a part of themselves. The moment of departure arrived, and after a most affectionate leave-taking between Mr. Dickens and myself, with a repetition of the sole instruction I had for the journey embraced in three words — "judge for yourself" — there came a general shaking of hands between him and my fellow-passengers; and, with the heartfelt wishes of all for his speedy recovery from his lameness, the tug bore him away back to Liverpool, leaving me, for the first time in my experience, to my meditations on an Atlantic steamer — outward bound; a loneliness which, however, I was not suffered long to feel.

That they had seen Mr. Dickens himself on the steamer was to the minds of the passengers conclusive evidence that he would read in America; and in their anxiety to do him honour, they vied one with another, in the cheeriest manner, in making the voyage as pleasant as possible to his representative; and upon this voyage I formed .many friendships among our "cousins," which still exist in all their cordiality.

On the tenth day from Liverpool (August 13th) at about 6 A.M., we steamed into the harbour of Halifax, in Nova Scotia.

The firing of the saluting cannon and the stopping of the screw caused everybody to get up to take a glimpse of *terra firma,* and very well worth the trouble of an early rise it was. It took a good hour to get the ship up to her wharf — where a curious medley of persons had congregated. The Java was a day overdue, having encountered some westerly gales in the latter part of the voyage to Halifax, and the signal gun had awakened the population of the little place. As we neared the wharf, English military officers in undress uniforms, and naval officers belonging to our own navy, were mingling with several officers belonging to a Russian monitor, which had encountered a gale of wind in the Bay of Fundy, on its way from Boston to some port in the Black Sea. This ironclad, which on the termination of the war had been sold to the Russians by the American Government, was as ugly a looking craft as it is possible to conceive, and had behaved so badly, nearly foundering in the bay, and knocking some of her men senseless with fright because they had to live below in perpetual darkness, that her commander had refused to take her any farther, and was now standing on the quay. Here, too, were landsmen of every kind and description, from officials in the employ of Mr. William Cunard — then representing the Cunard Company in Halifax — down to negroes and negresses.

The heat was tropical, and though it had not inconvenienced us at sea, when the steamer stopped it became painful, even at that early hour of the morning. Everybody wore white trousers (even the English General in command of the troops stationed there, who had honoured the arrival of the Java with his presence), and those who were not in naval or military uniform also wore white Panama hats and white cotton suits, the whole forming a *coup d'oeil* of the most picturesque description.

The mail cart, with sluggish-looking mules harnessed to it, was there to receive the mail bags. The mail agent, who all the voyage had been engaged with his assistant in sorting the letters, went ashore in his best uniform, and, taking a carriage, followed the mail cart at a short distance to the Post Office. The mails being landed, and the mail agent having been got rid of, the passengers who wished so to do were allowed to go ashore, and the shore people allowed to board the ship to see the remainder of the passengers from England take an early breakfast in the saloon — a privilege they availed themselves of very freely; for in those days (and that seventeen years ago) only one "Cunarder" a fortnight went into Halifax (though none go there now), and whether she arrived there in the early morning or late at night there was always the same public interest. The business of the ship — unloading cargo, taking in fresh provisions, fruit, butter, &c., for the remaining two days of the voyage to Boston — demanded a stay at Halifax of some six or seven hours, during which time nearly all the passengers went ashore; and very extraordinary and amusing were the sights that presented themselves. High change was being held in the market-place, and evidently there had been not only a great fruit season in Nova Scotia, but a most extraordinary "take" of lobsters as well. All the merchants seemed (when not smoking, chewing, or spitting) to be eating raspberries, strawberries, melons, peaches, or lobsters. Peaches were selling at 10 cents (5d.) a bushel, and other fruits at a proportionately low rate. Lobsters — large ones — were 5 cents (2½d.) each, or 60 cents (2s. 6d.) for a wheelbarrow full. Nobody seemed to eat anything but the claws of the crustaceans, for the bodies were lying about in all directions; everybody was eating something and throwing something else away, while the *débris* of peach stones, lobster bodies, claw shells, and melon rinds was far from improving either to the boots or dresses of the elegantly-attired lady passengers of the *Java.*

Amongst the passengers on the ship were two Nova Scotians with their families (one of whom was an alderman, and the other a town councillor — most agreeable companions and excellent men), who, neglecting their own private affairs for some little time after their arrival, did the honours of Halifax to a select few of the new acquaintances they had made upon the voyage, and showed them all that there was to be seen in the place, which, however, did not amount to very much; but, as I had the privilege of being included among the select, I can only pay tribute to the intention with which the hos-

51

pitality of the place was offered — a hospitality which doubtless would have been very acceptable to every one had there been more time to enjoy it, but, as "time and tide wait for no man," a return to the ship and an early lunch were indispensable (except fruit and lobsters there seemed to be no available food in Halifax, and not even a good hotel). Aboard the *Java*, a deputation of such of the municipality as could be got together awaited me, their object being to request that, in the event of Mr. Dickens visiting America, he would break his voyage at Halifax and give a Reading there. Money was no object, and if I would but give a promise that their wishes in this respect should be fulfilled, they would "plank" any sum that I might name before the *Java* left the port, or, if preferred, lodge it in the hands of Mr. William Cunard. Thanking the deputation and my friends, the alderman and councillor, for their good intentions, I told them that, in the then uncertain state of affairs, it was impossible for me to give any promise; and so, after several bottles of champagne had been disposed of, and a great deal of handshaking and "Godspeeding" had been got through, the deputation withdrew, and the *Java* pursued her headlong course through the Bay of Fundy to the "Hub of the Universe" — as Boston is familiarly called. I may here remark that the Russian Admiral had not nearly "worn out the gale," but had left behind him a much larger quantity for the *Java* passengers than they expected or desired.

The good ship was first-rate at rolling on the Atlantic in a gale, but she went through entirely new motions and gambols in the Bay of Fundy, rendering the 14th August, 1867, a remarkably disagreeable day to all, but notably so to the ladies. The next day, however (the day of arrival in Boston), was all that could be wished, or would have been so, perhaps, had the mercury in the thermometer been a trifle lower, for when the steamer "lay to" some hours before reaching Boston to receive the pilot, the heat had become almost intolerable.

This shipping of the pilot caused great excitement. Immediately the pilot-boat was sighted some miles ahead bets were offered and taken as to her number, whether the pilot would put his left or his right foot first on the deck, and whether he would wear a tall hat, or a black satin waistcoat, or both, or neither. Such bets were not "square," as in those days the pilots always wore the articles of costume mentioned. Then the pilot-boat came up, the pilot stepped on board (looking pretty much like an undertaker), walked straight up to the bridge without even saying "good morning" to the officers awaiting to receive him on the gangway, but paying Captain Moodie the compliment of saluting *him;* and when he reached the bridge proceeded straight to business, which was to take the ship to her wharf at East Boston. The solemnity with which he conducted this part of the task had something very comical about it. The ship had been under weigh again but a few moments when the pilot seemed to have forgotten something, and, hailing a passenger with a familiar "Say!" felt in his pockets and produced a huge bundle of the latest Boston and New York papers, which he threw carelessly amongst a group of passengers to be scrambled for — producing an effect

52

more resembling a "scrap" in a game of football than the action of a lot of sober citizens returning to their homes after the holidays. But of this the pilot took not the slightest notice.

On this day at noon the *Java* was on her best behaviour, and so she ought to have been, for she was dressed in her best bunting. She steamed grandly into the Bay of Boston, and for the first time I saw the American flag in its native air, beautiful in its simplicity, floating proudly over a fort. Delightful as the voyage had been, with every augury of success before me in the kindness displayed by my fellow-passengers, the moment had arrived for immediate action, and there before me lay the mother city, as it were, of future success or failure, and I had determined it should be one or other entirely.

The greater number of the passengers were busy with their own affairs in preparing to leave the ship, packing up their state-room boxes, travelling bags, and valises, paying wine bills (on that voyage some of them were of rather inordinate amounts), giving gratuities to state-room and saloon stewards, and putting on "shore clothes" to meet the friends awaiting them upon the wharf. While this was going on I was left comparatively to myself, feeling almost a stranger in a strange land, leaning over the rail on the lower bridge, thinking of home and the dear ones there, and of the man}' kind friends left behind; speculating, too, on the chances of success in the great task before me, and gazing all the while on the flag, be it confessed, with a lump in my throat. These and other thoughts were crowding through my brain, when suddenly the ship's cannon was discharged as a salutation to the flag at which I had been so intently gazing, a discharge that was fired from a porthole immediately underneath the point where I was standing! My first idea was that I had suddenly become a nonentity, and next that America, or certainly that part of it known as Boston Harbour, had exploded and "gone up;" both ideas, however, were dispelled by the cheery voices of the doctor and purser who were standing by, and the inquiry of, "How's that, Dolby?" — a question which I was totally unable to answer (not so much as knowing at first what it was) until the doctor had taken me below and administered a dose of brandy "cocktail." Going on deck again, there was more excitement, for the Custom House tender was coming alongside with Judge Russell and his staff of officers, some of whom became intimate friends of both Mr. Dickens and myself during the Boston campaign undertaken later on. These gentlemen were received by their friends on board in a cordial manner, and their first inquiry was, "Which is Dolby?" "Dolby" was not difficult to find, and having been formally introduced by a fellow-passenger (Mr. Howse, of Boston), an adjournment was made to the saloon, where a welcome to America was tendered in their own names and that of the Boston citizens and my fellow-passengers on the voyage. A message was moreover sent to me from Mr. Fields and his firm to the effect that they were waiting for me on the wharf to give me — as the representative of my chief — a fitting welcome; and Judge Russell further intimated that the hospitality of the Customs Department allowed my baggage to pass without examination, a privilege that many of the passengers on board doubtless wished had been extended to them, as, at that time, the duties on foreign goods were almost prohibitive, and the well-stocked trunks with Parisian and London novelties in articles of dress and jewellery were a source of many a pang to the heart and spasm to the pocket of the generous paterfamilias, or loving and confiding husband, who seemed to think, when he got into the clutches of the Custom House officers in his native land, that coming home after a pleasant voyage was not so funny after all.

Much correspondence had taken place between Mr. Dickens and Mr. Fields on the subject of the Readings in America, as has been already mentioned; and, although I had never before seen Mr. Fields or any of the partners of his firm, the letter of introduction sent to that gentleman by post the week prior to the sailing of the *Java* announcing my coming, was of such a character as to prevent any constraint or raise any doubts as to the nature of my reception; and the kindly greetings on the steamer, while yet some distance from the landing-place, justified me in my anticipations.

As the steamer neared the wharf I could not help speculating and conjecturing in my own mind as to which among all the crowd of well-dressed people assembled there was Fields. Everybody on shore and on the steamer seemed to be waving handkerchiefs, and I settled it in my own mind that those who were not waving handkerchiefs would be the representatives of the firm of Ticknor and Fields, arguing, at the same time, that the fact of my not waving a handkerchief would point out to the firm that I was the Dolby they were expecting — forgetting entirely that the firm had other friends in the steamer than myself who were more worthy, in their estimation, of the white cambric salute than I might be.

All was confusion on the shore. People were rushing about; some shouting themselves hoarse in the vain endeavour to send a message to the ship in the form of the ridiculous inquiry whether "so-and-so" had been sea-sick; others asking whether "so-and-so" had been seen in Paris or Rome; in fact, all sorts of questions hurtled through the air that might have been kept for a more convenient time, and certainly until the *Java* had made up her mind to behave herself, either by being obedient to her commander in going where he wanted her to go, or by not making such a bellowing with her steam-pipe as to prevent the people on shore and the passengers on the ship from hearing anybody say anything.

In all this confusion and noise it was impossible to make out anything, and it was only after a lot of tugging and hauling, and a lot of nautical shouting and apostrophizing, that the *Java* was brought alongside and made fast to the wharf. Then I was brought face to face with my new friends, James T. Fields, Howard Ticknor, and James R. Osgood, who represented the firm, and who did their best by their kindly welcome to make me feel at home.

All preliminaries having been got through agreeably and satisfactorily, there came many injunctions from my late fellow-passengers to the firm to use their best endeavours to "get Dolby to induce Dickens to come *out*," injunctions that were quite unnecessary to them, for they had been working on the idea for several months previously, being most desirous to have Mr. Dickens once more amongst them, for his presence in America was calculated to give an additional value to his works, the only authorized American edition of which was published by Messrs. Ticknor and Fields. Moreover, there was a faint hope that his visit might lead to the much-desired International Copyright Act.

Arrived at the Parker House Hotel I prepared for an early dinner at which I was to present my credentials, and at the same time to hand over the MS. of a new story, the "Holiday Romance," which Mr. Dickens had written for Messrs. Ticknor and Fields.

It is needless to say that the dinner was a most enjoyable one, not only on account of the cordiality of my hosts, but also on account of the novelty of the dishes. "Gumbo" soup, "sheep's head," fish, stewed terrapin, "grass" birds, "Reed" birds and "peeps," yams, sweet potatoes, and "green corn" — the latter a most delicious vegetable which I soon learned to gnaw off the "cob."

At this dinner the future plan of action was decided upon, and as I was consigned to the firm, I had no hesitation in accepting the proffered services of Mr. James R. Osgood as travelling companion, on the tour of inspection I had undertaken.

This arrangement was an inestimable advantage to me, inasmuch as Mr. Osgood was, and is, one of the most popular men in America. It was decided that the remainder of the week should be devoted to resting after the voyage, and only such operations should be carried on as involved sight-seeing and making the acquaintance of the many distinguished literary men and artists of Boston. Most of them were absent, however, at their various places of resort during the holiday season. Fields himself was supposed to be in New Hampshire; Professor Longfellow was at his beautiful retreat at Nantucket; Professor Agassiz was somewhere, nobody knew where, but wherever he was everybody supposed he was pursuing some scientific research for the benefit of his fellow-man. Mr. James Russell Lowell was *somewhere* in Europe, and other notabilities were "somewhere else;" so that the literary family of Boston, so far as the celebrities were concerned, was considerably dispersed; still there were left behind such worthy representatives as Mr. Emerson, and the no less worthy and distinguished Dr. Oliver Wendell Holmes, to both of whom I speedily had the pleasure of an introduction. There were lesser planets, also in Boston, ready and willing to contribute to my personal enjoyment, amongst whom may be mentioned Donald Mitchell ("Ike Marvel"), Mr. Aldrich, the "Bad Boy," and author of several most charming poems, and Henry Clapp, the man who said the funniest things imaginable (for which Artemus Ward got the credit).

To judge by the expressed opinion of these men of experience, there was no need to have any doubt, certainly so far as Boston was concerned, as to the success of the Readings; and the only thing to be done there was to find a suitable hall or theatre in which to give them.

Accordingly the various halls and theatres had to be inspected; the first to engage our attention being called the "Music Hall," in which is erected the finest and largest organ — next, perhaps, to the one at Haarlem — in the world. This hall is a magnificent one, but much too large for Reading purposes, albeit for musical entertainments it is perfection. The Boston Theatre was next visited, and the same drawbacks, only in an exaggerated form, presented themselves; for Drury Lane or Covent Garden Theatre in London could easily be placed inside of this one, and with space enough left to admit of a good-sized audience as well. As far as the principal theatre and the principal hall were concerned there was nothing to be done but give them up as being unsuitable for the purpose, or take them and ruin the enterprise by reducing the number of Readings in Boston, each of which would be given at a disadvantage.

There was another hall capable of holding a large number of people, but everybody said it was old-fashioned — that nobody would go to it since the Music Hall had been built, and everybody doubted if Boston could be induced to go to it even to hear Charles Dickens. This hall had to be seen, however, and it was seen; and, in my estimation, possessed all the requisites necessary for the success of the business in hand. It was called the Tremont Temple; it held over two thousand people, and the seats were so arranged, on a gradually rising floor, that every one in the house had a good view of the platform, and would be able not only to hear distinctly, but also to enjoy all the facial effects of the reader, without which Mr. Dickens's Readings would lose so much. Fashion then had to be sacrificed, for I at once decided that no other place in Boston than the Tremont Temple would suit the purpose; a decision that did not turn out very erratic, when it is considered that twenty Readings in all were given in this hall within five months, with an average receipt of $3,000 each Reading.

The Globe Theatre, then in course of construction, was one of the handsomest and most elegant theatres in the world. There was always a good stock company there, and when Mr. Dickens could get an evening to himself in Boston it was his habit to spend it in this theatre. In the great Boston fire of 1872 this charming theatre was destroyed, but it has since been rebuilt in, if possible, a more costly and more lavish style than before its destruction.

Boston being disposed of for the present — so far as the purpose of my visit was concerned — arrangements were made for "the road;" and in a few days Mr. Osgood and myself were on the "tramp," but not before Boston had endeared itself to me so much as to cause me ever after to look upon it as my American home; and to the present day I regard it as such, notwithstanding that many dear and valued friends have "gone over to the majority" since I was last there.

Before starting on the journey I had one pleasure, without which a visit to Boston would indeed have been incomplete. I went to Nantucket to see Longfellow. He was not in good health at the time, and a letter had been received from him, expressing his regret at "not being able to travel to Boston to pay his respects to Dickens through his representative." Accordingly, on a bright summer's day, I repaired to his house in company with Messrs. Fields and Osgood. This was the first railway journey I had taken in the States. I must confess that the travelling did not strike me as being very comfortable. In those days there was but one class and fare, everybody paying at the same rate. The Pullman system had not then been brought to its present state of perfection, at least for the short routes. At this time all classes travelled together in a long car, built to carry fifty-two passengers: there were thirteen seats on each side (with reversible backs to seat two persons each; and a broad passage-way ran up the centre to a door at each end, giving the traveller an opportunity of walking the whole length of the train. At each end of the car was a stove, kept almost at a red heat during the winter months; on the opposite side to the stove was a tank of iced water, a great luxury in hot weather; for the dust at that time is terribly troublesome, as it comes in in clouds with the restlessly peripatetic dealers in newspapers, books, pamphlets, ivory pincushions, "pop corn," who give the traveller really no peace of mind on his journey, and make him long for its termination.

Nantucket is a beautiful spot, and the position of Mr. Longfellow's place was worthy of its owner. The house (standing in its own grounds, which sloped gradually to the sea) is built somewhat in the Swiss style — and covered with Virginia creeper and wistaria — having verandah and balconies all around it overlooking the sea, on which Miss Longfellow's boat was riding jauntily, ready to convey its owner on an excursion. On the arrival of the carriage at the house, the party were received by Mr. Longfellow

James R. Osgood

and his daughter; the dear old poet, bareheaded and looking like a veritable patriarch with his beautiful long white hair streaming in the balmy afternoon breeze. After a hearty welcome from himself and his daughter, we took a walk round the grounds, and then a repast at which was served some of the much-coveted "soft-shell crab" then in perfection.

The interest taken by Mr. Longfellow in the idea that Mr. Dickens would read in America gave every one sincere pleasure. I had to answer questions as to every detail of Mr. Dickens's health, whether his mode of life was at all altered since Mr. Longfellow visited Gad's Hill, and all sorts of inquiries about Miss Dickens and Miss Hogarth, and every member of the family, the servants, and even the horses, dogs, and birds. Before leaving, I had charge of all kinds of affectionate messages to my chief, added to the strictest injunctions and warnings as to the inadvisability of my ever showing my face again in Boston, at any future time after my return to England, except to announce that Dickens was coming over.

Mr. Longfellow has been so often described, and his portrait is so familiar to the public all over the civilized world, that any lengthened description of him is quite unnecessary. Suffice it to say that in appearance he was as unlike a poet, or the accepted ideal of what a poet should be like, as man could possibly be. Speaking of this on the return journey, Fields told a story which will bear repeating here. Ticknor and Fields had engaged the services of a new shop-boy, a regular New England lad. On one occasion, when the other members of the establishment being away at their midday meal, this lad was left in charge of the store, a white-haired gentleman entered and inquired, "Is Mr. Fields within?" "Guess he ain't," replied the boy, without looking up from the book which he was reading. The gentleman modestly inquired if the boy could give him any idea when "Mr. Fields was likely to be in." As the boy "guessed he couldn't," and manifested symptoms of impatience at being disturbed in his reading, the gentleman requesting the boy to "kindly give *that* to Mr. Fields on his return," handed him a card. The boy stared at the card with the utmost indifference for a moment, but when his retina had clearly defined the words upon the card, "Professor Longfellow," he jumped off his office-stool, and, staring hard at the owner of the card, said: "Say, old man! do you mean to say you are *really* Longfellow?" Mr. Longfellow assured him that such was the fact; the boy replied, in a half-soliloquy, "Wall! I wouldn't have thought it!" adding in louder tones, "Now, how old was you when you wrote 'Evangeline'? that's what I want to know." Having been satisfied on this point, he proceeded with his reading, leaving the visitor, more amused than angry, to find the way out of the store as best he could.

Having enjoyed the rest in Boston, Mr. Osgood and I started on our tour. The places to be visited included New York and intervening cities, as far south as Washington; but as the war had terminated not long before, and matters financially were in a very troubled state, the people were indisposed to patronize amusements, so we decided that it would be useless to go further south. To the westward we were to go as far as Chicago, if necessary calling at the intermediate cities, and arrangements were made to visit the smaller cities in the New England States.

After many adieux of the friendliest kind — generally taking the form of "Good-bye, old man; come back soon, and bring Dickens with you!" — we travelled as far as New York, on the "Bristol Route," the pleasantest of journeys in summer, for only some three or four hours were spent in the train, the rest in one of those extraordinary floating palaces of steamboats. The steamer that conveyed us from the railway station, or "depot," at Bristol (Mass.), was an enormous "three decker," looking like a private hotel on a large scale. The main deck resembled a noble entrance-hall to a house, and was well carpeted with a thick velvet-pile carpet. Round this hall, and approached by a wide staircase — also carpeted, and having massive walnut wood banisters and balustrades — ran balconies. From these balconies passages led to the state-rooms, which were furnished in the most elegant style, some of them even having great "four posters" of carved oak. Then there were other balconies outside the vessel, where again were other state-rooms, most comfortable in hot weather.

Below were hot and cold baths, barbers' shops, cigar and newspaper stands, book-stalls, and hosiery establishments.

The saloons and retiring-rooms — not forgetting the drinking bars, where everything, from a bottle of champagne to a cocktail and "eye opener," could be obtained — were all fitted in a costly manner; while the restaurant department would have done credit to the largest hotel on shore. The inevitable nigger, too, in the white cotton suit, making the most attentive and amusing of waiters.

A walk on deck, in the enjoyment of a cigar after supper, the liveliest of *compagnons de voyage,* and sometimes songs, glees, and madrigals, filled up the time until the hour for "turning in" arrived. There is a very mixed class, though, on these steamers, and with all the vigilance of the detectives, who are constantly travelling to and fro, robberies do sometimes occur. It is imprudent to go to sleep without first making the door of the state-room safe. If this precaution be not taken, especially in the outside rooms — one of which Mr. Osgood and I conjointly occupied — the passenger must not be astonished if, on dressing in the morning, he finds that some ingenious hotel or steamboat thief "*has gone through his pockets.*" This very nearly happened to us, for on nearing New York, at an early hour in the morning, I awoke, with an impression strong upon me, that some one was trying to push down the little green jalousie blind in front of the state-room window, which we had left open during the hot summer's night. Silent observation soon showed that my impression was not ill-founded; so, reaching out for a bundle of sticks and umbrellas, and placing them, as noiselessly as possible, within reach, I feigned to be asleep, and waited patiently until Mr. Hotel Sneak should have succeeded in letting down the blind. This he soon accomplished, and a long arm appeared, feeling at the sides of the room where the clothes were supposed to be hanging up. A smart rap with the umbrellas and sticks, over the intrusive wrist, and a howl of pain and disappointment from the outside, had the effect of awakening Mr. Osgood from his slumbers; but he, on being informed as to the cause of the noise, merely remarked, "Oh, it's only a watch collector!" and proceeded to finish his night's rest. As it was then about six in the morning, I took advantage of the "early call" — so unceremoniously given — to get up, take a walk on deck, and catch my first glimpse of New York City, and its beautiful harbour, of which I had heard so much. The sun was shining brilliantly, and, as it was Sunday, the ships at the wharves were displaying their best bunting, in honour of the day. What a sight the city presents under these circumstances! Flags of every nationality, streaming out in bold relief against the clear blue sky, which gives a power and tone to the bright colours that no other sky in the world (in my experience) can produce.

The city looked as if it were fast asleep, but it was not — and *never* is! The New Yorker is ever on the alert, for business or pleasure, and this being a pleasure day, as all Sundays are in New York, the streets were found, even at that early hour in the morning, to be quite alive with people hurrying to meet a steamer, or to catch a train in Jersey City, or elsewhere, to carry them off to the pretty country around Englefield, or some other equally charming spot, or to take them up the famed Hudson River — one of the most beautiful in the world.

The steamer was brought to at the wharf, as quietly as if she had a fear of waking up her living freight, most of whom were fast asleep, and, in some cases, snoring, in the comfortable state-rooms; for on these vessels the passenger can remain in his room as long as his inclination dictates, and when he does get up, he has all the luxury of an hotel to fly to for his creature comforts.

Mr. Osgood, with his usual consideration, sacrificed his own comfort, and was up betimes to conduct me to our hotel on Broadway — the "Metropolitan" — of which, as being a fair specimen of an American hotel, conducted on American principles, I had heard so much. Though we arrived here at the early hour of eight in the morning, everything was in full swing, the hotel being as busy at that hour as an English hotel at midday; for, on entering the breakfast-room, there were some sixty or seventy persons partaking of their morning meal. Mr. Osgood had his own house in New York, and it was only to gratify a whim on my part that I was allowed to put up at the "Metropolitan." There was another reason, however, for my staying there, inasmuch as a distinguished member of Congress, who was also a newspaper proprietor in New York, made this hotel his home, and with this gentleman Mr. Dickens had made an agreement to write the original story with the manuscript of which, as I have already said, I was entrusted. For "George Silverman's Explanation," the sum of £1,000 (gold) was to be paid on the delivery of the MS. Inquiries made in Boston as to the status of the paper and its proprietor, led to the suspicion that it would be as well not to part with the story except on the strictest business principles; so, in order to give the member of Congress a fair chance in this respect, and to see the workings of one of the largest American hotels, Mr. Osgood's kind invitation to stay with him was declined. To what extent I was successful with the Congressman will be seen later on.

Left to myself, in the early part of the day I took a turn in the streets of New York, and, be it confessed, was greatly disappointed with their general appearance? notably with that of the far-famed Broadway. Its style of architecture, or rather its absence of style, gave it a kind of "higgledy-piggledy" look. Mr. Dickens described it as "a sort of elongated New Cut." The pavements were horribly laid, no two stones having, apparently, been set by the same man; or, if they had been, that man must have had very crude or very advanced ideas of the art of levelling. The carriage road was worse than the pavement, or "side walk," as it is locally termed. Here were to be found large holes, which gave one the impression that the stones had, at some time, been required for a particular purpose other than that of road-making, and that those in the road way, being the readiest to hand, had been summarily appropriated. These holes gave the most disagreeable wrenches to carriage-springs, to say nothing of the discomfort of the people "enjoying" the drive; and this is the more to be regretted as the carriages in New York City, both public and private, are of the most luxurious and elegant description — and so they ought to be, for they are dear enough! But nobody ever thinks of expense in New York; only give the people what they want, and they will pay anything for it in the most ungrudging manner; but offer them what they do not want, and your dearest friend will avoid you. There is no poverty visible in New York, or any other American city, and a beggar in the streets is comparatively unknown; everybody is well dressed, in the best of materials, and it is a marvel where all the money comes from to support so much luxury as is everywhere to be met with. At the time of which I am writing — just after the war — gold was at thirty-nine per cent, premium and everything except articles of food was excessively dear. A hat cost (in English money) £3; a great coat, or a morning or dress suit, £10 to £12; a pair of walking boots, £4, and everything else in proportion. At Delmonico's Restaurant, and at the other first-class establishments of the same kind, a glass of brandy cost two shillings; and a carriage drive of, say three miles, would cost as much as £1; but, with all these drawbacks, elegantly dressed ladies and gentlemen were to be seen driving about as if the charges were as moderate as in European cities. The excessive charges for carriage driving may be due, in a measure, to the tramcar system, which is as cheap as the other is expensive, five cents (2½d.) being the charge for any distance, long or short; but even this has its drawbacks, in the way the cars are overloaded, there being no regulation of the number of passengers.

In the Central Park, which is too familiar to need description, no one is allowed to ride or drive at a higher rate of speed than five or six miles an hour; and, as the possession of a fast trotting-horse and "buggy" is much coveted by the wealthy inhabitants of New York, this prohibition renders a public road — where the owner of the "mare and buggy" can test the quality of his cattle— a necessity. Outside the park there is a long, straight, and wide road, where the New Yorker, as soon as he reaches it, lets his horse "go." Here disported themselves the late Commodore Vanderbilt, and other distinguished patrons of the turf, with their fast trotters, ready for a race with any one worthy of a tussle; and many were the collisions generally resulting in the collapse, or "folding-up," of one or more buggies, while the occupants were considered fortunate if nothing more serious happened to them. This road is the resort on Sunday afternoons of the *elite* of New York society, who linger about on the long steps, or in the verandahs of the many restaurants at each side, the *tout ensemble* presenting a scene of animation and vivacity far exceeding anything of the kind either in the Bois de Boulogne, in Paris, or in Hyde Park. Returning to the city from the park, through the fashionable quarters of the Fifth Avenue, and the squares in its neighbourhood, I had reason to change my opinion respecting the street architecture of New York City (judging it, as I had done, from a Broadway point of view), for here is nothing but order and regularity in the arrangement of the streets, this part of the city being as unlike that part of Broadway from Castle Garden to Union Square as is Lancaster Gate to the purlieus of the New Cut.

It was arranged that we should get to work early next morning to obtain the opinions of the leading literary men and politicians then in New York. This enterprise promised a mixture of sentiments and ideas almost inexhaustible. New York City being regarded as the test place, by reason of the variety of opinion which prevails there. The first person we sought was Horace Greeley, then editor of the "New York Tribune," whose opinion — based upon his knowledge of the country and its people, on the one hand, and his admiration and personal affection for Mr. Dickens, on the other — rendered him the most fitting authority on so important an enterprise as the second visit of Charles Dickens to America. His reception of Mr. Osgood and myself was most cordial — that is, for him, for he was not a man of the most enthusiastic sort (which, perhaps, slightly enhanced the value of his opinion), and he soon made up his mind upon the point in question, expressing the belief that from a monetary point of view, the success would eclipse that of Jenny Lind. In a leading article in the "Tribune" he wrote: "The fame as a novelist which Mr. Dickens has already created in America, and which at the *best* has never yielded him anything particularly munificent or substantial, is become his capital stock in the present enterprise."

The next person consulted was William Cullen Bryant, the poet, and editor and proprietor of the "Evening Post." This veteran was as enthusiastic as Horace Greeley, and freely placed his paper at the service of the undertaking.

Another element had now to be sounded, the "New York Herald." The founder of this remarkable property, Mr. James Gordon Bennett, was then alive. This gentleman made an appointment with me for the purpose of talking matters over in connection with the "second coming of Dickens," as the "New York Herald" called it; but it must here be remarked that Mr. Bennett's opinion had no weight with me, either one way or the other; and it was only a little curiosity to make the acquaintance of so remarkable a man that led me to "interview" him at all.

When the meeting took place, Mr. Bennett pretended to take the greatest interest in the subject, declaring that if "Dickens would *first apologize* to the American public for the 'Notes' and 'Martin Chuzzlewit,' he would make a large amount of money;" but that even failing his inclination to do this, there was a possibility of his succeeding, if "he was in good hands," notably in those of Mr. Grau, who, Mr. Bennett had been given to understand, had made Mr. Dickens a very handsome offer.

I thanked Mr. Bennett for his disinterested opinion, and promised to forward it to the proper quarter together with his advice "not to charge a cent less than ten dollars (!) a ticket to see and hear Dickens." The following morning's issue of the "New York Herald" was looked for with no small

amount of curiosity; the surprise, however, was far greater than was anticipated, and amounted to a sensation; Mr. Bennett, with native liberality, had
presented the New York public with a reprint of the "American Notes," *as a
"special," free of cost!* — an attention which I felt bound to acknowledge as
speedily and handsomely as possible. This suggested to the enterprising
mind of Mr. Osgood the idea of reproducing an edition of the "Notes" in a
cheap form, which subsequently realized an enormous sale at the moderate
price of twenty-five cents a copy. This edition was to be found on every
bookstall, tramcar, and steamboat in the country; and, for the first time, the
"Notes" were read by the then living population of the United States, and did
more to cement that feeling of amity and friendship between Mr. Dickens and
the American people (a friendship which, in his opinion, had never been sev-
ered) than anything else could have done.

The "New York Times" (one of the most ably conducted newspapers in
America) said on this subject: "Even in England Dickens is less known than
here, and of the millions here who treasure every word he has written, there
are tens of thousands who would make a large sacrifice to see and hear the
man who has made happy so many homes. Whatever sensitiveness there
once was to sneering criticism, the lapse of a quarter of a century, and a profound significance of a great war, have modified or removed."

The newspaper and political elements having been consulted, and their
opinions having been "boiled down," there was one other class still left,
whose opinion would be well worthy of consideration, viz., the "showmen,"
as the managers of the theatres and caterers for public amusements are pop-
ularly termed. Foremost amongst these was Mr. P. T. Barnum, the evergreen
showman, whose opinion on all matters connected with public life is price-
less. Then came Mr. Bateman (the "Colonel"), who was busily engaged at the
time with a French Opera Bouffe Company, and who, in later years, became
the lessee of the Lyceum Theatre in London, and the discoverer of our now
justly celebrated Henry Irving. Harry Palmer was also in New York, making
arrangements for the opening of his theatre (Niblo's Gardens) with his great
spectacle of the "Black Crook," out of which he amassed an enormous fortune. Lafayette Harrison, the proprietor of Irving Hall, had to be consulted,
and John Brougham, the most versatile of actors and authors, and a warm-
hearted Irishman, was also taken into council, and swelled the chorus of approval with which the enterprise was greeted.

Being thus armed with encouragement by men of good business talent, and
judges of what would succeed and what would not, I felt that New York was
certainly safe, if only a good room could be found for the Readings. The
Cooper Institute was visited first, but the faults of the Boston Music Hall, Boston, were manifest here. Irving Hall was too small; the theatres were all engaged, and the only available hall was the Steinway Hall, the property of the
celebrated pianoforte makers of that name; and this was eventually secured
for the purpose.

Of the other cities which I visited at this time, Washington presented the greatest novelty. Willard's Hotel was in those days the resort of officials from all parts of the civilized and uncivilized world; members of Assembly, Congressmen, Indians from the prairies —trying to look like other people in the coat, waistcoat, and trousers, and the tall hat of civilization. which last they generally wear at the back of the head, for no other reason that I could make out than to make the war paint on their faces appear more conspicuous. Add to these the loafer generally found about American hotels, and a more than usually large number of hotel thieves, and the reader can form some idea of what a large Washington hotel is like. The hotel thieves at "Willard's" evidently included a considerable proportion of the guests, for they were important enough to have large printed notices posted about on the staircases, lobbies, and in the rooms, headed, *"Caution to Hotel Thieves,"* and informing them that, if caught in the exercise of their "profession" in *that* hotel, they would be confined in a cage kept for the purpose, and placed in a conspicuous part of the building, where they would be "on view" for a few days before being handed over to the police! This was no idle notification either, for there was one of the fraternity holding a *levée* in the cage at the time of my visit. Had there been any doubt as to the success of Mr. Dickens's Readings in America, it would have manifested itself in this "city of magnificent distances," and, thanks to the energy of Mr. Franklin Philp, an Englishman holding a high position in Washington, the best advice was obtained, showing that Washington would prove no exception to the other cities which we had tested.

According to my judgment, there was no necessity to pursue the inquiries any further, and certainly no occasion to travel so far west as Chicago and the other western cities, especially as the newspapers in those places were filled with words of welcome to Mr. Dickens and his representative. Moreover, I was anxious to get back to England and settle the matter; so I decided to call at New York, and collect the £1,000 in exchange for "George Silverman," or, at all events, to give the Congressman the chance of paying the money, and then go on to Boston, take leave of my friends there, and sail for home in the Cunard steamer *Cuba,* the week after leaving Washington.

When I arrived at New York, I did not return to the "Metropolitan," but went to the Westminster Hotel, at the corner of 14th Street and Irving Place, in which Harry D. Palmer had invested a large amount of money. This hotel became the New York home of Mr. Dickens on his subsequent visit to America, and was as comfortable and as quiet as any private house could have been. During the few days' stay in New York, frequent letters were written to the Congressman, informing him of my intention of returning to England in the course of the following week, and asking for his views with regard to the MS. This had, apparently, no effect on the legislator, as he never gave any signs of life until the very moment when I was about to leave the Westminster Hotel for the Bristol boat, when he suddenly appeared in the sitting-room at the hotel, where a farewell party was being held, and, throwing a bag

— *supposed* to contain one thousand sovereigns — on the table, claimed the MS. The Congressman's reputation being patent to the company then assembled, there were indications of a "row;" but I prevented this by informing him that it would take more time to count one thousand sovereigns, and to test their genuineness, than I had at disposal; and, handing him back the bag with the intimation that Messrs. Ticknor and Fields had, in my absence, kindly undertaken to complete the business portion of the matter, the Congressman withdrew, saying "he would send a banker's order to Boston," which, it is almost unnecessary to add, he never did; but in all probability used the sovereigns in playing *faro,* a game to which he was so devoted that he actually kept an establishment in which to gratify his taste, and that of any person who happened to be passing by, any time of the day or night, especially the latter. The MS. eventually became the property of Messrs. Ticknor and Fields, and was published by them in the "Atlantic Monthly," and re-published in "All the Year Round," in the early part of 1868, while Mr. Dickens was in America.

Chapter Five - Preparations for the American Tour

I SAILED from Boston in the *Cuba,* under the command of Captain Stone, on Wednesday, the 11th September. Before I left Boston, it was agreed with Messrs. Ticknor and Fields that a telegram containing either "Yes" or "No" was to be the pass-word for future action. If the former word, then Mr. Osgood had undertaken to secure such halls as had been agreed upon for the dates arranged, and so save any waste of time that might occur in communicating by mail; if the latter, then to abandon the idea at once and for ever.

A splendid run of a little over eight days, brought the *Cuba* safely to Queenstown, whence I telegraphed to Gad's Hill, announcing my arrival, and requesting that instructions as to future and immediate movements might be sent to the "Adelphi" at Liverpool, to await my arrival there on the following (Saturday) morning. The telegram in reply was characteristic of Mr. Dickens's good-nature and thoughtfulness: "Welcome back, old boy! Do not trouble about me, but go home to Ross first and see your wife and family, and come to me to 'Gad's' at your convenience." This entailed another telegram, to the effect that Mrs. Dolby was then on her way to London to meet me, and asking if the office, or "Gad's," would be the more convenient to talk matters over with the Chief on Monday morning. A prompt reply was awaiting my arrival in London: "Come on to 'Gad's' this afternoon with your wife, and take a quiet day or two's rest, when we can discuss matters leisurely." This was accordingly done, and within a few hours of landing in Liverpool, I was cordially shaking the hand of my genial and loving friend at Higham Station, on the North Kent Line, whither he had driven in the basket carriage, escorted by a sufficient number of large dogs to have taken the prizes at all the dog shows in England.

After all the work and excitement of my visit to America, the pretty Kentish country looked prettier than ever, and was well worth crossing the Atlantic for, independently of the greeting awaiting myself and wife at "Gad's" from the kindest women in the world, Miss Dickens and Miss Hogarth, who were standing under the porch to give a welcome to the traveller. Dinner was ready, and the gong was announcing this fact as we drove up to the house, a circumstance which amused us all very much, suggesting, as Mr. Dickens said, "real show business;" so the ceremony of dressing was dispensed with. Mr. Dickens was more intent on giving the news of theatrical, musical, and social events that had taken place during my absence, than in talking of matters of so much moment to himself, except so far as inquiring earnestly after the welfare of his old friends in America.

Nothing, however, would induce him to enter on the most interesting subject, for he preferred, as he said, to give *that* a rest for a day or two, or at all events to defer it for a walk on the following day to Cobham village and through Cobham Park, returning by the "Leather Bottle," the inn where Mr. Tupman took refuge after his adventure with Miss Wardle. During this walk it was arranged that I should make an official report on the following day, or the day afterwards — at my convenience — which report would be forwarded to his friends, Mr. John Forster, Mr. Wills, and Mr. Frederic Ouvry (his solicitor), for *their* opinions, Mr. Dickens reserving the right of pleasing himself eventually. The report was a very voluminous one, and included plans of the various halls in the country; also calculations as to results at various prices of admission, and calculations of expenses on a liberal scale. Then there was the consideration that gold was then at thirty-nine per cent., which would necessitate a great loss in the conversion of greenbacks into gold, unless Mr. Dickens chose to turn speculator in American securities by purchasing "Five-twenty Bonds," then bearing interest at six per cent. — as he was strongly recommended to do by sagacious business friends in America, and holding them until "matters pulled themselves round," as they undoubtedly would, and did.

As it was not possible, or convenient, to send the report with all its details to Messrs. Forster, Wills, and Ouvry, and as they could not be brought together conveniently (for Mr. Forster was at Ross, in Herefordshire; Mr. Wills was at his house at Dorking; and Mr. Ouvry was, if I remember rightly, in Scotland), an idea occurred to Mr. Dickens to make a condensed report, for the consideration of these gentlemen, embodying all the features of the lengthened one; and this he dictated to me, over the morning cigar, on the day after the first report had been handed to him. "The case in a nutshell," as he called it, tells the story so completely, that it would be an injustice to the reader not to give it in full, though it has already been published.

"**1.** I think it may be taken as proved, that general enthusiasm and excitement are awakened in America on the subject of the Readings, and that the people are prepared to give me a great reception. The 'New York Herald,' indeed, is of opinion that 'Dickens must apologize first,' and where a 'New York Herald' is possible, anything is possible. But the prevailing tone, both of the press and of the people of all conditions, is highly favourable. I have an opinion myself that the Irish element in New York is dangerous — for the reason that the Fenians would be glad to damage a conspicuous Englishman. This is merely an opinion of my own.

"**2.** All our original calculations were based on one hundred Readings. But an unexpected result of careful inquiry on the spot, is the discovery that the month of May is generally considered (in large cities) bad for such a purpose. Admitting that what governs an ordinary case in this wise governs mine, this reduces the Readings to eighty, and consequently at a blow makes a reduction of twenty per cent, in the means of making money in the half-year, unless the objection should not apply in my exceptional instance.

"**3.** I dismiss the consideration that the great towns of America could not possibly be exhausted, or even visited, within six months, and that a large harvest would be left unreaped; because I hold that a second series of Readings in America is to be set down as out of the question; whether regarded as involving two more voyages across the Atlantic, or a vacation of five months in Canada.

"**4.** The narrowed calculation we have made is this: What is the largest amount of clear profit derivable, under the most advantageous circumstances possible as to their public reception, from eighty Readings, and no more? In making this calculation the expenses have been throughout taken on the New York scale, which is the dearest; as much as twenty per cent, has been deducted for management, including Mr. Dolby's commission; and no credit has been taken for any extra payment on reserved seats, though a good deal of money is confidently expected from this source. But, on the other hand, it is to be observed that four Readings (and a fraction over) are supposed to take place every week, and that the estimate of receipts is based on the assumption that the audiences are, on all occasions, as large as the rooms will reasonably hold.

"**5.** So considering eighty Readings, we bring out the net profit of that number remaining to me, after payment of all charges whatever, as £15,500.

"**6.** But it yet remains to be noted that the calculation assumes New York City and the State of New York to be good for a very large proportion of the eighty Readings; and that the calculation also assumes the necessary travelling not to extend beyond Boston and adjacent places, New York City and adjacent places, Philadelphia, Washington, and Baltimore. But if the calculation should prove too sanguine on this head, and if these places should *not* be good for so many Readings, then it may prove impracticable to get through eighty within the time, by reason of other places that would come into the list lying wide asunder, and necessitating long and fatiguing journeys.

"**7.** The loss consequent on the conversion of paper money into gold (with gold at the present ruling premium) is allowed for in the calculation. It counts seven dollars to the pound."

After the "Case" had been sent off, I decided to return to my house at Ross, in which town, by an odd coincidence, Mr. Forster was staying for the benefit of his health. So arrangements were made for a meeting to take place between us in ten days after my arrival there,

Up to this time, I had only met Mr. Forster at the social gatherings at "Gad's" and at the office; and, before the interview at his hotel at Ross, had not met him in a business capacity. Being perfectly aware of the intimate relations existing between Mr. Dickens and Mr. Forster, I regarded this interview with considerable anxiety, as, in my opinion, much depended on the view Mr. Forster should take of the matter. This anxiety was not allayed by the discovery that he had in the most unreasonable manner, and without any knowledge of the subject that I could see, made up his mind that the enterprise was *not* to be; and a red rag could not have made a mad bull more ferocious than the discussion of the clauses in the moderate and business-like "case in a nutshell" made the biographer of the novelist. He had made up *his* mind, and there was an end of the matter. He urged that ever since the Staplehurst accident Mr. Dickens had been in a bad state of health, and that a sea-voyage was the very worst thing in the world for him. He had a personal dislike to America and the Americans ever since the Forrest-Macready riot; and as everybody in America knew of the intimacy between Dickens and Macready, the riots, he believed, would be revived. He was certain there was no money in America, and, even if there were, Mr. Dickens would not get any of it; and if he *did,* the Irish (by some means I could not quite understand), and the booksellers, between them, would break into the hotel and rob him of it. Even if the money were deposited in a bank, the bank would fail on purpose.

Then the calculation of £15,500 profit in eighty Readings was, in Mr. Forster's opinion, all nonsense, as the halls were not large enough, and, even if they were, there were not people enough in America to produce such a result. Mr. Dickens's desire to increase his property in such a short space of time, and in such a way, was unworthy of him, or, in fact, of any man of genius, as the business of *reading* was a degrading one. Besides, had not the Americans taken Mr. Dickens's books without paying any author's fees; and why should they not do the same thing with the Readings?

The unreasonableness of these arguments, and the manner in which they were laid down, produced such an unpleasant effect on my mind that I felt relieved when Mr. Forster suggested that there "was no reason why the interview should be prolonged," as he had "fully made up *his* mind that Dickens should *never go to America again.*"

It was with a sense of relief that I heard the hotel waiter announce that luncheon was served, and with a much greater sense of satisfaction that I declined an invitation to partake of that meal, and so ended a most disagreeable colloquy.

As for Forster, his parting assurance was: "I shall write to Dickens by tonight's post, and tell him how fully I am opposed to the idea, and that he must give it up."

Leaving the oracle to his reflections and his lunch, I proceeded at once to the telegraph station, and sent the following telegram to Mr. Dickens: "I can make nothing of Forster; he is utterly unreasonable and impracticable. Come down here and stay at my house, and we will tackle him together."

Mr. Forster had kept his word and had sent his manifesto to Mr. Dickens, who on receipt of it telegraphed to me that he would come to Ross by the afternoon train, as suggested; but would stay with Forster at the hotel for fear of wounding his feelings.

I met Mr. Dickens on the arrival of the train, and conducted him to the hotel, leaving him in the care of his friend Forster, who displayed a considerable amount of chagrin at the action I had taken.

Next morning I learned from Mr. Dickens that Mr. Forster had conducted himself in the same unreasonable manner as before, leaving the matter where it was on the previous day.

It may be mentioned that Mr. Dickens had received a letter from Mr. Wills, taking a sensible business view of the case, and suggesting that everything should be left entirely in my hands, relieving Mr. Dickens of all responsibility, on the understanding that all precautions would be taken to make the enterprise a success.

When we returned to Mr. Forster he remarked at once, "I see it's of no use for me to say anything further on the subject, for by your faces it is plain you have made up your minds." Being assured that such was the case, he resignedly ordered lunch, and nothing more was said about the matter on that occasion. Later in the day Mr. Dickens returned to London, and then a sudden change came over Mr. Forster's spirit. These good qualities which had endeared him to Mr. Dickens's heart began to manifest themselves, leaving an impression in my mind that the churlishness displayed at our first interview was the outcome of his love and affection for Mr. Dickens and of an anxious desire for his welfare. The objections to the American tour were heard no more; but when Mr. Forster was leaving Ross, he gave me at the railway station a parting injunction to take care of Mr. Dickens, which would have been really comic, but for the earnestness with which it was delivered.

The word "Yes" was cabled to Messrs. Ticknor and Fields, and I was left to make the most speedy arrangements for my return to America, to carry out the work in which I took so much pleasure.

About three weeks sufficed for the necessary arrangements for my departure. All casualties in the future, so far as the American enterprise was concerned, had to be provided for; and as Mr. Dickens did not wish to be embarrassed with the details of money matters during the tour, he, with characteristic liberality, made such provisions for my requirements in this respect as would leave him free from monetary cares until the conclusion of the engagement.

On Saturday, October 12th, I left Liverpool in the Cunard steamer *China,* having secured for Mr. Dickens the second officer's room on the deck of the *Cuba,* which was to sail on the 9th November, under the command of Captain Stone. To Mr. Forster this arrangement was communicated early in October: "The *Scotia* being full, I do not sail until Lord Mayor's Day, for which glorious anniversary I have engaged an officer's cabin on deck in the *Cuba.* I am not in very brilliant spirits at the prospect before me; and am deeply sensible of your motive and reasons for the line you have taken; but I am not in the least shaken in the conviction that I could never quite have given up the idea."

So far as my voyage to America was concerned, it had no particular novelty about it, until the arrival of the *China* at Halifax. The enthusiasm of the American passengers was far in excess of that experienced in the first voyage, for now the Reading tour in America was a settled fact; and as the scheme had been largely discussed not only in the States, but amongst Americans in all parts of Europe, the excitement was unbounded; and many were the offers made in the *China* by men of position to "take a hand" in the speculation.

At Halifax, the alderman and councillors having heard of my arrival there, and that Mr. Dickens had determined to revisit America, again waited on me in the hope of extracting a promise that he would give one or more Readings in their city. It was not possible to give any definite premise, so the deputation decided to wait on Mr. Dickens personally, when they had an opportunity.

The *China* arrived at Boston at seven on the morning of Wednesday, October 23rd; and early as the hour was, all the old friends, with the "firm" at their head, were in waiting at the wharf to give me a hearty reception, and over a private breakfast on the steamer many sanguine hopes were expressed, which were happily fulfilled to the fullest extent.

During my absence from America, and during the return voyage, some ridiculous paragraphs had appeared in the English and American papers about Mr. Dickens's health, and also about an imaginary "interview," reported by the London correspondent of the "New York Tribune."

My reception in Boston was of the most encouraging character, and was really demonstrative on my appearance (as an invited guest), at the opening of the late Mr. Arthur Cheney's theatre (called Selwyn's Theatre, but since rechristened the Globe), on the Monday evening after my arrival; where men of every class and denomination in literary and art life, not only in Boston, but from New York and the other large cities in America, were represented.

On the receipt of the cablegram with a cabalistic "yes," Messrs. Ticknor and Fields (through their energetic partner, Mr. Osgood) had nearly perfected the tour arrangements, so far as securing the most important halls in the most important cities was concerned, leaving only matters of detail concerning the smaller cities, the advertisements, the printing of tickets, and the distribution of them, to be attended to. In the matter of printing the bills and posters, an unexpected difficulty presented itself in the fact that no paper of Mr. Dickens's favourite colour (a light orange) was to be found in America; and as he always used this paper in all his English enterprises, whether for the "contents' bills" of "All the Year Round" or for reading purposes, I (being desirous of making him feel that the Readings in America were identical with those in England) was naturally anxious to have all the familiar details reproduced as far as possible.

After a diligent search amongst the factories of the principal paper-makers, for the desired colour, and finding it was not to be obtained, a calculation was made as to the quantity likely to be required, and an order for two tons was given. This was quite unnecessary, for after Boston and New York had been "billed" for the first series of Readings in those cities, not a bill or poster was printed the whole of the American tour; and on its termination the unused stock was sold for more money than it originally cost.

The question of prices of admission had here to be taken into consideration, and as this matter was one on which a great deal depended in the future result of the enterprise, it was necessary to treat it with a great deal of caution. One authority gave it as his opinion that any charge over fifty cents a ticket with twenty-five cents extra for a reserved seat would be fatal to the success of the enterprise. Mr. James Gordon Bennett, as I have already said, believed, or affected to believe, that the public would eagerly fill every room in the country at ten dollars a ticket. Other persons suggested five dollars as being the proper price to adopt, and so on; until at last it became so evident that no one had any practical basis on which to found his calculations, that I decided on adopting a medium course, and fixed two dollars a ticket, to include a reserved seat, a decision that met with general approval as the results produced made clear.

The intervals of travelling and making advance arrangements for the coming tour, so as to leave me comparatively free when Mr. Dickens should arrive, were pleasantly spent in Boston, in constant meetings with such delightful men as Longfellow, Agassiz, Emerson, James Russell Lowell, Oliver Wendell Holmes, Dr. Hayes, Donald Mitchell, Bret Harte, James T. Fields, Osgood, Howard Ticknor, and all the other representatives of the firm. The time passed away in the most agreeable manner until the date announced for the first sale of tickets in Boston, which was fixed for Monday, November 18th, and two days before Mr. Dickens's expected arrival.

Since my parting with Mr. Dickens, many letters were received from him, either by myself or Mr. Fields; and in one of these, written before sailing, to Mr. Fields, he says, in reference to the banquet, already mentioned, and in connection with the various rumours afloat as to his intentions in revisiting the States: "You may have heard from Dolby that a gorgeous repast is to be given to me to-morrow, and that it is expected to be a notable demonstration; I shall try, in what I say, to state my American case exactly. I have a strong hope and belief that within the compass of a couple of minutes or so I can put it with perfect truthfulness in the light that my American friends would be best pleased to see me place it in. Either so, or my instinct is at fault."

Chapter Six - The Commencement of the American Tour

GREAT as was the excitement, on the announcement being made that Mr. Dickens would read in Boston, the fixing of the date for the first Reading, viz., Monday, December 2, 1867, seemed to increase that excitement tenfold; and especially when it was known that the first sale of tickets would take place at the publishing house of Messrs. Ticknor and Fields, No. 12, Tremont Street, Boston, on Monday morning, November 18th, at nine o'clock. Vague rumours were in circulation, and fears were entertained, that in the great excitement the general public would get no chance of buying tickets, for that the speculators, not only of Boston, but of New York, were making their plans to purchase all the tickets they could get, in the hope of selling them at a premium. These rumours caused a considerable amount of pressure to be put upon every one connected with the enterprise, by friends and acquaintances who wanted to have tickets beforehand, or at all events to have their places marked before the sale commenced; and so great was the demand in this respect, that Mr. Fields had on his list, on the night prior to the sale, orders for nearly 250 tickets for each of the first four Readings, and every one else connected in the firm was in a proportionately similar position. As such a course would have been obviously unfair to those persons who had no private influence with the "powers," I most distinctly declined to allow the sale to be conducted in any but a fair and straightforward manner, and decided that tickets for the course of the first four Readings only were to be sold the first day, and if any were left they were to be sold as required on the following days.

In addition to the private demand for tickets, I was beset in every conceivable manner, not only through the post, but by personal application from people who were, or who pretended to be, afflicted in a variety of ways, by deafness, blindness, paralysis; and all were anxious to avoid the trouble and annoyance of purchasing their tickets in the usual course. Strange to say, in consequence of their various afflictions they all wanted front seats, a demand it was impossible to comply with. I came to the conclusion that the afflicted ones formed a large proportion of the population of Boston.

On the evening prior to the sale, I was sleeping on the sofa in my room at the hotel, when a stranger suddenly burst in, and walking straight up to the sofa, proceeded to shake me violently. When I was thoroughly aroused, he commenced yelling, as if in the greatest pain. Then taking a chair, he consented to state his case, in the intervals of shouts and shrieks of the most horrible and painful description. He said that from childhood he had been subject to pains in his back, which rendered exposure to the cold air a dangerous operation. Under these circumstances, he considered it would be inhuman to expect him to take his place in the line in the morning, for the purpose of buying his ticket; and as he had a great desire to hear Mr. Dickens read, and as his family was large, it would be a great convenience to him and his family if he could have his tickets there and then.

Suspecting that the pains in the back were only a pretence for something else, I inquired how many persons his family consisted of, and expressed the hope that they were not similarly afflicted; suggesting that perhaps one of his sons (if he had any) could save the parent the pain of exposure in an inclement atmosphere, and so obtain the tickets for him.

He had no sons he could depend upon, he informed me, for such a duty; in fact his family were "mostly all" girls.

"How many tickets do you want for each Reading?" I inquired.

"Wall I guess I'll take a dozen for each Reading, or more, if you'll let me have them," he replied, "and pay right away for them."

On being informed that such a proceeding was impossible, and would be unjust to the persons who were purchasing tickets in the ordinary course, in fact that his request could not be complied with at all — pains in the back or no pains — but that if he would leave his address the tickets should be sent to him after the sale had commenced on the following day, he rose to retire, a proceeding that brought the pains back again with the accompanying shrieks, which continued all along the corridor of the hotel.

About an hour afterwards, the invalid was in perfect health at the bar of the hotel, and invited me to "take a drink" with him.

The invitation being declined, he informed me that he had come all the way from New York to buy tickets, and under the circumstances he thought it "mean" not to have supplied him considering his infirmity (here the pains in the back returned). Some of my friends being at the bar at the time, I joined them, cruelly leaving the sufferer to his pains and Bourbon whiskey. This beverage evidently had the effect of curing him, for at the sale of tickets on the following morning he was one of the earliest purchasers, and turned out to be one of the advance guard of the New York speculating brigade.

A timely notice having been given that no private applications for tickets on the first day's sale would be attended to, a crowd assembled on the night preceding the sale in Tremont Street, Boston, such as has never been seen before on an occasion of the kind. Intending purchasers sent their clerks, servants, and others to take their places outside the store of Messrs. Ticknor and Fields, as early as ten o'clock on the Sunday night, supplying each of them with a straw mattress, blankets, food, and in many cases with tobacco and creature comforts of an alcoholic description. As all sales of tickets for places of amusement and for railways in America are conducted as in France (*en queue*), the proceedings were of a most orderly character.

By eight o'clock in the morning the *queue* was nearly half a mile long, and about that time the employers of the persons who had been standing in the streets all night began to arrive and take their places. Some idea of the extent of the sale may be formed when it is mentioned that the sale lasted over eleven hours, and until every ticket for the first course of four Readings was disposed of. The receipts amounted to $14,000 (or in English money, allowing for the depreciation in greenbacks in converting them into gold, nearly £2,000), and but for the fact that for these first Readings in America a great many tickets had to be given away to the representatives of newspapers, not only all over America, but over nearly the whole civilized world, the receipts would have been much larger.

In the midst of the sale of tickets a telegram was placed in my hands from Halifax, announcing the arrival of the *Cuba* in that city, *en route* for Boston, with Mr. Dickens on board. When this telegram was read to the crowd, there was a terrific *furore,* and the news had the effect of considerably enhancing the value of the tickets that found their way into the hands of the speculators. As has been said, the price of the tickets was two dollars, but some of them that had fallen amongst the speculators, and represented good positions near the platform, were sold for as much as twenty-six dollars.

As the *Cuba* was expected at her wharf early on the following day (Tuesday, November 19th), in order to save Mr. Dickens the inconvenience of a public reception on his landing, after the fatigues of a long voyage, I took advantage of the kindly offer of Judge Russell and Captain Dolliver to place the U. S. Customs steamer, the *Hamblin,* at my disposal that I might meet the *Cuba* in the bay, and land him at Long Wharf, where carriages would be in waiting to convey him to the Parker House Hotel. Messrs. Fields, Ticknor, and Osgood were invited to join the party, and at about midday we started off on what may be called a winter's yachting excursion. As there was considerable uncertainty as to the precise time that the *Cuba* would appear, it was necessary to lay in some stores and creature comforts for the trip. The weather was terribly cold, the first herald of what proved an exceptionally hard winter. Hour after hour passed away and no sign of the *Cuba* was apparent, and after some hours of knocking and buffeting about in the sea in search of her, it was decided, whilst the daylight still lasted, to land at the signal station at Hull, in Boston Harbour, to see if, by the assistance of the powerful telescopes in use at the station, we could discern the steamer.

Having landed and struggled up the side of the high hill on which the signal station is placed, we found ourselves in the presence of a large staff of newspaper men, who had been sent there to report the advent of the *Cuba.* These gentlemen were nearly frozen to death, and almost at starvation point, having been at their post since early morning with no house of entertainment within reasonable distance. Some one (it was Mr. Osgood, I think) suggested that in summer there was an hotel open about a mile away, and as the Cuba was nowhere to be seen, and as she could not under the most favourable circumstances (even if she appeared then) make the land where we were under an hour and a half, a pilgrimage to the hotel was decided on. Away we went, press-men and all, in search of the place, only to find on arrival there that the house was shut and deserted for the winter, the only sign of anything to eat being the brick kiln in which the "clams" were baked in the season.

Our stock of eatables on the *Hamblin* had long been exhausted, and only some liqueurs remained; two bottles of champagne had been reserved with which to drink Mr. Dickens's health on his arrival, and a little brandy remained. These with a few biscuits were all we had to give to the press gentlemen, and they very soon made short work of them, returning to their duties at the top of the hill. It was our time now to be starved, and after many conjectures as to what had become of the Cuba, whether Captain Stone had lost his way in the Bay of Fundy (for we knew he had left Halifax the previous day), or whether the ship had got into trouble, and what not, with night closing in upon us, matters began to look a little serious. Mr. Osgood, always equal to an occasion, suggested that, as I was intimate with Captain Moodie (whose ship, the *Java,* was lying in the harbour, having gone into the stream to make room for the *Cuba*), we should board his ship and ask for food and shelter until the *Cuba* came up to Boston. This suggestion was acted on, and in coming alongside the good old ship we were received by a greeting on the part of the officers on duty which could not have been more hearty or more sincere had we been shipwrecked mariners instead of hungry and half-frozen landsmen.

My first inquiry was, "Where is the captain?"

"In his room, aft, sir."

A procession being formed, we marched thither to find one of the best and most genial of men taking his last glass of grog before setting sail for home the next day (although they may be *bon vivants* on shore, most of the Cunard captains and officers are strict temperance men at sea). As all the party were personally known to Captain Moodie, it was only necessary to make our wants known to him for them to be instantly supplied; and it has been a marvel to me to the present day how so sumptuous a meal could have been produced in so short a time.

The saloon seemed to be lighted up, and the stewards in their places, as if by magic; indeed, we had scarcely time to finish a glass of grog with the skipper before supper was announced; and when we got well to work at it, and had time to express our opinion about anything, we all came to the conclusion that there never had been and never would be such another supper again. The captain, with his dear old beaming face, of course took the head of the table, and seeing that we were enjoying ourselves so much, went in for a second supper himself. The cloth having been removed, and the kettle of boiling water, with glasses and toddy ladles, with a bottle of fine old Scotch whiskey (a rarity in the States), having been placed on the table, the party settled themselves down to await the arrival of the *Cuba* with a considerable degree of resignation.

Scarcely had the first glass of toddy been disposed of, and a discussion commenced as to the advisability of tackling a second one (some of the party did not discuss the matter, but *took* it), when the look-out man reported the

"*Cuba* in sight." A rush was made for the deck, and for the *Hamblin,* and after hasty "good-byes "and thanks to Moodie, we cast away and steamed towards the *Cuba.* Moodie had made up his mind to be the first to salute his country-man Dickens on his arrival in America, and did so with a perfect shower of rockets as the *Cuba* passed his ship.

Whether Captain Stone was in a hurry to make up for lost time in the only half-mile he had yet to run before getting to his wharf or not, I cannot say, but he disregarded the signals of the Customs boat, and went along as if he were going to run Boston down. Away we went puffing after him, and mak-ing the harbour hideous by the shrieks of the *Hamblin's* steam whistle, all to no avail. The big ship looked like a floating village, with all her port-holes lighted up, and owing to her superior speed we had fears that we should not be able to board her after all, and so release Mr. Dickens before the *Cuba* got to her wharf. Fortune, however, favoured us, to the inconvenience of Captain Stone and his passengers, inasmuch as when he did slacken speed, and was within fifty yards of the wharf, the *Cuba* took a fancy to a mud-bank, and there she stuck for some hours! the passengers having to remain on board all night, much to the discomfort of their friends on the wharf, who were really within hailing distance of them.

As we came alongside the *Cuba* at last, I heard the old familiar voice calling me by name. Here was really my old Chief, who had an idea in his head, as he said afterwards, that "Dolby will pick me up from a pilot boat, or some other impossible place between Halifax and Boston." The *Cuba* was snorting, blow-ing off steam, backing and trying all she knew to get off the soft mud bed in which she was resting; and in all the confusion, it seemed a lifetime before the plank was lowered, to enable me and our friends to get on board of her. At last all was right, and I had the unspeakable delight of being once more face to face, after a hearty greeting, with the best and dearest friend man ev-er had. Nor was the greeting between Fields and Dickens less hearty, for they were old friends, and had a sincere love for one another. Then the party left the ship for the quiet wharf, where a carriage had been in waiting for some hours. There was an addition to our number in the person of a young friend of the late Lord Lytton (Mr. Lowndes), who had been recommended to the care of Mr. Dickens by his noble friend.

This gentleman only remained with us for a few days, having a diplomatic appointment which took him to British Columbia.

Arrived at the Parker House Hotel, there was a perfect ovation awaiting Mr. Dickens, for the news had spread to the city, and the disappointed ones on the wharf, having heard that Mr. Dickens had given them the slip, ran or drove to the Parker House, so as to catch a glimpse of him as he entered his hotel. Mr. Parker and Mr. Mills (the proprietors of the hotel) were there, as were also all the notabilities of Boston, besides the ordinary crowd to be found in a large American hotel in the evening. Through such a crowd as this, Mr. Dickens made his way, escorted by his friends, to his apartments, which, being in a quiet corner (high up) of the hotel, gave him immense satisfaction.

Messrs. Parker and Mills had provided an excellent supper, which, albeit it was the second most of us had partaken of that evening, was enjoyed immensely; and at an early hour our guests retired, leaving my Chief and myself alone to discuss matters over a tumbler of the old brew of punch and a cigar.

Home matters and news of home took precedence of everything else, as it always did with him. His domesticity and mine were the first things to be discussed; then came his account of the voyage, from the time of leaving London to the time of our meeting, with any theatrical and musical news which he thought would be interesting to me up to that time.

The voyage, but for the delay caused by head winds in the Bay of Fundy, between Halifax and Boston, would have been considered in those days a rapid one. Captain Stone and Mr. Dickens had become very friendly, a circumstance not to be wondered at but for the well-known reticence of the captain, who was known as "Silent Stone;" and to such an extent had Mr. Dickens conquered him, that on the last day of the voyage he not only induced the captain to sing several songs after dinner in the saloon, but persuaded him to take part with himself in the duet "All's Well," and to make a speech. He recounted to me in a comical manner (if such a term can be used in connection with the subject) the circumstances under which Church Service was held on the only Sunday of the voyage (Sunday, November 17th).

There was a very heavy sea, and the ship was rolling tremendously. It is usual for the captain or the doctor to read the service, unless there happens to be a clergyman on board, in which case he is invited to officiate. On this occasion a pale young curate was amongst the passengers, and, being requested to perform the service, he amiably assented, without in the least calculating on his sea-going powers, or even his sea-legs, to carry out his good intention. When the time for service arrived, 11 a.m. (and a most impressive time it is at sea, with the fore and aft bells going to call the passengers together), the officiating clergyman was brought into the saloon by two stalwart stewards supporting him (to use Mr. Dickens's own words) as if they were "bringing him up to the scratch for a prize fight."

The congregation (passengers, and such of the officers and crew whose watch it was below) were all seated, so that there ought to have been plenty of room on the floor of the saloon for the reverend gentleman and his supporters. Such, however, proved not to be the case, for the mizen-mast was unfortunately in the way, rendering it necessary to watch very carefully the rolling of the ship before this could be cleared. An opportunity presenting itself, the stewards took advantage of it to relieve themselves of their charge, and literally shot him between two tables to the reading-desk (consisting of some sofa cushions placed on the table). Then commenced fresh difficulties, for the clergyman found it hard to keep his legs (when standing up), added to which the reading-desk and the books kept moving about, and the congregation also began to roll off their seats, thus making what under ordinary circumstances is a solemn and impressive occasion exceedingly funny.

During the recounting of this episode in his voyage I could not but see that he was very depressed in spirits, which I ascribed to fatigue, and under ordinary conditions I should have bid him "good-night," but I was anxious to have a talk with him about the coming enterprise, a subject I found him reluctant to discuss. He had been annoyed at supper by the waiters leaving the door of the sitting-room partially open, that the promenaders in the corridor of the hotel might take a peep at him, through the crack between the door and the doorpost, whilst he was sitting at table. This curiosity made an unpleasant impression in his mind, and caused him to regret that he had not adhered to his original determination never to visit America again; for, he said, "These people have not in the least changed during the last five and twenty years — they are doing now exactly what they were doing then." But here I reminded him that he had not been three hours in the country, and that he had not seen the people or even a house in the daylight, and I begged him to withhold any criticism on the subject until he had had better opportunities of judging, when I felt sure his opinion would change. After this the prospects of the success of the enterprise were discussed, and although he had heard from the pilot, who had met the *Cuba* early in the morning, of the success of the first sale of tickets on the previous day, he was totally unprepared for the figures I placed before him, and was more than amazed at the result of the sale. His pleasure, as he stated at the time, was not attributable to any feeling of avarice, but the compliment paid to him by the American people — for up to that time very few (and only those who had heard him read in Europe) had any idea what the Readings were like. Until Mr. Dickens read in America the public idea of a Reading was of a person reading from a book the work of some author other than himself; and it was only fair to suppose that when the author himself pourtrayed his own creations in his own way (and the *favourite* author of the American people too), the excitement would increase, and that, great as were the prospects in Boston, they would be equally as great, and if possible greater, in every city we visited on the tour. With this flattering hope we parted for the night, and so ended the day of arrival in America of Charles Dickens in 1867, a day memorable not only to me, but to many dear friends he has left behind him there to mourn his loss.

In arranging the plan for the American tour, provision was made to enable Mr. Dickens to become acclimatized and to recover from the effects of his voyage before commencing hard work. For this purpose ten days were allowed from the time of his arrival to the date of the first Reading in Boston. Some slight misapprehension existed as to the reason why Boston was selected as the first Reading city in the States, in preference to New York. The reason was to be found in the fact that Mr. Dickens always regarded Boston as his American home, inasmuch as all his literary friends lived there, and he felt it to be only due to them that he should make that his starting-place, and especially so as it was on the earnest recommendation of his friends Messrs. Ticknor and Fields that he renewed and entertained the idea of reading in America.

As results proved, the ten days allowed for rest were quite unnecessary, and instead of being a relief to Mr. Dickens was a cause of some mental irritation to him, for he felt he was losing time and was eager to commence reading. His friends in Boston vied with each other to make the days pass pleasantly, and had it been possible to go to three or four dinner parties a day and as many breakfasts, luncheons, and suppers, these hospitalities would have been forthcoming. He felt, however, that the purposes for which he was in America were all important, and with a view to saving himself for those purposes he made a point of declining most invitations, accepting only those given him by his friends Fields and Professor Longfellow.

The day following his arrival, the latter called on him, as did also Messrs. Emerson and Agassiz and Dr. Oliver Wendell Holmes, all of whom he met the following day at a dinner party at the house of Mr. Fields. With this exception, he accepted no invitations for great dinners, but passed his time in long walks with Fields (to Cambridge, one day, to call on Longfellow) or in paying little visits to his friends, merely partaking of a luncheon with them, or joining them in a family tea.

Two days after Mr. Dickens's arrival, I had to leave him for New York, where the first sale of tickets for the first four Readings there was announced for the following week (Friday and Saturday the 29th and 30th).

On my arrival in New York, to make preparations for our first sale of tickets in that city, indications pointed to a still greater *furore* there than in Boston; and as a result of inquiry I ascertained that the speculating fraternity were making active arrangements for securing all the best seats in the house, when the ticket-office should be opened.

I had engaged a ticket clerk in Boston (one Marshal P. Wild), and taking him and my English agent in advance with me, proceeded to make preparations for the sale, a matter of no small importance, when it is considered that the Steinway Hall (in which Mr. Dickens was to read) seated two thousand five hundred persons. This hall, like every other hall and theatre in America, is perfect in its arrangements. Every seat in the house is numbered, and each seat is spacious and comfortable and provided with arms, so that it is not possible for two persons to take up the space of three, as in too many cases in England. The rows of seats are alphabetically arranged from A to Z, and then begin the double As, double Bs, and so on (the separate seats in each row being numerically defined). There are spacious passage-ways intersecting the hall, and the tickets are all marked R and L (for right and left), so that a ticket-holder knows exactly where to find his seat; thus preventing scenes of confusion such as are frequently witnessed in places of entertainment in England. This system necessitates the printing and numbering of each seat *separately,* and for this particular occasion ten thousand tickets were so prepared, and had to be checked and arranged in rows for each of the four Readings announced; in addition to this, each ticket had to be stamped with our own private stamp, as it had come to my knowledge that an enterprising individual had become possessed of a "proof" of our tickets, and had actually got some printed with the intention of imposing on the public. This information was given to me by the largest speculator in New York, who also supplied me with the name and address of the printer employed to print the bogus ticket. This printer was a highly respectable man, and on my representing to him the case I ascertained that he had been duped by an unscrupulous person, representing himself as my agent, and he instantly in my presence "broke up" his type and destroyed all the tickets he had printed (some thousands), and, appealing to the police authorities, made the unscrupulous one pay largely for his folly.

The arranging and stamping of our tickets became a matter of some days' labour for my little staff, but it was excellently done, and not a difficulty occurred from this cause at our first sale.

After a run back to Boston (a little journey of nine hours) to arrange some matters of detail in connection with the first Reading there, and to see how my Chief was getting along, I returned to New York with Mr. Osgood, who had kindly undertaken the duties of treasurer to the enterprise, and thus left me free to go and do as I liked, without being trammelled by account keeping.

The scene in Boston was as nothing compared with the scene in New York, for the line of purchasers exceeded half a mile in length. The line commenced to form at ten o'clock on the night prior to the sale, and here were to be seen the usual mattresses and blankets in the cold streets, and the owners of them vainly endeavouring to get some sleep — an impossibility under the circumstances; for, leaving the bitter cold out of the question, the singing of songs, the dancing of breakdowns, with an occasional fight, made night hideous, not only to the peaceful watcher, but to the occupants of the houses in front of which the disorderly band had established itself.

These ladies and gentlemen had my sincere sympathies; for my hotel was within fifty yards of the scene of action, and the shouting, shrieking, and singing of the crowd suggested the night before an execution at the Old Bailey, when executions were still public.

Under the circumstances it was not difficult to be up betimes in the morning, especially as all through the night I was receiving visits from the most prominent of the speculators, who were desirous to know what my plan of action was to be when the sale *did* commence: a subject I was not communicative upon (indeed, had no fixed plan myself, as will be hereafter explained). The anxiety of these gentlemen on the subject, and a friendly chat over a glass of brandy-and-water, convinced me that the speculative element was more largely represented in that line of human beings, certainly amongst those nearest the ticket-office, than amongst the legitimate purchasers, and decided me in taking my friend, Mr. Palmer (whose experience in such matters was invaluable), into my counsels, to consider the best mode of baffling, if possible, the speculators' designs, and giving the general public a fair chance of getting good seats.

The sale was announced to commence at nine o'clock; at eight I turned out with Mr. Palmer, Mr. Osgood, and Captain Garland (the police captain of the precinct), followed by such of our staff as could be spared, and the "boss" speculators, to walk along the line and to inspect the forces, in order to see who were speculators' agents and who were not. At this time merchants or their clerks began to arrive and take the places of those who had been keeping them warm (!) for them all through the night, thus changing the appearance of the force inspected from that of a rabble to that of a most respectable community.

We ascertained, from observation during the inspection, that certainly forty-five out of the first fifty men in the line were speculators' representatives, and a closer observation showed to us that nearly all these men wore caps. Here was an idea, suggested, I think, by Palmer. "Sell only at the first 'go off' six tickets for each Reading, to men in hats" (it may be mentioned that, as at Boston, tickets were only sold on the first day for the course of four Readings then announced), "and turn out those who come to the ticket-office in caps," a proceeding which seemed a little rough on the poor fellows who had been standing out in the cold the whole night; but at the same time necessary for the carrying out of Mr. Dickens's desire and principle of giving the public a fair chance in all matters in which he was concerned.

When the time for opening the ticket-office arrived, and the police passed the word along the line that "four tickets only for each Reading would be sold to each person, and those only to people in hats," the consternation amongst the speculators was great. They, however, were equal to the occasion, for in the lapse of a few moments they had collected all the hats they could from waiters and others in neighbouring restaurants and other places, and by means of changing a hat for a cap at the entrance-door to the ticket-office, the speculators contrived to get into their possession the greater portion of the first seven or eight rows of seats in the hall.

By two o'clock in the afternoon of the first day, every ticket was sold, and the amount taken was something over $16,000 for the first four Readings. At the last moment I had suppressed nearly four hundred tickets for each Reading; for, although the Steinway Hall is a very fine one, and perfect in every respect for musical performances, I did not feel sure of it for the purposes of the Readings, as at the back of the first and second galleries there were large square recesses, each of them holding four hundred persons; and my idea was, after Mr. Dickens had seen the hall, and had tested its acoustic qualities (in which operation he was an adept), that he would wish to have these recesses closed in, and by so doing improve the hall for speaking purposes, and also give it a more snug appearance from the platform. A suggestion to this effect was made by myself to Mr. Steinway, who, with characteristic liberality, at once entered into my ideas, and immediately gave an order for panelled shutters to be made, and to be in readiness for Mr. Dickens's arrival at the end of the following week.

The suppression of these four hundred tickets assisted the speculators' trade immensely, and before the sale had progressed two hours the speculators were selling the best seats at enormous premiums. One man (one of the first purchasers), who wished to be present at the first Reading only, sold the remaining three tickets for the first Reading and two tickets for the second, third, and fourth, for fifty dollars and a brandy cock-tail (about £7 10s.), a profit of ten dollars, not to mention the advantage of getting his ticket for the first Reading for *nothing,* with four tickets in hand for the other Readings.

On the following night, I returned to my Chief in Boston, so as to be ready for the first Reading there on the following Monday (December 2nd); but not before I had discovered myself to be, as Dickens described me, "the best abused man in America."

The Rush for Tickets for the Dickens Readings in New York
From a contemporary print.

Despite my precautions, the sale of tickets in New York had given universal dissatisfaction, the public connecting me with the speculators' trade, and without in the least taking the trouble to "look at home;" for the Wall Street brokers, merchants, lawyers, and private individuals became even greater speculators (with their surplus tickets) than the ordinary practitioners. Leading articles of the most abusive kind were written about me, notably in the "New York Herald" and the "World," the latter paper remarking, "Surely it is time that the pudding-headed Dolby retired into the native gloom from which he has emerged;" a suggestion which caused the greatest amusement to myself and Mr. Dickens, and gained for me afterwards (amongst our friends) the initials "P. H." The "Tribune," "Times," and other leading newspapers took no notice of the correspondence showered into their offices on this subject; for Mr. Horace Greeley had detected, with his usual astuteness, that the letters and articles were instigated by the speculators themselves, who, in view of a second sale of tickets about to take place after the first Reading in New York, for a second course of four Readings, would have been glad to get matters more into their own hands than they were able to do at the first sale; and the success attending their first effort had made them eager for the second, in proof of which, during the early part of the first day's sale, they were offering "twenty dollars for anybody's place" on the line (an offer which in no instance was accepted). All kinds of suggestions were made as to the manner in which the future sales should be conducted, and amongst others was one that the tickets should be sold (in sets) by auction (with a reserve price of two dollars, a ticket) a proceeding which would have greatly benefited the enterprise, but would have been inconsistent with Mr. Dickens's principle, never to receive more than the advertised price for the tickets, and would also have laid him or myself open to the charge of collusion with the speculators.

On my return to Boston, early on the morning of Sunday, December 1st, I found Mr. Dickens had been passing his time wearily (for him), and was looking forward to the following evening to commence the campaign. This weariness would have been unbearable to him but for the social intercourse with his friend Fields. The result of the sale of tickets in New York was an additional source of satisfaction to him, and he was immensely amused at the descriptions I gave him of the incidents of the sale, at the same time he had fears that the speculating mania would act prejudicially on the enterprise. At first he was greatly shocked and pained at the correspondence and the "leaders" in the newspapers; but this feeling gave place to one of hilarity when I explained to him the source from which the articles emanated, and, like myself, he regarded them as so much gratuitous advertisement.

A mass of correspondence was awaiting me, containing offers of engagement for Readings from Canada, Nova Scotia, and the outlying places in the far West, all of which had to be attended to and respectfully declined, for we had decided on not accepting any offer, no matter how brilliant. In addition to these, there were over two hundred letters, containing requests for Mr. Dickens's autograph. A quiet morning was devoted to the despatch of such business as could be got through; and in the afternoon, at the request of Judge Russell, a visit was made to the school-ship, where, after the afternoon service, Mr. Dickens made his first speech, on this his second visit to America, to the boys who were in training there, giving them words of encouragement and counsel as to their future lives, such as he only could give — words equally encouraging and hopeful to the elder members of the congregation, and bringing tears to the eyes of many, both great and small. On his departure from the ship, the boys manned the yards, and, notwithstanding that it was Sunday, they gave him a ringing cheer as the little *Hamblin* puffed away from her larger sister.

The day following was devoted to preparing for the evening's Reading, some hours being spent in the superintendence of the erection of the screen, gas arrangements, and the fixing of the little reading-table. The Tremont Temple had to be tested acoustically, a process that was always gone through in every new room in which he read.

The process was very simple, and was conducted in the following manner. Mr. Dickens used to stand at his table, whilst I walked about from place to place in the hall or theatre, and a conversation in a low tone of voice was carried on between us during my perambulations. The hall having been pronounced perfect, a long walk was undertaken; and after a four o'clock dinner (as in England) and a sleep of an hour or so, we went to the Tremont Temple for the great event of the day.

The Readings selected were, the "Christmas Carol" and the "Trial from Pickwick." The audience was of the most brilliant description, being composed of all the notabilities in Boston, literary and artistic, added to which New York had supplied its contingent from the same sources, and had further sent to Boston a staff of newspaper men to report, by telegraph, columns of description of the first Reading, so that on Tuesday, December 3rd, not only had all the Boston papers a full account, but so had also the New York papers — a compliment which was highly appreciated by Mr. Dickens.

The reception accorded to Mr. Dickens, in making his appearance at the little table, had never been surpassed by the greetings he was in the habit of receiving in Edinburgh and Manchester, and was calculated to unnerve a man of even greater moral courage than he was possessed of. Those who were not applauding and waving handkerchiefs were seriously "taking in" the appearance of the man to whom they owed so much, which up to this time they knew only by the bad photographs in the shop windows. These, by the way, were so wonderfully *unlike* him, that, later on, I prevailed on him to sit to Mr. Ben Gurney in New York, who succeeded in producing the only good photograph of him in existence. It was to this artist only, and then only once, that he gave a sitting in America.

When everything was quiet, and the deafening cheers which had greeted his appearance had subsided, a terrible silence prevailed, and it seemed a relief to his hearers when he at last commenced the Reading. The effect of the first few words (without any prefatory remark): "A Christmas Carol in four staves. Stave one, Marley's Ghost. Marley is dead to begin with. There is no doubt whatever about *that.* The register of his burial was signed by the clergyman, the clerk, the undertaker, and the chief mourner. Scrooge signed it, and Scrooge's name was good upon 'Change for anything he chose to put his hand to," placed the reader and his audience on good terms with one another, the audience settling itself down in rapt attention for what was to follow; and by the time the first chapter was finished the success of the Readings, certainly so far as Boston was concerned, was an accomplished fact.

During the progress of the Reading I was moving about in various parts of the hall and its galleries by the many entrance doors, watching the effect of the Reading on the audience, and gauging the acoustic properties of the Tremont Temple, reporting myself by arrangement at the side of the screen at the end of the second chapter, where a brief conversation, carried on in an "aside" during the applause, was held between the reader and myself:

Mr. Dickens. Is it all right?

Myself. All right.

Mr. Dickens. Hall good?

Myself. Excellent; go a-head, sir.

Mr. Dickens. I will, when they'll let me.

Myself. First-rate audience.

Mr. Dickens. I know it.

Brief and hurried as was this "aside," it seemed to give him greater confidence in depicting the scenes in the third chapter, and in all my experiences with him, I never knew him to read the description of the Cratchit Christmas dinner with so much evident enjoyment to himself, and with so much relish to his audience. When at last the Reading of "The Carol" was finished, and the final words had been delivered, and "so, as Tiny Tim observed, God bless us every one," a dead silence seemed to prevail — a sort of public sigh as it were — only to be broken by cheers and calls, the most enthusiastic and uproarious, causing Mr. Dickens to break through his rule, and again presenting himself before his audience, to bow his acknowledgments.

No one but myself (and his servant Scott) was ever allowed (except on rare occasions) to go into his dressing-room during the interval between his first and second Reading, but on this evening Fields had been invited to do so. He, on entering the room, exclaimed, "You have given me a new lease of life, for I have been so looking forward to this occasion that I have had an idea all day that I should die at five minutes to eight to-night, and be deprived of a longing desire I have had to hear you read in my country for the last nineteen years."

A hearty embrace and a glass of champagne convinced Fields that he was still in this life (would that he were so now!); and after a lapse of a few minutes (ten minutes only being allowed for the interval), Mr. Dickens returned to the table to make his audience shriek with laughter, and revel in the pourtrayal of the humorous characters in the far-famed Reading of the "Trial from Pickwick," which had been given by him so often in England, that he often strayed away from the actual text, and indulged in the habit of an occasional "gag." As nearly every line of "Pickwick" was as well-known to the audience as to himself (for in Boston nearly every man, woman, and child, was a "Pickwickian," certainly so far as their knowledge of the book was concerned), these occasional liberties with the text were the more enjoyed, and, being invariably taken on the spur of the moment, were regarded more in the light of a new edition, direct from the author, than anything else.

In this particular Reading, he had full scope for the impersonation of each of the characters he represented, and with his dramatic instincts he took advantage of the situation and gave himself up to the delineation of those characters, a circumstance which in one instance did *not* give entire satisfaction.

During the progress of this Reading, I was engaged in conversation with one of my staff at the foot of the stairs leading to the hall, when my attention was drawn to a gentleman coming down the stairs in a most excited state. Imagining him to be ill and wanting assistance, I said, "What's the matter with *you?*" From, the accent of his reply, I concluded that he was a "reg'lar down Easter."

"Say, who's that man on the platform reading?"

"Mr. Charles Dickens," I replied.

"But that ain't the *real* Charles Dickens, the man as wrote all them books I've been reading all these years."

"The same."

After a moment's pause, as if for thought, he replied, "Wall, all I've got to say about it then is, that he knows no more about Sam Weller 'n a cow does of pleatin' a shirt, at all events that ain't *my* idea of Sam Weller, anyhow."

After the delivery of this speech he clapped his hat on his head, and left the building in a state of high dudgeon.

The Reading being concluded, and the most enthusiastic signs of approval having been accorded to the Reader in the form of recall after recall, Mr. Dickens indulged in his usual "rub down," changing his dress-clothes for those he habitually wore when not *en grande tenue,* and a few of his most intimate friends were admitted into his dressing-room to offer their congratulations on the result of the evening's experiences, and great was their surprise to find themselves in the presence of a highly refined "Pegotty," rather than in that of the polished gentleman they had been listening to for the past two hours.

After the fatigue and excitement of the Readings in America (although on this particular evening he declared he was as cool and collected as if he had been reading in Greenwich), it was his great pleasure to have a few friends to supper with him at the hotel, and on this occasion Mr. and Mrs. Fields, and some others joined our supper party — friends whose judgment could be relied upon — when all agreed that never before had anything in Boston called forth such enthusiasm as that night's Reading had done, an assurance that gave Mr. Dickens the greatest satisfaction.

The following evening's Reading was, if possible, a greater success ("David Copperfield" and "Mr. Bob Sawyer's Party") than the Reading on the previous evening. Before the announcement of the Readings in Boston, an intimation had reached me that the "pirates" had decided in sending shorthand writers to the Readings to "take them down" as they progressed, with a view to their reproduction and sale — an intimation which was conveyed to Messrs. Ticknor and Fields; and they promptly anticipated such a proceeding by at once issuing the Readings (taken from Mr. Dickens's own reading books) in small volumes, and selling them at their store at such a price as made it impossible for the "pirates" to get anything out of their publication.

It is not necessary to go through in detail the features of the first four Readings in Boston. As in England, only four Readings were given in each week, viz., Mondays, Tuesdays, Thursdays, and Fridays; leaving Wednesday, Saturday, and Sunday for rest when no travelling had to be done. Later on in the tour, it not unfrequently happened we had to travel, as in England, on the day a Reading had to be given, but this only when short journeys had to be undertaken (from three to four hours), towards the end of the tour. Letters containing offers of engagements kept pouring in, and the autograph nuisance became greater than ever. As each of the autograph hunters enclosed a postage stamp affixed to an addressed envelope for reply, it became absolutely necessary that some notice should be taken of the application.

This difficulty was overcome by means of a printed circular, signed by myself and sent to the applicant, informing him (or her) that "compliance with the request contained in the letter received was not reasonably possible."

Before adopting this plan, I consulted a well-known and highly popular author in Boston as to what course *he* pursued under similar circumstances. He replied, "I invariably, when the writer of the letter is not known to me, throw the letter into my waste-paper basket, and use the stamp enclosed for my personal correspondence; and it is surprising how soon this fact becomes known, and how few letters of a similar kind I receive now."

The success of the Readings in Boston, and the prospects of the same success repeating itself in New York, decided us in changing our plan of tour. A reference to the "Case in a Nutshell" will show that the original idea was to give eighty Readings in all in America, these to include Canada and Nova Scotia, whence it was intended to set sail for England. The early success, added to the prophecies of the "knowing ones" in matters of weather (notably. Dr. Hayes the Arctic explorer, who was one of our constant associates), that the winter would be one of unexampled severity; the facts that Mr. Dickens had caught a severe cold thus early in the proceedings, and that the discomfort in travelling was not calculated to improve his condition; — all these things decided him to limit our scene of action as much as possible, and not to go farther south than Washington, farther west than Chicago, or farther north than Portland, taking in the New England cities *en route*. This plan included Albany, Syracuse, Rochester, Buffalo, and a pleasure trip to Niagara, and was designed to induce the public to come to Mr. Dickens rather than that he should go to them. The comparatively small number of Readings that had to be given, with the prospects of success, justified us in thus cutting down the tour list.

Chapter Seven - Christmas and the New Year in the States

ON Saturday, December 7th, we left our kind friends in Boston for our first railway journey to New York, and great was the crowd to say "good-bye" to the one they all loved so dearly. This journey was undertaken by the Shore Line Route, the most convenient as to the hours of departure in the morning, a matter to be thought of when it is considered that the distance from Boston to New York is about 240 miles, and the time occupied in performing this journey (by express train) is nine hours. This time would be considerably reduced if the train had not to cross two wide rivers, one at Stonnington and the other at New London, this causing a delay of certainly one hour on the journey; although everything is done to make the inconvenience as light as possible, by running the train on to the ferry boat (in which is an excellent restaurant), and conveying it across the river bodily, without troubling the passengers to move from their seats, unless they wish to do so.

New York was reached at six in the evening, Mr. Dickens being very tired, and his cold showing signs of taking an influenza turn.

I had secured a suite of apartments for him at the Westminster Hotel, where he was hospitably received by my friend Harry Palmer, and his partner, George Roberts; and an excellent dinner having been disposed of, we took a little turn round in the gas-lighted streets, just to refresh his memory, if possible, of New York, and to see if he could make out in what part of the city he was located; all to no avail, for in the twenty-five years which had elapsed since his first visit there. Union Square and Fourteenth Street scarcely existed.

The mass of correspondence awaiting me, not to mention the preparations for another sale of tickets on the following Wednesday, suggested an "all night sitting" by myself in the hope of getting through some of the work before the morrow, when I knew I should have to be on duty with my Chief the whole day. I found a hundred or more letters from the autograph collectors, which for the time being had to be put on one side, to make place for the enormous correspondence consequent on so gigantic an enterprise. And as Mr. Dickens, during his stay in America, made it a rule of never opening a letter addressed to himself (except his European letters, and those addressed in the well-known handwriting of one of his friends), my labours were at times a little perplexing; especially as, if at any time I referred any matter to him, he invariably met such reference with the remark, "Do as you like," which did not in the least ease my mind.

After breakfast the following morning, the first thing to be done was an inspection of Steinway Hall, about which he had evinced the greatest curiosity and anxiety, not feeling at all sure that he would like it, from the description I had given of it. I had said nothing to him about the provision I had made for enclosing the recesses.

The hall being reached, it did not in the least surprise me that he was very dissatisfied with it, declaring that it was next to impossible to produce any effect in so large a place, especially with those big open recesses at the back of the galleries, where all the sound would go and stop when it got there. The first feeling of disappointment and annoyance having passed off, we proceeded to test the acoustic properties of the hall in the usual way, and, to Mr. Dickens's amazement, it was found to be *perfect;* and depressed as he was in spirits on first seeing the hall, his spirits rose immense when I told him of the arrangements I had made for shutting in the objectionable recesses; and but for the attack of influenza from which he was suffering, the prospect of success, in his imagination, would have been as great in New York as it had been in Boston.

We spent a quiet day together in walking about the city and in driving in the Central Park, which was a source of great pleasure to him. He was very much struck with the alterations that had taken place in the city since his first visit there, and especially in the extension of Broadway, pointing out to me that the spot where Wallack's Theatre (now the "Germania") stood was quite a suburb at the time.

His delight in the Westminster Hotel was unbounded. Mr. Palmer, with thoughtful consideration, had hired specially a French waiter for our service, and had "told off" a boy to be in attendance outside the sitting-room door in order to prevent intrusion on Mr. Dickens's privacy; and, in addition, had arranged that he was to have the exclusive use of a private staircase leading from a private door, so that he could come in and go out without fear of molestation. No wonder then that the Westminster Hotel, in Irving Place, became our postal address for all our correspondence, and our domicile whilst in America. The apartments were furnished to suit Mr. Dickens's taste, and two writing-tables with lock-up drawers were placed side by side (one for Mr. Dickens and one for myself), so that we could work together without the inconvenience of running from room to room, in the event of any question having to be referred.

The success of the Readings in New York far exceeded Mr. Dickens's most sanguine expectations, and but for the extra exertion in reading in so large a hall as the Steinway, under the burden of an influenza cold, everything would have been in the highest degree satisfactory. He described the New York audience as being "far better than that at Boston," which was saying a great deal for them.

On Wednesday, December 11th, the second sale of tickets was held in New York for four more Readings announced for the following week, when the same features presented themselves as on the occasion of the first sale, only in a more exaggerated form, with the additional inconvenience to those who had to stand out in the streets all night to secure good places in the line. They were in position long before the Reading of Tuesday evening the 1oth was over. The thermometer had fallen to several degrees below zero (Reaumur), and signs were not wanting that a heavy fall of snow was imminent. The speculators were in greater force than ever, the New York brigade being augmented by contingents from Brooklyn, Philadelphia, and Jersey City, all of whom had taken temporary offices in New York, for the disposal of the tickets at handsome premiums. Some of these gentry had attired themselves in fancy costumes, one of them being made up like George Washington — wig, three-cornered hat, and all. He was a very old man, and would have looked the part well had he been a little less stout and less like Mr. Pickwick.

When the ticket-office opened, I changed my plan of action, and instead of commencing to sell the seats in the front rows, gave orders to the ticket clerks to commence selling at the tenth row, in the hope of getting the least good seats into the hands of the speculators, and after the first fifty or sixty purchasers in the line had been supplied, of commencing to sell the front rows to the general public. This, of course, again gave general dissatisfaction to the speculators, but was greatly approved of by those who got the seats nearest to the platform. It unfortunately happened that amongst the earliest purchasers were two clerks employed in a commercial house in New York, and they having been supplied with tickets for seats far back in the hall, became greatly exasperated at my treatment of them, and would listen to no explanation, although I had offered to change their tickets for seats near the platform.

This offer was accepted by one of the malcontents, but the other would listen to no reason, and immediately repaired to the police-office, and took out a summons against Mr. Dickens for obtaining money under false pretences. At dinner that evening, Mr. Dickens was personally served with the summons by the Marshal, whose astonishment was great, first to find himself in the presence of Mr. Dickens, and secondly, at Mr. Dickens's polite invitation to join him in a glass of champagne in recognition of the gentlemanly manner in which he had performed a most unpleasant duty. The Marshal was so overcome by this attention that he gulped down the wine in a great hurry. This led to a fit of coughing and a hasty exit from the room.

The summons was handed over to our legal advisers in New York, and the circumstance having been brought under the notice of the employers of the enterprising clerk, he was dismissed their service for speculating in tickets, and had to withdraw his action, paying all the costs himself. When we heard of this I gave him better seats than those he had purchased, and Mr. Dickens personally waited on his employers and interceded for him. The result was that he was reinstated in his position, after promising that he would never again (whilst in that employ) speculate in tickets for places of amusement.

Handsome as had been the abuse of me in all the smaller papers of New York on the occasion of the first sale of tickets, it literally paled before the attacks which were made now. Mr. Dickens described me as "the most unpopular man in America (and for no reason that I can see except that he cannot get four thousand people into a room that holds two thousand), and so he is reviled in print every day. He takes it very coolly though, and does his best."

The number of persons "in the line" on this particular occasion exceeded three thousand, and the *queue* was over three-quarters of a mile in length. Long before noon all the tickets were disposed of, and many had to go away ticketless. The receipts exceeded the proceeds of the first day's sale.

All the money taken was in paper (greenbacks), and necessitated a considerable labour in sorting and checking it, and making it up into packets for the bank; and Mr. Dickens's amusement was great on my return to the hotel, when he saw me turn out of my pockets on the table what he called my "stuffing." "Dolby," he wrote, "has just come in from our ticket sales, and has put such an immense untidy heap of paper money on the table that it looks like a family wash." Amongst this "untidy heap" were greenbacks for all sorts of amounts, from 25 cents (about is.) up to $50 (£10).

The climate of America is so even that those accustomed to it have no difficulty in predicting any change. The prophecy of a snowstorm turned out to be quite correct, for early in the evening the snow commenced to fall, and continued falling the whole night, the ground being covered on the following morning with a mantle eight inches deep, and, in places where it had drifted, considerably more, rendering the streets impassable. This continued all through the day, and it was only late in the afternoon of Thursday that the tramlines were cleared sufficiently (by means of steam snow-ploughs), to enable the traffic to be resumed. The snow by this time had fallen to the extent of from sixteen to eighteen inches. Americans are always practical and equal to an occasion, and it was surprising to see with what rapidity every kind of conveyance which only the day before had been running on wheels had suddenly become transformed into a sleigh. Not a wheel, except on the tramcars, was to be seen in the city after midday. Up to this time only the traffic was entirely suspended, and having to walk "down town" in the blinding snow to our bankers' agents to send to England our first remittance of £3,000, with the "family wash" done up in a brown paper parcel, I felt a considerable security against being knocked down and robbed in the fact that from Union Square to Wall Street (a distance of three miles) I saw but three persons in Broadway. The walk was not an unpleasant one, except that from the feet to the knees I was wet through, and was an experience I would not have been without, if only to satisfy my mind that I should not make a good Arctic traveller.

On my return to the hotel, I found my Chief in a state of despondency, standing at the window watching the still falling snow, literally streaming at the eyes and nose from the effects of his influenza, and propounding a theory to himself as to the utter futility of attempting to read that evening, even if his influenza would enable him to do so, as he was under the impression that there would be no one to listen to him in the immense hall in which he was advertised to read that night; forgetting for the time that the tickets were all sold and the money banked, and that if there were any loss at all it would devolve on the speculators who had so eagerly bought the tickets, and that they stood a chance on this occasion of being "stuck."

The operations of the ticket speculators on the evening of any performance are carried out on the pavement (or side-walk as it is called in America), in front of the theatre, circus, or hall in which the performance or lecture takes place. On this occasion they were in front of Steinway Hall in full force, willing to sell at any price so as to "get out." The public, taking advantage of the snowstorm and the resumption of the tramcar traffic, came in goodly numbers, fully bent on getting the best of the speculators for once in their lives. Long before the time for opening the doors most of the speculators had "sold out" at considerable reductions, taking in some instances seventy-five cents and a dollar, or a dollar and a half for a ticket that had cost them two dollars, thereby incurring heavy losses. The more astute of them, however, seeing the way things were going, "held their stocks" until a quarter of an hour before the time advertised for the commencement of the Reading, in many cases realizing handsome profits— one speculator getting at the last moment as much as ten or twelve dollars for a ticket, thus realizing as much as if there had been no storm at all. I felt that as the speculators ran the risk, they were entitled to the profits the public were willing to pay, rather than be put to the same inconvenience, and that as I could not give satisfaction to the aforesaid public I had no right to attempt to spoil the market of our chief supporters by giving them only the worst seats in the house, an opinion entirely endorsed by Mr. Dickens after the experience we had in the snowstorm.

Mr. Dickens was amazed on going to the platform to find himself in the presence of an audience as brilliant in every respect as on the two previous occasions, and, as is frequently the case under similar circumstances, the effects of his influenza was not observable in the delivery of the Reading. The only person inconvenienced was himself, but he got through manfully, as he always did, to the immense delight of the audience.

After having sold their tickets for the Reading on this evening, the principal speculating firms repaired to Boston, where a second sale of tickets was to be held on the following morning. Mr. Dickens being unwell, I had to remain in New York with him, but sent my ticket clerk and another member of the staff to Boston, to assist Messrs. Ticknor and Fields in the conduct of the sale. One of the New York speculators had telegraphed to Boston to have fifty men placed in the line, and to be in waiting for his arrival at six in the morning; but as the country was many inches deep in snow the train was late. His advance agents had been equal to the occasion, however, and he arrived in Boston at about ten in the morning to find himself a purchaser of three hundred tickets for each of the two Christmas Readings announced for Monday, December 23rd, and the following evening (Christmas Eve). He returned to New York to superintend the sale of his equally large stock of tickets for the four Readings to be given the following week.

This enterprising individual made a point of staying in the same hotel with ourselves, so as to be able to move as we moved; and he took the utmost pains to ascertain our movements in advance, that he might be ready for emergencies; the only city where he did not "operate" being Washington, in which he had no faith.

Mr. Dickens's cold and the inclemency of the weather kept him confined to the hotel, which he quitted only to go to the hall in the evening to read. The monotony of his life was greatly relieved by the timely arrival in New York of Mr. and Mrs. Fields, Mr. and Mrs. John Bigelow, and occasional visits from his friends Horace Greeley and William Cullen Bryant.

Here were guests enough for a dinner party on the following Sunday, and a cheerful conclusion to a week of hard work, bad weather, and great anxiety. On this occasion, and in consideration of his state of health, the guests retired earlier than usual, in the hope that Mr. Dickens might enjoy a good night's rest, so as to strengthen him for another hard week's work. Their intention was good, but it was frustrated by a wholly unforeseen circumstance. Having parted with him for the night, at about eleven o'clock, and not being disposed for rest myself at that hour, I went down to the bar of the hotel (fitted up more like a smoke-room of a club than an ordinary bar-room) to see if any friends were about.

Walking straight up to the marble counter, and calling for the bar-keeper, I became aware of a brass helmet emerging from under the counter, and in an instant, instead of a bar-keeper, I found myself face to face with a fireman, looking very much perplexed.

"What's the matter now?" I inquired.

"Well," said the landlord, "we didn't want you here at all to-night, for, to tell you the truth, the house is on fire, and we can't find out where the fire is; and until we can do so we don't want Mr. Dickens to be disturbed."

I inquired how long it was since the discovery had been made, to which the landlord replied that he "guessed about five or six hours." That the place was on fire somewhere there was no doubt, for clouds of smoke now began to come out from between the wainscotting boards forming the wall of the bar; the paint was beginning to blister, and the smoke to rise through the stair-case boards.

As matters were now looking a little more serious and business-like, it occurred to me that I would go and report to Mr. Dickens, whose apartments were at the farther end of the house, to prepare him for any emergency.

I found him on the point of getting into bed.

"What do you want?" he inquired.

"The hotel's on fire."

"I know it," he said.

"How do you know it?"

"I can smell it," he said. "What are you going to do about it?"

"I don't know," I replied,

"Where is the fire?"

"Nobody knows; but they guess it's somewhere at the other end of the building."

"When do you suppose it will get here?"

"Well," I said, "at the pace it has been going for the last five or six hours, I should say some time before breakfast in the morning."

Here a council of war was held as to the best thing to do under the circumstances. To go to bed with a view to a night's rest was out of the question, not to mention that we had a lot of valuables about us, in the way of papers, jewellery, and money (there were over $5,000 in greenbacks in my writing-table drawer), all of which had to be taken care of.

We decided on arousing Scott and George (the gasman), the other men being in Boston. This being done, Scott had instructions to pack one suit, his master's dress clothes, and the reading-books, with his jewellery, in a small portmanteau, and to place it, with the despatch boxes, near the window in the sitting-room, from which he could easily escape in case of necessity, and then to proceed to pack up as many of Mr. Dickens's other matters as time would allow.

George was told off to assist me in like operations, and as I was in evening dress, I had to make an entire change suitable to the exigencies of the climate and the situation.

All these preliminaries having been disposed of, and the luggage having been piled up close to the window, I proceeded to "stuff" myself with the paper money, and to put my jewels and papers in my pockets; then we went downstairs to see how the fire was getting on, Mr. Dickens, in his pea-jacket and blue sailor's trousers, with a thick muffler round his neck, looking more like a pilot than ever.

By this time the smoke had left no doubt in the minds of the other guests as to what was going on, and the passages and staircases were one mass of confusion, ladies and children only half dressed rushing about in the wildest dismay, while the gentlemen were busy packing and hauling about their large American trunks.

Mr. Dickens's entry into the burning bar was hailed by the landlord with delight, and he thereupon insisted on our joining in a "drinks round," to pass the time until the actual seat of the fire could be discovered.

The firemen and hotel servants were chopping away at the floors, ripping up boards in every likely and unlikely place in the hope of finding out the fire, and for some time to no avail, until an idea struck one of the firemen that the cause of the smoke might be in a distant part of the house.

He commenced his investigations in a sitting-room (the ladies' reception-room) close to our apartments, and there was the cause, sure enough. The wing of the hotel in which we lived had been but recently built, and under a new fireplace in the ladies' reception-room was a large wooden beam, which had become ignited. The smoke having no vent had travelled along under the first floor of the hotel, and had found an outlet in the bar. When once discovered, the mischief was easily remedied, and much of the night was passed in jovial congratulations all round, the whole entertainment winding up about two o'clock in the morning in Mr. Dickens' sitting-room.

Two weeks in New York, without the inconvenience of travelling, had a most beneficial effect on Mr. Dickens's influenza. The elegant carriage I had hired for him had been replaced by a most comfortable and equally elegant sleigh, and we used to take long rides in this every day, with an exhilaration of the spirits such as is not to be produced by any other means.

Having a spare evening on Wednesday, December 18th, and the influenza being much better, Mr. Dickens accepted the invitation of Mr. Palmer to visit his theatre (Niblo's), where the great spectacle of the "Black Crook" was presented; and as Mr. Dickens was little disposed to be the subject of popular enthusiasm, as he would have been had he sat in the front of the house, Mr. Palmer had an armchair placed for him in the prompt entrance, a position from which everything could be seen on the stage, with the additional advantage that he was able to move about behind the scenes, and enjoy a friendly chat with the artists engaged.

The "Black Crook" had been running for over sixteen months, and had netted to the proprietors, Messrs. Jarrett and Palmer, a considerable fortune. Not one of the actors or actresses engaged in the piece had even been able during all this time to discover what it all meant, and the only intelligible thing that could be said of the representation Mr. Dickens described in the following words: "The people who act in it have not the slightest idea of what it is about, and never had; but after taxing my intellectual powers to the utmost, I fancy that I have discovered 'Black Crook' to be a malignant hunchback leagued with the Powers of Darkness to separate two lovers, and that the Powers of Lightness coming (in no skirts whatever) to the rescue, he is defeated. I am quite serious in saying that I do not suppose there are two pages of 'All the Year Round,' in the whole piece (which acts all night); the whole of the rest of it being ballets of all sorts, perfectly unaccountable processions, and the Donkey out of last year's Covent Garden pantomime."

The shortness of the ballet skirts was a source of considerable surprise to Mr. Dickens. He thus describes them in a letter to his friend Mr. Macready: "Having some amiable talk with a neat little Spanish woman, who is the *première danseuse,* I asked her in joke to let me measure her skirt with my dress glove. Holding the glove by the tip of the forefinger, I found the skirt to be just three gloves long, and yet its length was much in excess of the skirts of two hundred other ladies whom the carpenters were at that moment getting into their places for a transformation scene on revolving columns, or wires and 'travellers' in wire cradles, up in the flies, down in the cellars, on every description of float that Wilmot, gone distracted, could imagine!"

Mr. Dickens's presence in America, and the success attending his Readings, naturally prompted the various theatrical managers, not only in New York, but all over the country, to reproduce adaptations of his books in the form of plays, and for the time being *opera bouffe* and the lighter pieces so popular in America were put on one side to make room for these productions — some good, some indifferent, and some bad. Mr. Dickens could not be prevailed upon to witness any of them, and with the exception of Niblo's Theatre and Lent's Circus he did not visit any of the theatres in New York.

We left New York on Saturday, Dec. 21st; starting by a midday train in order that Mr. Dickens might not be hurried in the morning, and in the hope that he would obtain some relief from the effects of his cold, which at the time was causing him many sleepless nights.

The railway line had been cleared of snow, and our train was but very little late in arriving at Boston, where a delightful surprise was awaiting us at the hotel, the result of the affectionate thoughtfulness of Mrs. Fields and of Captain Dolliver — Mrs. Fields had decorated our rooms with flowers and English holly, "with real red berries," festoons of moss dependent from the looking-glasses and picture-frames; and Captain Dolliver had sent to England for some enormous boughs of mistletoe (a great rarity in America), so that the rooms presented such a homely Christmas appearance that we were both deeply affected by it. Our Christmas letters from home were in waiting for us, and it must be confessed that at our late dinner on that evening we were less conversational and more thoughtful than even the depressing effects produced by the Chiefs influenza had made us for some days past. After dinner we sat round the fire and talked of nothing but home and the dear ones there, until the early hours in the morning, when we went to bed thoroughly worn out. Of the thoughtful kindness of our friends that day, Mr. Dickens wrote, "In such affectionate touches as this the New England people are especially amiable."

By this time four Readings had been given in Boston, eight in New York, and all the tickets sold for the four Christmas Readings in Boston, and four more Readings in New York announced for December 26th and 27th and January 2nd and 3rd in the New Year; giving a vacation of five days to enable New York to recover from the effects of keeping Christmas and the New Year, and also to give Mr. Dickens a little rest, in which to combat with the influenza which, in the severity of the climate and the discomfort of the travelling, was literally keeping him down.

The successful issues of the Readings already given had proved to us that, in future operations, there was no necessity to take the smaller cities of America except for the purposes of breaking long journeys, and we also became convinced that when these smaller places were touched the holding capacity of each hall would be tested to the utmost. Mr. Osgood, whose knowledge of the country and whose connections in it were universal, undertook the formation of the plans for our new tour, making such alterations in existing arrangements as would entail the least travelling and discomfort to Mr. Dickens.

The only place to which we were actually bound was Philadelphia, for eight Readings (in four visits, of two Readings each), and in the new route Brooklyn, Baltimore, Washington, Cincinnati, Chicago, and St. Louis were included, also Providence (R.I.), Worcester, New Haven, and Springfield in the New England States, and Rochester, Buffalo (*en route* for Niagara for our pleasure trip), Syracuse, and Albany, in the State of New York. As Mr. Dickens was under the impression that the value of the Readings in New York and Boston would be greatly enhanced by not being overdone, we decided on closing up in New York in the middle of January, and not going there again except for five farewell Readings in the month of April. Boston was to be treated in the same way, with the exception of one other visit in the last week in February, for four Readings only, and as circumstances afterwards proved, this decision was a very wise one.

The Readings in Cincinnatti, St. Louis, and Chicago, were never given, much to the disappointment of the inhabitants of those places, and as much speculation existed in the public mind as to the cause which determined Mr. Dickens not to read in Chicago, it may be as well here to state that his reasons were entirely of a private character with which the general public have nothing whatever to do. That he fully intended reading there is shown by the fact that I twice started for Chicago, only to be recalled from Pittsburg; and on the third occasion I contrived to evade the telegram I felt sure would be awaiting me in Pittsburg, by passing through that place without staying there, even for a night's rest, being as desirous myself that he should reap the harvest awaiting him in the West, as the Western people were that he should pay them a visit.

A hard day's work in our own rooms at the Parker House, in re-arranging our route, with the valuable assistance of Mr. Osgood, was pleasantly relieved by a dinner party at the house of Mr. and Mrs. Fields. This was our Christmas dinner, for on Christmas Day we had to travel from Boston to New York. A most brilliant company had been invited to do honour to the occasion, and all the well-known features of an English Christmas dinner-table, in the shape of roast beef and turkey, were placed before us, even to the plum pudding, made in England, and sent over specially for this entertainment. All feeling of depression at being away from home at such a time was dissipated by the geniality of our host and hostess, and the guests invited to meet Mr. Dickens; and there was universal regret when the hands of the clock pointed to the small hours in the morning, suggesting most painfully that the time for breaking-up had arrived.

These Christmas Readings at Boston were, if possible, more brilliantly attended and more enthusiastically received than any of the previous ones had been, especially the reading of the "Christmas Carol" on Christmas Eve. The circumstances under which the Reading was given, and the subject itself, on such an occasion, producing a profound sensation.

On Christmas Day we left our friends in Boston for New York; Mr. Dickens suffering from the most acute depression, consequent, in a great measure, on the return of the influenza, and the necessity of having to leave Boston and to travel on such a day. At the station, early in the morning, were Mr. and Mrs. Fields, Longfellow, Agassiz, Oliver Wendell Holmes, Ticknor, and a host of other friends who, with the kindest of intentions, had come to say "good-bye," and to present their Christmas greetings. These were a signal failure, and the kindly wishes ended in a perfect break-down in heart and speech to him who had done so much to keep Christmas green in the hearts of Englishmen.

Under these circumstances the journey to New York was anything but a pleasant one. During the early part of it not a word was spoken on either side. Nor was this feeling alleviated by an unlooked-for compliment which awaited us in the crossing of one of the rivers on the steam ferry. On this river is stationed one of the men-of-war belonging to the United States Government, under the stern of which the ferry had to pass. The captain in command of this vessel had attended some of the Readings in Boston, and, knowing that Mr. Dickens would be in the ferry, he had determined to give him a greeting. As the ferry-boat passed the war vessel the band on board struck up "God save the Queen," and at the same time the British flag was unfurled on the mizen-mast, and a wreath of holly and evergreens "run up" immediately beneath it. Our fellow-passengers knew the meaning of this tasteful tribute, and set up a ringing cheer with "three times three and a little one thrown in," which had the effect of rather increasing the depression from which we were both suffering.

Never before or since had we experienced so gloomy a journey, and we were delighted to find ourselves once more in New York. Very little was said about Christmas, the only reference to it being made by Mr. Dickens in proposing the health of all our dear ones at home, finishing with his favourite quotation from "Tiny Tim." It was with some sense of relief and pleasurable anticipation that we looked forward to the end of the Readings, which were announced for the two following nights, that Mr. Dickens might take a few days' rest, of which he stood so much in need.

New Year's Day is strictly observed in New York, and as everybody is either paying calls or receiving visitors (as in Paris), it is considered, and is, a bad night for theatres and amusements of all kinds. The amount of self-denial the ladies especially display is surprising. At the time we were in America, it was the fashion for ladies to wear a very different kind of *coiffure* from the present style, and as first-class hairdressers were very scarce, the few that did exist and had any *clientèle* were greatly in request, having, in order to get through their commissions, to commence as early as eight o'clock in the evening on New Year's Eve, thus entailing on the customer the inconvenience of sitting bolt upright all through the night for fear of disturbing the work of the artist in hair before the time for receiving visits the following day. This process commences early in the morning, the ladies receiving guests, whilst the gentlemen are rushing frantically about from house to house, making calls; the more wealthy of them using carriages for this purpose (the rate of fares on this particular day being raised to an almost prohibitory price), the poorer ones being compelled to walk from house to house. As a slight thaw had set in on New Year's Day of 1868, the pedestrians spent a "good time" in the streets.

In every reception-room in each house is a *buffet,* and the gentlemen are supposed to take a glass of something to wish the household prosperity and happiness on the coming year, a habit that is a little trying and inconvenient to men with a large circle of friends. Citizens who are teetotalers all the year round, yield to temptation on New Year's Day, and the effects of the Bourbon whiskey make themselves apparent early.

Nobody is in the least shocked at these proceedings, and everything passes off with the utmost good-humour, the only ill effects being swelled heads the following day, the whole city seeming to suffer from an unquenchable thirst, allayed only by frequent potations of brandy-and-soda; and as the ladies have to be recompensed for their labours of New Year's Day, the suffering cavaliers have to escort them to the theatres and other places of amusement; the only persons benefiting by this arrangement being the managers and proprietors of the various houses of entertainment and the irrepressible ticket speculators.

The few days' rest had a most beneficial effect on Mr. Dickens's cold, and the New Year's Readings passed off as successfully as the others.

The tour list by this time being completed, I took advantage of the recess to perfect all my plans, as far as possible, for the execution of all matters of detail in connection with it; and as the checking and stamping of so vast a number of tickets formed no inconsiderable item in this respect, it became necessary to increase our staff of clerks. Some idea may be formed of their work, when it is stated that, in addition to the Readings announced for the first week in the New Year (in Boston and New York), I had to prepare for sale in the course of the next few weeks nine thousand tickets for Philadelphia, eight thousand for Brooklyn, eight thousand for Baltimore, and six thousand for Washington.

This work, in addition to the correspondence, looking after advertisements, account-keeping, travelling, and visiting, with many minor matters of detail (together with my anxieties about Mr. Dickens's health), gave me but little rest, but it was a labour of love, and so it came comparatively easy.

On Monday, January 13th, the real travelling of the tour commenced; and as the superintendence of the sale of tickets in each city visited became a matter requiring careful manipulation (in order to frustrate as much as possible the designs of the ticket speculators), it was arranged that I should, as far as was consistent with my being occasionally present at the Readings, take this department entirely under my own supervision. In order to enable me to do this, Mr. Osgood kindly undertook to "mount guard" over the chief, and to attend to the duties of a travelling life. Accordingly, during the run of the two last Readings in Boston and New York, I went to Philadelphia and Brooklyn to sell the tickets for the Readings announced there; and rough as had been the crowd in New York, it was nothing in comparison with the crowds in these two places.

Arriving in Philadelphia on Sunday evening, January 5th, 1 went to one of the smaller and private hotels, for the New York speculators were in a body

at the Continental Hotel, some twenty or thirty in number. The hotel I selected was an excellent inn, but a circumstance occurred here which made me
regret that I had not faced the band at the "Continental." A supper party with
some friends was very enjoyable whilst it lasted, but the following morning's
reflections were the reverse, for I became aware of the unpleasant fact that I
had been poisoned: the symptoms being of a most unpleasant nature, a doctor was sent for, and in a comparatively short time I had sufficiently recovered to attend to my duties at the ticket-office at twelve the following day,
having had to delay the sale of tickets for some hours. The cause of the poisoning was for some time a mystery, and would probably have remained so
until now had not an American friend unravelled it. I had eaten some partridge at supper. The snow lying deep on the ground, the birds cannot get
their usual food, and for the time being they subsist on some kind of berry
which does not injure them, though the poison permeates their flesh, and
harasses the persons who eat them.

This discovery having been made only after I had been twice poisoned by
partridge at supper, it is unnecessary to add that for the remainder of the
winter in America a black line was drawn through the name of this delicate
bird, whenever it was submitted in a bill of fare.

When I arrived at the Music Hall in Philadelphia to superintend the sale of
the tickets, I found the usual line of speculators and purchasers. The weather
was bitterly cold (the thermometer (Reaumur) being eighteen below zero)
and the snow deep on the ground. The straw mattresses, blankets, and whiskey bottles were there as usual ("George Washington" and all), but I noticed
an unusual number of police and detectives in plain clothes. The doors of the
ticket-office having been opened, a rush took place to secure the front seats,
followed by a scrimmage between the police and the would-be purchasers.
The former, with their batons, most unceremoniously routed the latter,
whilst the "plain-clothes men" took their places in the line and turned speculators! This caused the greatest dissatisfaction, with the usual abusive correspondence in the newspapers, reflecting unpleasantly on myself, and connecting me with the *ruse* that had been played on the purchasers, of which I
was quite innocent. So great was the demand for the tickets that they were
all sold off in about three hours, and I was only too pleased to return to New
York, to nurse myself and to prepare for the sale of tickets at Brooklyn, announced for two days afterwards. There were no drawing-room cars in those
days on the New York and Philadelphia line, and the travelling for an invalid
was anything but pleasant, fifty or sixty persons being closely packed in an
ordinary car, with a great stove at each end almost at red heat, and no venti-
lation. The windows were closed, but a rush of cold air, with gusts of snow,
smoke, and cinders from the locomotive, was continually forced into the car
by the incessant opening and shutting of the doors at either end by baggage-
men, express-men, breakmen, and vendors of all sorts of articles, from sugar-
candy to a newspaper, not to mention the passengers who are perpetually
walking from one end of the train to the other, and seemingly taking a savage

delight in banging the doors with all their force. In good health these drawbacks do not so much force themselves on the mind, but as I was ill the discomfort of that journey was indescribable, and so was the relief of finding myself again in the ferry-boat, plying from Jersey City to New York.

Plymouth Church, Brooklyn
Lent by the Rev. Henry Ward Beecher for the Dickens Readings.

The only available place for a Reading in Brooklyn was the Rev. Henry Ward Beecher's church (Plymouth Church), and by the courtesy of the reverend gentleman this was secured; but a difficulty presented itself as to the manner in which the tickets had to be distributed, and many were the suggestions offered with a view of overcoming this difficulty.

In an ordinary hall or theatre the matter was comparatively simple, and I used my own discretion as to how few or how many tickets I issued to each person, but in a church, which was arranged in pews, each varying in its holding capacity, the difficulty seemed almost insurmountable. It was suggested that Mr. Beecher's system of disposing of the pews should be adopted, viz., to fix the price of each pew at the rate of two dollars a ticket (as a reserved price), and to sell the premium on each of the pews in the best positions by auction.

This Mr. Dickens objected to as laying him open to grave charges in receiving more money for his tickets than the established rate. The only way then was to sell the pews entire at the rate of two dollars each seat.

This plan evidently gave the greatest satisfaction to the speculators and the public, and on my arrival at Brooklyn to sell the tickets, I was greeted with hearty cheers and a great deal of "chaff" by the mob in waiting. "The noble army of speculators," as Mr. Dickens described them, were in greater force than ever. They had been in the line since ten the previous evening, and during the whole night had kept up an enormous bonfire in the street, sleeping around it in turns on their mattresses, and enjoying their supper of bread-and-meat, with potations of Bourbon whiskey. Early in the morning, and just about daybreak, a body of police appeared on the scene, an idea having suddenly occurred to them that in a narrow street, composed entirely of wooden houses, a bonfire was a source of considerable danger to the whole of that part of the city. On my arrival there at eight o'clock in the morning, with my ticket clerks and the tickets packed in a small portmanteau, in Mr. Dickens's carnage, lent for the occasion, I was greeted with "Holloa, Dolby!" "How's Charley this morning?" "Look alive, old man!" "Let me carry the portmanteau for you." "So he's trusted you with the carriage, has he?" "We're frozen to death waiting for you. and will buy you *right up,* carriage, horses, and all if you like — anything to get away from this darned cold."

At this time the police made a raid on the bonfire, the mattresses, 'and speculators, and a terrific combat ensued, in which the people farthest off in the line took the most prominent part, until they saw that those nearest the door were being routed, and then with broken heads and bleeding noses rushed into the good places, bringing with them their mattresses, and hanging on to the iron railings round the church to keep possession of the places they had so gallantly fought for. The New Yorkers got the worst of the fight, and the Brooklyn men got the best of the tickets. Many arrests were made, and amongst the arrested ones was poor old "George Washington," who, however, was "Met off" on promising not to come to Brooklyn any more for ticket speculation, certainly in tickets for Readings in a church.

The plan I had decided on adopting for the sale of the tickets in the church was a little more tedious than the plan adopted at other sales, and the purchasers would have been great sufferers from the cold, but for their ardour in the matter. This sale in about four hours produced nearly $20,000, and I returned to New York to meet Mr. Dickens on his arrival from Boston, to give him an account of the morning's proceedings.

Although appreciative of the humorous side of these transactions, he always entertained an opinion that the speculators' trade would eventually tell against the receipts of the Reading, and but for the precautions we had taken in the change of our route, "closing up," as it were, in New York and Boston at the right time, and only revisiting those places for the farewell Readings, such would undoubtedly have been the case. The public would not protect themselves, as they could have done in refusing to pay the exorbitant demands of the speculators, and without taking the trouble to go to the root of the evil, abused the system of selling tickets which I had adopted.

Our arrangements did not give satisfaction to the public, and great were the complaints in the newspapers when the discovery was made that there were to be no more Readings in New York until the middle of April.

The visit to Philadelphia was a successful one in every way, and although Mr. Dickens was again suffering from the effects of a fresh attack of influenza, produced undoubtedly by standing with the breakman outside the cars in travelling, in the hope of getting rid of the noxious air inside the car, still everything was done by our friends in the city to make him forget the inconvenience from which he was suffering. Mr. and Mrs. Barney Williams were staying at the Continental Hotel with their pretty little "child daughter," who was a source of the greatest amusement to Mr. Dickens, and Mr. George William Childs, the proprietor of the "Philadelphia Ledger," and the American correspondent of the London "Times," was indefatigable in endeavours to entertain him.

It may truly be said that, notwithstanding the discomfort, the first Philadelphia visit was always regarded as amongst the pleasantest of our American experiences.

Prior to our visit to Philadelphia, Mr. Osgood had prepared a statement of his accounts, up to and including the date of the last Reading given in New York, which completed a little over a quarter of the number intended to be given in America. After paying all the preliminary expenses of every kind, on my return to New York on January 15th, I had been able to remit to Messrs. Coutts's Bank in London, to the credit of Mr. Dickens, £10,000, and had over £1,000 in hand after doing this "to go on with."

Although Mr. Dickens was totally devoid of avarice, he could not but be well pleased at the result of his labours thus far; and this circumstance, together with the cheery news he had received from his friends, Wilkie Collins and Fechter, of the success of the dramatisation of his Christmas number ("No Thoroughfare"), at the Adelphi Theatre, all had the effect of putting him into excellent spirits for the return to New York for the Brooklyn Readings. In writing to his friend Fields from Philadelphia before leaving there he says: "The cold remains just as it was (beastly), and where it was (in my head). We have left off referring to the hateful subject, except in emphatic sniffs on my part, convulsive wheezes, and resounding sneezes. Philadelphia audiences ready and bright. I think they understood the 'Carol' better than 'Copperfield,' but they were bright and responsive to both. Dolby is in Washington, and will return in the night. Osgood is 'on guard.' He made a most brilliant appearance before the Philadelphia public and looked very hard at them. The mastery of his eye diverted their attention from his boots, charming in themselves, but (unfortunately) *two left ones*!"

There was a novelty in the Brooklyn Readings, inasmuch as they were given in a church, and unusual means had to be resorted to in order to render the platform available for the purpose. The pulpit was in the way and had to be removed, and so had the readingdesk — alterations which Mr. Beecher obligingly allowed to be made. Although an enormous building, and capable of holding over two thousand people, Mr. Dickens pronounced it to be perfection; and although his influenza (by this time dignified with the title "American catarrh," which he always said he hoped, for the comfort of human nature, was peculiar to only one of the four quarters of the world) had taken such hold on him, he found it scarcely required an effort to speak in it. At one of the Readings Mr. Beecher himself was present, and paid Mr. Dickens a visit in the vestry on its termination, much to Mr. Dickens' satisfaction; and to judge by the congratulations which were exchanged, the meeting was one of pleasure to both. Of course I have no idea what Mr. Beecher's sentiments with regard to Mr. Dickens may have been, but those of Mr. Dickens for Mr. Beecher were expressed in the following words: "I found him an unostentatious, evidently able, straightforward, and agreeable man; extremely well informed, and with a good knowledge of art."

During our stay in New York for the Brooklyn Readings, Mr. Horace Greeley had accepted an invitation to dine with Mr. Dickens at the Westminster Hotel on Saturday, January i8th; and in expressing his delight at the success of the Readings took occasion to question the advisability of Mr. Dickens reading in Washington, giving as his reasons that the political horizon was a little hazy, and that "trouble" with the President (Andrew Johnson) might accrue at any moment, in addition to which the "rowdy" element was more largely represented than usual in the city at that moment, in view of the supposed difficulties with the President. It was his opinion also that the "rowdies" would make themselves obnoxious to Mr. Dickens. I had just returned from Washington, and had secured the only available hall there (the Carol Hall), which held but seven hundred and fifty or eight hundred people, and intended charging five dollars a ticket for the Washington Readings; a proceeding Mr. Dickens disapproved of at first, but to which he eventually yielded on my pointing out to him that there were more people in New York, Boston, Philadelphia, and Brooklyn than there were in Washington, and that these people on an average paid (thanks to the "noble army of speculators") that price to hear him in those cities. As to the "rowdy" element, I thought nothing of that, for in my experience they were too much occupied in "bar-loafing" and "office-seeking" to part with such a sum as five dollars to gratify an imaginary wrong, even if they had ever heard of it, or, what was more improbable, if they had read the books to which Horace Greeley referred. My arguments had their effect both with Mr. Dickens and Mr. Greeley, and nothing more would have been thought or said on the matter had not an influential friend and politician paid us a visit later on in the evening, who reiterated Horace Greeley's fears. It was arranged that I should go to Washington the following night, to judge (if possible) for myself as to the chances of any difficulty in the event of Mr. Dickens visiting Washington, the matter being left entirely in my hands either to go on with the arrangements there or to give the place up entirely. On re-visiting Washington, I became convinced (thanks to the assistance I received in my inquiries from Mr. Franklin Philp, a gentleman whose knowledge of Washington was indisputable) that Mr. Greeley's fears were groundless, the only alteration in the original plan for that place being that I (under pressure) resolved in making the price of the tickets three dollars instead of five dollars, a result that I telegraphed to Mr. Dickens; and took advantage of his absence to slip off to Chicago to make arrangements for that place (only to be re-called at Pittsburg), joining him again in Philadelphia, after calling at Baltimore to sell the tickets for four Readings announced for that city.

Chapter Eight - Further American Experiences

ON my return to Philadelphia, I found Mr. Dickens still suffering so much, that he was compelled to decline all offers of hospitality tendered to him by his friends in Philadelphia; feeling that if he took advantage of these offers, he would be totally unfit for the labour of the Readings. In his weak state of health, he was desirous of seeing me, to confer as to the advisability of taking so long a journey as that to Chicago, a distance of nearly fifteen hundred miles. He also had fears as to my staying power, or, as he expressed it in a letter to his son (Mr. Charles Dickens), "If Dolby holds out well to the last it will be a triumph, for he has to see everybody, to drink with everybody, sell all the tickets, take all the blame, and go beforehand to all the places on the list. I shall not see him after to-night for ten days or a fortnight, and he will be perpetually on the road during the interval."

What he underwent from the effects of his cold, it is impossible to describe. He could not sleep at night, and rarely, if ever, got up before twelve o'clock in the day. He had to abandon his breakfast, and dine at three, and could take no food until after the work of the evening was over, and then only something very light, in the shape of quail or a devilled bone. The champagne had to be given up during the Readings, and in its place I prepared an egg beaten up in sherry for him every night, to take between the parts; this seemed to do him good, and to refresh him wonderfully.

The abandonment of the Western journey caused the greatest disappointment and annoyance to the Chicago public, as indeed it did to all the friends of the great Western country, amongst them Mr. Childs, of Philadelphia; who, in his desire to impress on Mr. Dickens the importance of visiting Chicago, said that if he did not read in that city "the people would go into fits," to which Mr. Dickens replied that he would rather they went into "fits" than that he did.

The Baltimore sale of tickets took place in the same bitter cold weather as those of Brooklyn and Philadelphia, but was a remarkably quiet one by reason of the absence of the New York speculators, who had but little faith in the success of the enterprise in Baltimore. The results, however, proved that the New Yorkers were wrong. The hall I had taken was the Concordia Hall, which gave Mr. Dickens the greatest pleasure, being built like a theatre. The public, too, were quite to his liking, being a bright, responsive people.

Not only were Chicago and the West abandoned, but also the Readings in Canada and those in Nova Scotia, the latter in consequence of the withdrawal of the Halifax steamer from that port by the Cunard Company. The tour list had again to be changed, and in view of Mr. Dickens's continued ill-health, the number of Readings had to be considerably reduced. An idea struck us (Mr. Osgood and myself), that a walking match between ourselves, to take place at the end of February, in Boston, would be a source of amusement to Mr. Dickens. He entered heartily into the scheme, volunteering to draw up the articles of agreement, to act as trainer, and to write a "sporting narrative" of the match after it had taken place. The match was fixed to take place in Boston, on Saturday, February 29th. "Beginning this design in joke," he writes, speaking of Osgood and myself, "they have become tremendously in earnest, and Dolby has actually sent home (much to his opponent's terror) for a pair of seamless socks to walk in. Our people are hugely excited on the subject, and continually make bets on 'the men.' Fields and I are to walk out six miles, and 'the men' are to turn and walk round us. Neither of them has the least idea what twelve miles at a pace is. Being requested by both to give them a breather yesterday, I gave them a stiff one of five miles over a bad road, in the snow. I took them at a pace of four and a half miles an hour, and you never beheld such objects as they were when we got back — both smoking like factories, and both obliged to change everything before they could come to dinner. They have the absurdest ideas of what are tests of walking power, and continually get up in the maddest manner to see how high they can kick the wall— the wainscot here in one place is scored all over with their pencil marks. To see them doing this—Dolby a big man, and Osgood a very little one— is 'ridiculous beyond description.'"

If we had been professional pedestrians, instead of amateurs, Mr. Dickens could not have paid more attention to our "coaching" for the great event.

During our stay at Baltimore, I received a visit from the Governor of the Maryland Penitentiary, who, knowing the interest taken by Mr. Dickens in prison matters in England, was anxious to conduct him over the establishment under his control; an invitation which Mr. Dickens accepted with the greatest readiness, especially as the governor had given me to understand that this prison was regarded as the model prison of the States.

Our reception by the governor and his officials was all that could be desired— the governor himself acting as guide— and as the prison happened to be more than usually full at the time of our visit, it became doubly interesting, as illustrating the system adopted in it. All the prisoners were allowed to work at their trade, not confined in separate cells as in England, but in comfortable workshops provided for them, these workshops being warmed by large stoves and hot-water pipes. Some prisoners were brush-making, boot-making, tailoring, and mat-making, and in one large carpenter's workshop there were as many as fifty men (and amongst them half a dozen men convicted of murder), busily engaged making door-frames, panels for doors, window-frames, &c., having the free use of the usual carpenter's tools, and with no guard over them other than one warder (in plain clothes, and smoking cigars the whole time), perched up at a high desk with no other means of defence (in the event of an *emeute*) than a six-barrelled revolver. It must be explained that at the time of Mr. Dickens' second visit to America, there was a strong feeling against capital punishment for murder, as indeed there is at the present time; and that these murderers, although sentenced to be hanged, had by some peculiar vagary of the law been respited during the pleasure of the Government. On inquiry, we ascertained that the warder was not placed there so much for the purpose of preserving order, as to prevent the prisoners from making an improper use of the materials supplied them for their trade, notably those who had a talent in working in metals, making hinges, locks, &c.; for, as a result of experience, it had been discovered that these worthies applied such materials, "on the sly," to the manufacturing of skeleton keys, with which they supplied their friends in the burglary trade "outside," on visiting days.

A strict account was kept with each prisoner of the result of his labours, one-third of the proceeds going towards his own maintenance whilst in prison, a third for the support of his family during his "absence" from home, and the remaining third was safely banked as a reserve fund for his own use when the time arrived for his liberation. This arrangement, which at the time gave the greatest dissatisfaction to the legitimate tradesmen in Baltimore, as the prison labour being untrammelled by rent or taxes, became a strong opposition and competitive agency with the honest and industrious shopkeeper or manufacturer; and as the winter was unusually severe, and in consequence work was very scarce, the extraordinary number of inmates in the house was fully accounted for, especially as the scale of dietary was most liberal. The "long term" prisoners and the murderers had a capital bill of fare (for a prison), — cocoa, coffee, or tea, with a choice of fish and bread-and-butter for breakfast; soup and meat for dinner; and cocoa, coffee, or tea, with bread-and-butter, for supper. The "short term" men were supposed not to require so much, and their bill of fare was less sumptuous, although far more luxurious than the condition of affairs would seem to warrant, especially as the number of inmates of this class was far in excess of either workshop room or tool appliances, to enable them to earn anything.

This struck us very much when we were conducted into a large room in which were over five hundred unemployed men, all seated on forms arranged like the seats in a lecture room, with a passage-way up the centre for the warders — cigar in mouth and revolver in belt — to promenade up and down. (Negroes on one side of the room and white folks on the other, the whites refusing to associate with the niggers.) The heat of this room was insufferable, and as the prisoners had no work to do they were not allowed to talk, but at intervals between meal times were allowed to sing, the whole presenting such a scene of depression and misery that it was a source of the greatest relief to us to be once more in the comfortable quarters of the governor, to smoke a cigar, and to have a talk with him about the lenient system he was introducing, in the hope of diminishing crime in the State of Maryland.

Looking over some of the prison books, Mr. Dickens noticed the word "pardoned" against the name of every man, a few days, and in some cases weeks and months, before his term of sentence had expired. The governor explained, "If he had served his term out, the prisoner would have been disfranchised and the State would have lost the votes!"

The governor was desirous of knowing how his establishment compared with the prisons in England, and was surprised to find that nothing of the kind was in existence there. Mr. Dickens remarked at the same time that the Maryland Penitentiary was more like a "huge hydropathic establishment, without the privilege of going out for a walk," a tribute which gave the kindhearted governor such an amount of satisfaction, that on our return to the hotel (after two hours' training for the walking match), we found handsome presents, the product of prison labour, awaiting us.

Nothing has been said about the Baltimore hotels, neither would any reference to them be necessary except for the benefit of any one who has never visited Baltimore, and who might propose doing so. But for Mr. Dickens' state of health, he would undoubtedly have stayed at Barnum's Hotel, then, as now, the oldest and one of the best and most liberally conducted in the South; but it was considered prudent to put up at a smaller and more private house. This hotel was "Guy's," where I found I could secure a sufficient number of rooms for our requirements, en suite, and be out of the way of the noise and turmoil of a larger hotel, and where I could get more care and attention in the preparation of delicacies with which to tempt Mr. Dickens's appetite — such delicacies as are not to be appreciated in any other city in the world, Baltimore being the home of the far-famed canvas-back duck, the terrapin, and the Blue Point oyster. These luxuries are to be found in other parts of America, but away from Baltimore (or perhaps Washington) they are *not* the same, and to the *gourmet* it is almost worthwhile to make a pilgrimage to this city, to indulge in these freaks of nature, either at Barnum's Hotel, or "Guy's," where there is an excellent restaurant.

During the visit to Baltimore, I went to Washington (a journey of only about an hour and a quarter) to superintend the sale of the tickets for the Readings there, returning to Baltimore after transacting this business. There being no speculators here from New York, everything passed off quietly, and it was satisfactory to find no evidences of either "rowdyism" or discontent on the part of the public at the raised prices. My only regret was that I did not adhere to my original plan of charging five dollars a ticket instead of three dollars. The receipts in Washington did not come up to the average of other large cities in America, but there was full compensation in the associations of the place, which would have been greatly enhanced had the climate of Washington been a little more genial, and had Mr. Dickens been less a sufferer than he was from the effects of his "American catarrh."

His spirit and determination were of the most indomitable character, and under the most trying circumstances he would be the most cheerful. On many occasions in America, I had been fearful that he would not be able to give his Readings, and but for my knowledge of him and his power of "coming up to time" when "time" was called, I should often have despaired of his physical capacity. It was only by a most careful observation that any one could form any idea of the extent of his sufferings, for he made it a rule, in the unselfishness of his nature, never to inflict his own inconveniences on any one else; and as for the public, he held it as a maxim that "No man had a right to break an engagement with the public if he were able to be out of bed."

As he had lost all appetite, took little or no food, and could not sleep for more than three or four hours out of the twenty-four, I was greatly embarrassed to know what to do for the best with regard to an hotel in Washington. Willard's Hotel was closed, and even if it had not been, with its *clientèle* of bar-loafers, swaggerers, drunkards, and "axe grinders" (a class of politician peculiar to Washington hotels), it would not have been the place for Mr. Dickens in his state of health, which demanded that he should have peace and quietude, with the greatest amount of comfort attainable.

All the other hotels were inconveniently situated, and presented the same undesirable features as "Willard's" did, so in my extremity I took my friend Franklin Philp into my counsels, as to the advisability of taking a furnished house for our whole staff, during our stay in Washington. It being High Session, this could not be satisfactorily arranged, and although invitations were not wanting, Mr. Dickens's rule of accepting no invitations to stay with friends precluded his acceptance of them, for he said, "I came for hard work, and I must try to fulfil the expectations of the American public."

Mr. Philp was equal to this occasion, as indeed he was to almost any occasion, and after tendering the offer of his establishment to Mr. Dickens, Mr. Osgood and myself did the very best thing possible under the circumstances, by making an arrangement with Mr. Whelcker (a German), the proprietor of the best restaurant in the city, who re-furnished some of his private dining-rooms to suit our requirements; and as the house was a comparatively small one, and we had one wing entirely to ourselves, with excellent French waiters and a *cuisine* that would have done credit to Champot or Vachette in Paris, or Delmonico in New York, I congratulated myself on the discovery, and was grateful to Franklin Philp for the interest he had taken in the matter. Mr. Dickens was highly pleased with the arrangement, and everything looked well for a pleasant week in Washington, during which I had no travelling, save for a couple of days, during which I had sales of tickets in Baltimore and Philadelphia for the final farewell Readings there; and with the exception of having to attend to the ordinary routine of our travelling life, had very little to do but to avail myself of the goods the Washington gods provided, and to give my attention to training for the great "walking match," in which Mr. Dickens took so much interest.

I had one more journey to make before entering on this week's pleasure, viz., to New York, to attend to some business matters there. It was far from a pleasant experience, as there were considerable doubts as to the possibility of getting through, for another heavy snow storm had occurred, and the road in some places was supposed to be "blocked;" but beyond the inconvenience of arriving at my journey's end some hours late, no other annoyance was felt. Mr. Dickens, always solicitous for my safety and comfort, writes on January 30th: "The communication with New York is not interrupted, so we consider the zealous Dolby all right. You may imagine what his work is, when you hear that he goes three times to every place we visit. Firstly, to look at the hall, arrange the numberings, and make five hundred acquaintances, whom he immediately calls by their Christian names; secondly, to sell the tickets — a very nice business requiring great tact and temper; thirdly, with me. Pie will probably turn up at Washington next Sunday, but only for a little while; for as soon as I am on the platform on Monday night, he will start away again, probably to be seen no more until we pass through New York in the middle of February."

Mr. Dickens at the time of writing this had no idea of my intention of spending as much of the week with him as I could spare; indeed he knew nothing of my intended movements at any time, giving me *carte blanche* to do as I liked, and never questioning any of my acts with regard to business matters. He never gave me an order to do anything in connection with our affairs, but always suggested his wishes by saying, "Don't you think *we* had better do," &c., and if on any occasion I consulted him in times of difficulty, his frequent reply was, "Do as you like, and don't bother me."

As he conjectured, I returned to Washington by the Sunday night train from New York, to find him completely prostrate with his cold, and on hearing of my decision to spend the greater portion of the week with him, he expressed his pleasure, especially as his birthday would occur during the week, and he was anxious to have me with him for the occasion, so that our domesticity might not be entirely broken up, away from all he loved. Great were the preparations, in which Mr. Osgood vied with myself to make the coming February 7th a pleasurable day to him, with the slight drawback of having to appear before an audience on the evening of the day, instead of receiving his friends at our apartments at Whelcker's Restaurant — where, as in New York and Boston, everything was done by the proprietor in the hope of tickling his appetite by the preparation of some delicate dish, but all to no avail.

I found on my arrival in Washington, on talking matters over at the breakfast table, that Mr. Dickens had been compelled to break his rule as laid down, and had accepted an invitation from Mr. Charles Sumner (an old friend of his), to dine with him on that Sunday evening, and had stipulated that there was to be no party. The only other persons present were Mr. Secretary Staunton (War Minister) and Mr. Sumner's private secretary; and although Mr. Staunton had been previously unknown to him, Mr. Dickens was greatly interested in his new acquaintance, who was gifted with a remarkable memory, and famous for his knowledge of Mr. Dickens's works.

The Chief being out for the evening, Mr. Osgood and I were left together to compare notes as to business matters that had transpired during my absence; and Mr. Osgood's account of Mr. Dickens's health was such as to cause me the greatest anxiety, and make me feel glad that I had changed the plan of the tour, by giving up the idea of going West.

On Mr. Dickens's return, he gave us a most interesting account of the way he had spent his evening at the house of his friend Mr. Sumner. He was specially pleased with his intercourse with Mr. Staunton, who on being started with a chapter from any of Mr. Dickens's books, could repeat the whole of the chapter from memory, and, as the author confessed, knew more about his works than he himself did. This was accounted for by the fact that during the war, when Mr. Staunton was Commander-in-Chief of the Northern forces, he never went to bed at night without first reading something from one of Mr. Dickens's books, a habit which engraved them on his memory.

The Washington Readings were amongst the most brilliant of any given in America. At the first Reading every class of society was represented, the President himself being present, with his family, and not only the English ambassador, but all the ambassadors representing other countries, and a large proportion of Congressmen, and those connected with the Legislative Assembly. Under these circumstances, it is not surprising that the Carol Hall presented a spectacle which would have been perfect, but for the badness of the gas. This caused Mr. Dickens to depart from his usual rule, by making a preliminary speech, in which he said that he must trust to the brightness of the faces before him for the illumination of his own. Expectation was on its tiptoe, whatever that might be, and Mr. Dickens had partially recovered from the effects of his cold, a change produced possibly by the geniality of the Washington climate on this particular day; although it must not be understood that the climate of Washington is always genial, for as a rule in the winter season, the four seasons are represented within the twenty-four hours, a fact which caused poor John Brougham to remark that, "in Washington, there was a Congress of climates, as well as a Congress of legislators."

Here, a slightly unpleasant incident occurred. A member of Congress, a military man of high distinction, had partaken rather too freely of the good things of this life at dinner, before coming to the Reading, and this preliminary exhilaration had the effect of creating in him a bad attack of anglophobia. As was my habit, I was talking to Mr. Dickens behind the screen, the house being by this time quite full, and all the people in their seats, when our attention was attracted by an unseemly noise in the body of the hall. One of the assistants rushed round to me, requesting my presence in the front of the house (before Mr. Dickens made his appearance), and I was ushered into the presence of the military gentleman, who was indulging in language not usual in good society. Being personally known to a great many people in the hall, my presence was hailed with, "Quite right, Mr. Dolby, we are very glad to see you here; this man is making use of language not fit for ears polite. If he is allowed to remain in his seat, the Reading will be spoilt." I remonstrated with the obnoxious person, and requested him to leave the hall. He pleaded that he meant no offence, offering the excuse for what he had said, that he had been dining with some friends, and scarcely knew what he was about, and he distinctly refused to leave his place, promising not to repeat the disturbance. I had taken the precaution to place two policemen in the hall, at the far end, with instructions to them to come to my assistance if necessary. As the military person refused to leave I had no other course left, but to call the policemen, and order them to remove him. The sight of the constables had the effect of subduing the disturber's ardour, and so, to ensure his good behaviour, I arranged that a policeman should sit on each side of him, with instructions that, if he moved hand or foot, or raised his voice, he was to be immediately ejected. Having done this, I went back to Mr. Dickens, and told him that all was quiet, and that he could commence his Reading.

His reception was most enthusiastic, and as he afterwards said, "resembled more the receptions given him by Manchester shillings, instead of Washington half-sovereigns." The Reading was the "Christmas Carol," and after the pause at the end of the first chapter, the military gentleman seemed to have had enough of it, and looking on either side of him at his guardians, decided that, after all, Readings were not in his line, and rolling more like a ship at sea, than a human being leaving a hall of well-dressed people, he retired amidst the jeers and laughter of the assembly to their immense satisfaction.

After this came the canine comedy which Mr. Dickens has himself described. By some means or another, a stray, comical-looking dog had contrived to force his way into the hall, unseen by the police and the ushers in attendance. During the Reading of a comic portion of the "Carol," this dog suddenly made his appearance from under the front seat, and stared intently at Mr. Dickens. It was fortunate that this happened during a comic scene, or Mr. Dickens, with his love of humour, would have had his gravity considerably upset, feeling sure, as he did, that the dog would take advantage of any applause that might ensue, to set up a bark. The public being too intent on the reader, did not notice the dog; but one of the ushers observing him, took an early opportunity of having the dog removed, a process which was quietly effected; but a little later the animal contrived to return to his former position, where he indulged in a prolonged howl, as if in great pain. This had such a ridiculous effect on Mr. Dickens, that he could not help laughing. Everybody laughed, but the dog was most unceremoniously ejected, receiving miscellaneous kicks and raps over the head from sticks and umbrellas. Strange to say, he returned the next night, but on his way into the hall, he indiscreetly knocked his head against Mr. Osgood's leg. That gentleman was too quick for the dog; seizing him with both his hands, he threw him over his shoulder, and he was caught like a ball at a cricket match by the ushers, and passed on from one to another, until he found himself in the street.

He was not, however, to be got rid of in this manner, for on the occasion of the third Reading he came again accompanied by another dog; but the staff were on the look-out for him, and he did not get in, much to his disappointment, for, as Mr. Dickens said, "he had evidently promised to pass the other dog free."

Not the least pleasant episode connected with our sojourn at Washington, was a private audience given to Mr. Dickens by the President (Mr. Andrew Johnson). He, with his family, had been present at all the Readings, and had twice requested Mr. Dickens's presence at the White House. On the first occasion this was rendered impossible by reason of a previous engagement; but, on the second occasion, Mr. Dickens and myself had the honour of waiting on him. Our cards being sent in to the President by his secretary, we were kept waiting in the ante-room of his private audience-chamber but a very few moments, during which we were able to note the simplicity with which this apartment was furnished, being greatly amused by a printed notice, stuck upon the walls of the chamber, requesting gentlemen to "kindly use the spittoons."

We were most cordially received by the President, who seemed to be impressed by the presence of his distinguished visitor, and for some moments sat looking at him, as if uncertain how to commence a conversation. He warmed up, however, in congratulatory expressions as to the effect the Readings had produced on him. This gave Mr. Dickens an opportunity of saying a few kindly words to his distinguished host, touching lightly on political matters, which just then were assuming rather a serious aspect, resulting eventually in the well-known impeachment of Andrew Johnson.

Many bitter things had been said by the political enemies of the President as to his habits of life, especially his alleged intemperance, all of which, to judge by his appearance and frank manner, were unjust. In a letter to Mr. Fields, Mr. Dickens gave his opinion of Andrew Johnson:

"I was very much surprised by the President's face and manner. It is, in its way, one of the most remarkable faces I have ever seen. Not imaginative, but very powerful in its firmness (or, perhaps, obstinacy), strength of will, and steadiness of purpose. There is a reticence in it, too, curiously at variance with that first unfortunate speech of his. A man not to be turned or trifled with. A man (I should say) who must be killed to be got out of the way. His manner is perfectly composed. We looked at one another pretty hard. There was an air of chronic anxiety upon him; but not a crease or a ruffle in his dress, and his papers were as composed as himself."

On leaving the President, after a most agreeable interview, Mr. Dickens was met by Sir Edward Thornton, who had arrived in a State sleigh, to present his credentials as English Ambassador; and in the anteroom adjoining the President's audience-chamber was an old friend of Mr. Dickens's awaiting an audience. This was General Blair, who so greatly distinguished himself during the war. This meeting was particularly pleasant to Mr. Dickens, being the means of renewing an acquaintance formed twenty-five years previously, on the prairies.

The day chosen for the interview with the President was Friday, February 7th, Mr. Dickens's birthday, which, at its commencement, did not bid fair to be a very happy one, for the "catarrh" was worse than ever, and but for the appointment at the White House, the day would undoubtedly have been spent by Mr. Dickens in his room. But his indomitable courage here again came to the fore, and he bestirred himself as usual to keep his engagement.

The occasion was to have been kept a secret, but by some means the newspapers got wind of it, and so from early morning visitors were continually calling with letters of congratulation, cards, birthday presents, and baskets of the most exquisite flowers, with which our room was literally covered. Telegrams and letters, radiant with good wishes from far-off places all over the country kept pouring in, and amongst these was a cablegram to myself from Ross, in Herefordshire, announcing the birth of a son. Mr. Dickens declared that the christening of the youngster ought to be postponed until after our return to England, that he might stand sponsor to him; a wish that was gratefully appreciated as another proof of the affectionate regard he had for me and mine.

In the afternoon, amongst other distinguished persons who called to offer their congratulations, was Mr. Charles Sumner, who, being an old friend, was admitted into Mr. Dickens's apartments, to find him covered with mustard poultices and apparently voiceless. Mr. Sumner, turning to me, said —

"Surely, Mr. Dolby, you are not going to allow Mr. Dickens to read to-night?"

I assured him it was not a question of my "allowing" him to do so, but a question of Mr. Dickens's determination to read if he were alive.

"I have told Mr. Dickens," I said, "at least a dozen times to-day, that it will be impossible for him to read; and but for my knowledge of him and of his wonderful power of changing when he gets to the little table, I should be even more anxious about him than I am.

I was right in my conjecture, for he had not faced his audience five minutes before, as usual, his powers returned to him, and he went through his evening's task as if he had been in the most robust health. The frequent experience of this return of power, when called upon, was a source of the greatest consolation to Mr. Dickens, and saved him a great deal of anxiety; and as his general health was not in the least affected by the "catarrh," it was very satisfactory to his friends that matters were no worse. The great fear for the time being was that his strength would give way, in which case he would have sunk altogether, especially as he had contracted the habit of taking little or no food, and suffered from sleepless nights.

None of these drawbacks were perceptible to the general public, when Mr. Dickens made his appearance before them, and as audiences vary in their aspect, in the same way as does a landscape under the influence of sun or cloud, so was Mr. Dickens affected by the appearance of his audience, which on this occasion was worthy of the day they came to honour. Some unknown hands had gained possession of the hall during the day, and had decorated it, especially the little table, with costly flowers. Amongst the audience were the President's family, Ambassadors, Secretaries of State, Judges of the Supreme Court, the naval and military authorities in full uniform, and every notability in Washington, with a perfect bouquet of ladies, whose toilettes resembled

114

those of a State ball or of a grand night at the opera. These circumstances all helped to distract Mr. Dickens's mind from his own immediate sufferings, and when the cheering had subsided, it was only to those who knew him the best that there was any lack of voice even in the few first words he uttered.

When the Reading was over, the whole audience stood and cheered, the ladies throwing their bouquets to him, and the gentlemen the "button-hole" flowers out of their coats, causing Mr. Dickens to return to the platform to make a little speech of grateful acknowledgment, which was highly appreciated by his audience.

The following day (our last in Washington) was spent in the reception of friends who came to say "good-bye" to him they so loved and honoured; for it was well known that in his state of health he could not leave his apartments to call on them, even had the climate allowed him to do so.

Mr. Osgood and myself, who, to use his own expression, were "always doing some ridiculous things to keep me in spirits," had been out in the snow settling accounts and making farewell calls. On our return we perceived Mr. Dickens standing at the sitting-room window of our apartments, and, being still some distance from the house, we put on a tremendous spurt, pretending we had been in training for the walking match, and, rushing madly up the staircase, and bursting into the sitting-room, where Mr. Dickens was apparently writing at his table, we sat down on the floor, gasping for breath, much to his amusement, whilst he administered to each of us a cool brandy-and-soda before we could be induced to give any account of ourselves or the Washington Readings just completed.

Before leaving Washington I had received a friendly intimation from a gentleman in a high position in the Internal Revenue Department, that it was barely possible that the "rowdy" element, although absent from Washington, might manifest itself in the western part of the State of New York, and as our tour included the cities of Syracuse, Rochester, and Buffalo, I was naturally anxious as to the form the rowdyism would take.

My friend explained to me that the greater proportion of the collectors and the heads of departments in his bureau in this part of America consisted of Anglo-Americans and Irish-Americans, nearly all of whom suffered from anglophobia. At this time there was an Act of Congress which provided that all theatres and permanent places of amusement in the States should pay not only income tax to the Government (which was rated at five per cent, of the income), but in addition there was in each city a Mayor's license to be obtained and a city tax of two and a half per cent, on the gross receipts. But there was a clause in this Act of Congress to the effect that "occasional concerts and lectures were excepted;" and as Mr. Dickens's Readings clearly came under the head of this exemption, my friend suggested that, in the event of any molestation from the local authorities, it would be well to have an official authority for the non-payment of the charges in Mr. Dickens's case. He also proposed "I should see the Chief Commissioner of Internal Revenue in Washington, and get him to send instructions to the smaller places we were about to visit.

There were other reasons for this precaution being taken, as the political atmosphere was daily becoming more murky, and the impeachment of Andrew Johnson was regarded as a certainty. In that event the officials under his government would in all probability not be employed by any new government which might come into power — a prospect that would make the existing officials the more assiduous in the execution of their duty.

At the suggestion of my friend I made an appointment with the Chief Commissioner to talk the matter over with him, and was received by him and his secretaries with the utmost courtesy — a courtesy that is always present in official dealings in America — and as the interview was a lengthy one, the conversation incident to it being interspersed with pleasant chat on other matters, the time passed on far into the luncheon hour. Finding this to be the case, I invited the general and his secretaries to lunch with me at Whelcker's — an invitation which was accepted as being the readiest means of disposing of the question without the loss of any more *official time*.

During lunch the general suggested that I should supply him with my tour list, that he might communicate officially with each city. But, as it not unfrequently happens that in the very best regulated official departments, accidents do sometimes happen, I proposed that as my tour list might be again changed, it would answer the same purpose if he gave me an official general order or travelling letter, containing his views in the matter, which, in case of necessity, might be shown to the local agents, and so save not only some trouble to them, but in all probability some inconvenience to Mr. Dickens or myself.

After some little deliberation this was assented to, and within an hour of our separating I was the recipient of the much-desired order, which I found useful on an occasion which will be referred to later on, when the rowdy element *did* assert itself.

A novelty in official routine presented itself to the notice of Mr. Dickens while he was confined to the house during his illness, in the shape of crowds of well-dressed ladies leaving the Treasury Department (a magnificent white marble structure nearly opposite) every afternoon at about half-past three, and a large crowd of well-dressed gentlemen in waiting for the ladies, conveying an impression to his mind that the men had not all the legislation to themselves, and that in the Treasury Department there was a house of Congress for the ladies as well as the men.

Having an invitation from Mr. Sumner to visit the various Government Offices, we were taken through this same Treasury Department, where, to our astonishment, we found that all the clerks employed for copying and official work were ladies. Mr. Sumner explained to us that since the termination of the war, and, indeed, during the latter portion of the time of the war, the mothers, widows, and sisters of the officers, and of some of the men who were killed in battle, and on whom they were dependent for support, were employed to do such work as had previously been done by male clerks — an arrangement thoroughly in keeping with the thoughtfulness and good-nature of the American character, and one which impressed itself strongly on Mr. Dickens's mind, at the same time persuading him that the Government were not only performing a kind and humane act, but that they were unconsciously "running" a matrimonial agency, for he had opportunities of watching the friendly greetings that took place every afternoon, and the little exchanges of love tokens, in the shape of flowers, gloves, and sweetmeats.

On Sunday, the 9th of February, we took our departure from Washington, with many regrets at leaving so many kind friends and pleasant companionships behind us. It was my intention to proceed direct to the New England cities, viz. New Haven, Hartford, Providence, and Worcester, to superintend the sale of tickets in these places for the Readings announced for the week commencing on the 17th, but Mr. Dickens being desirous I should remain with him for the farewell Readings in Baltimore and Philadelphia, I, contrary to my own feeling in the matter, consented to do so. I had my fears lest the "noble army of speculators" should make their appearance again in these cities, and should they do so, I felt sure (knowing the inhabitants of those places as I did) that their appearance would have a prejudicial effect on our receipts, and for this reason I was desirous of being on the spot myself to frustrate as much as possible their plans. Mr. Dickens attached no importance to my fears in this respect, and, insisting that I wanted rest, over-persuaded me to remain with him, and allow my English ticket agent to sell the tickets in my stead. I had my misgivings that this arrangement would not act satisfactorily, and in carrying out my Chief's wishes in the matter telegraphed to my English agent in New York that I should not be with him until the end of the week.

The morning after our arrival in Baltimore was devoted to making preparations for the evening's Reading. After these Mr. Dickens proposed that he should take Mr. Osgood and myself out for our daily "breather," as he used to call it — a walk of about twelve miles — for as the time drew nearer to the date of the match the training was more severe. The "breather," however, was not of the duration Mr. Dickens had intended, for the snow and ice, with a freezing atmosphere, made walking a great difficulty, and after many falls, our "trainer" decided he would take "his men" home. There a surprise of a most unpleasant kind was awaiting me in the Baltimore evening paper just published.

My attention was first attracted on opening the paper with the following sensational lines:

Riot at the Sale of Charles Dickens's Tickets
At New Haven! Dickens's Agent and New York Speculators
Arrested! The Mayor Telegraphs to the Mayor of Hartford to expose the Swindle!
Great Excitement in New Haven: Indignation Meetings to be held!

When I drew Mr. Dickens's attention to these pleasing items, and regretted that I had been led away by his kindness in his desire that I should remain with him, he, after reading the paragraphs, simply remarked: "Well, what are you going to do about it?" There was but one thing to do, in my opinion, and that was to go to the scene of trouble, and, if possible, make out for myself the real state of the case. It was an eighteen hours' journey — unpleasant at most times, but doubly so with eighteen inches of snow on the ground all over the country. Arriving in New York, and calling at the Westminster Hotel, I found a gentleman who had just come from New Haven, and who was a witness of the previous day's proceedings. From him I learned the facts, which were very simple. The New York speculators had accompanied my agent *en masse* to New Haven, and by some means or another had prevailed on him to distribute amongst them the eight front rows of seats before commencing the sale to the public. Such an act of folly, not to say dishonesty, became apparent the moment the sale commenced, resulting in a free hand-to-hand fight in the street, the English agent making his escape as best he could, leaving a large proportion of the New York speculators, with poor old "George Washington" amongst them, in the cells of the police station.

The case was of so unusual a character, as reported to me, that I resolved on returning to Baltimore, to consult with Mr. Dickens as to what was the best course to pursue. We decided that it would be better that I should return to New Haven, and if the case really was as it had been represented to me (and I had no reason to doubt it), then the New Haven Reading should be given up, and the money returned to the holders of tickets, no matter what the amount might be. Before proceeding on my journey back to Baltimore, I had telegraphed to a personal friend at Hartford to send me an account of the day's proceedings there, my agent not being aware that I was in possession of any information with regard to his own shortcomings. The information from Hartford being of a highly satisfactory character, and all the tickets in New Haven, in the meanwhile, having been sold at a bookseller's shop in the city, I journeyed thither more leisurely than otherwise I should have done, arriving on Wednesday evening, the 12th of February.

I reached the hotel about eight o'clock in the evening — a time when the American hotels are generally crowded. I found myself suddenly the object of much abuse. As an indignation meeting had been advertised to take place that same evening at nine o'clock in the large room of the hotel, I volunteered, with the kind permission of the promoters of the meeting, to form one of the indignant public, a suggestion which seemed to meet with general approval.

The Mayor was in the chair, and I must confess that, in the whole of my experience, I never came across a man who was so unfit to be a chairman of any meeting, indignant or otherwise, leaving alone his apparent incapacity to hold such high office as Mayor of so important and thriving a city as New Haven. He stated the case as well as he could, premising his remarks with a statement that until then he had never heard of Mr. Charles Dickens in his life, consequently could have no personal feeling in the matter. He had, on general grounds, a great objection to all places of entertainment and recreation, and an utter abhorrence of anything in the shape of a swindle; and admitted, that although he knew nothing of the merits of the case then under discussion, he had felt it to be his duty not only to caution the Mayor of Hartford as to what *might* occur in *his* city, but to preside at the meeting then being held.

Another orator intervened and took the matter ruthlessly out of the Mayor's hands. Addressing myself, and not the meeting, he stated the case so clearly that I had only one course left me, and that was to act on the lines laid down in my last interview with Mr. Dickens, and great as was the indignation at the treatment the New Haven people considered they had received at the hands of the agent, it was small as compared with their frenzy when I informed them that I had determined not to allow Mr. Dickens to read in New Haven at all, and that at ten o'clock on the following morning I should be only too pleased to refund the money paid for the tickets at the advertised prices. Here a new difficulty presented itself, for some of the persons in the room had bought tickets from the speculators, for which they had paid large premiums. Others suddenly became satisfied with the position of their seats in the hall, and felt it to be a hardship that they should be deprived of the pleasure of hearing Mr. Dickens read. As these gentlemen represented the larger proportion of those present, I was at a loss to understand for what reason they were all thus assembled. The Mayor could not understand either, and speedily vacated the chair to beat a hasty retreat, and be seen no more until the following day, when I had enlisted his services to superintend the return of the money for the tickets already purchased. Finding me to be inexorable, the meeting became more indignant than ever, leaving me so far the master of the situation, but with a loss of $2,600.

After the meeting, and over a friendly cigar with some of the indignant ones, I became convinced that the New Haven public had a real grievance, and it was perhaps a "little steep on them" (as one of the gentlemen present expressed it) that the Reading should be given up, and particularly so on those who had bought of the speculators. At the same time, I had Mr. Dickens's feelings in the matter to consult, which to me were all-important, and I felt sure that when it came to his knowledge that one of our own people had been in the pay of the speculators in New Haven, the amount of money he would lose by not reading there would not trouble his mind.

On the following morning I met my friends, and had the novel sensation of returning money in America instead of receiving it, and it was with the greatest reluctance that such of the public as kept the appointment I had made at the meeting, or through the medium of the newspapers, consented to receive their money back. The Mayor was present, and, for having assailed me previous to my arrival in New Haven on a charge of false play in the selling of the tickets, he was profuse in his apologies for the part he had taken in the matter. He proposed that a deputation of the leading citizens should wait on me with a view to induce Mr. Dickens to give another date to New Haven, should I have one at disposal, that the town of New Haven might not be entirely left out in the cold.

The Mayor's apologies were accepted, and a seeming friendship struck up between us (or, as Mr. Dickens afterwards expressed it, "Dolby and the Mayor of New Haven alternately embrace and exchange mortal defiances"). I promised him I would submit his recommendation to the consideration of Mr. Dickens, and, if time allowed, would use my utmost endeavours to appoint another evening for the purpose he proposed. After waiting in New Haven nearly the whole day, while but few persons came to claim their money (less than six hundred dollars being returned in all), I took advantage of the circumstance of being in the neighbourhood to call on Mr. Donald Mitchell, perhaps better known by his *nom de plume,* "Ike Marvel," who was said to hold some tickets for the Reading in New Haven. Mr. Mitchell's house was situated at the top of a high and steep hill some miles from New Haven, and in my journeying thither I experienced the delight of a long sleigh ride, and its exhilarating effects, after the worry and anxiety of the past few days. During the previous night a furious gale of wind had lifted a large tree from the spot on which it grew, and deposited it immediately opposite the entrance door to the house, missing the porch (fortunately), by a few inches.

The greeting given me by Mr. Mitchell took place across the tree, over which I had to scramble before I could enter the house. My course of action with regard to the abandonment of the Readings was highly approved by my host; at the same time he expressed the hope that the efforts of the deputation to obtain another date would meet with success.

After leaving New Haven, I journeyed to Philadelphia to attend the farewell Reading in that city, where I found that the local speculators had been holding out for such high prices that the public had held out also, and that at the last moment the former were glad to sell at half the cost price, and even at this rate the public would not buy, being under the impression, as at Baltimore, that the announcement of "Final Farewell Reading" was nothing but a *coup de théâtre* on my part, and that later on there would be some more "farewells." They inquired of me on leaving the hall—

"When will Mr. Dickens read here again?"

"Never," I answered.

"What! not come back again after such a business as you are doing?"

"No, sir," I replied; "Mr. Dickens's time is all filled up."

"Well now that is too bad," joined in the ladies; "and those horrid speculators got hold of all the tickets and some of our friends couldn't afford to buy any; and there were several empty seats in the hall tonight!"

I explained that the loss was the speculators' in this respect, and that Mr. Dickens regretted that his time would not allow him to appear even "once more" (as an enthusiastic lady admirer had pleaded), to so delightful and appreciative an audience as that one in Philadelphia.

On my way through New York, I had telegraphed to the erring ticket agent, who was then in Worcester (Mass.), to rejoin me in New York on Sunday morning, and not to go to Boston for the sale of tickets there as arranged. He was in ignorance of my movements during the past week, or that I knew anything of his New Haven escapade; and meeting me, according to my instructions, was much surprised at the information I possessed on the subject. Finding that excuses would avail him nothing, he explained that the speculators had plied him with Bourbon whiskey, and that, not knowing what he was about, he had fallen into their net, and, as I afterwards proved to him, out of his situation, for he was instantly dismissed. His passage for England being secured for him by the following Wednesday's steamer, he left the shores of America a wiser and a sadder man.

Mr. Dickens would frequently, on troublesome occasions, remark that he felt sure I should be bereft of my senses (as he would be bereft of his, if the situation were not sometimes so comically disagreeable), and he used frequently to point as a proof of this theory of his to a printer's error in one of the advertisements, which immensely delighted him. It ran thus: "The reading will be comprised within *two minutes;* and the audience are earnestly entreated to be seated *ten hours* before its commencement." As will be seen, the printer had transposed the minutes and the hours, the mistake causing me to be chaffed on all sides, not only by Mr. Dickens and our friends, but in the newspapers also — the latter never being backward in taking advantage of any item that may come under their notice, especially in connection with the doings of any public man or woman in America.

Mr. Osgood having returned to Boston to make arrangements for four more Readings there, I was left alone with Mr. Dickens to travel to Hartford, Providence, and Worcester with him; and as the New Haven Reading was given up, we had Monday, February 17th, on our hands. This was devoted to making up accounts, and the remitting of money to Coutts's, after which Mr. Dickens took me out for a "breather," or, as he termed this one, a "buster," our walk being from the Westminster Hotel along the Fifth Avenue, and round the Central Park (altogether about eight or nine miles); and as both Mr. Dickens and myself were well known in New York, and as the newspapers had frequent references to the walking match, the pace at which we went along the fashionable quarter of the city created some little amusement. The following morning we were much interested to find this paragraph in one of the daily newspapers: "Dickens and Dolby are in town, and had a walking match yesterday in the park. They were afterwards seen taking dinner at Delmonico's, and as Dolby paid for the dinner, we know who *lost the match.*"

As a matter of fact we did not dine at Delmonico's, but at our own hotel, for in the evening we travelled to Hartford, to be in readiness for the Reading on the following evening.

Beyond referring to Hartford as a pleasant city, pleasantly situated, with a good hotel (the Alleyn House), and a delightful hall (the Alleyn Hall), in which all the gas jets are lighted by electricity, and where there are the most electrical of audiences, no incident worthy of record took place here. The Mayor of Hartford had taken no notice of the telegram sent him by the Mayor of New Haven, being himself an enlightened man, who felt assured that if the incidents had occurred in New Haven of which the Mayor of that city had complained, such occurrences were entirely without the knowledge or approbation of either Mr. Dickens or myself.

The following day we travelled to Providence (Rhode Island), and were greatly surprised on our arrival there to find a crowd of some thousands of people awaiting Mr. Dickens at the railway station, just to get a peep at him. It was Mr. Dickens's habit, when the weather permitted, to walk to his hotel from the "depot" (as the railway stations in America are called), and without imagining that the crowd would accompany us as far as the hotel, we started off as usual, leaving our men behind to see after our baggage. On leaving the station the whole crowd followed us through the streets, some of its component parts occasionally darting out in front of Mr. Dickens to have a good look at him, whilst others requested the honour of shaking him by the hand. Two policemen standing in the street saw that Mr. Dickens was being inconvenienced by this, and at once took charge of us, one walking by the side of Mr. Dickens, and the other by my side, until we reached the hotel, when the crowd filed on each side of the steps, up which we marched, Mr. Dickens remarking to me: "This is very like going into the police van in Bow Street, isn't it?"

The crowd were very well behaved, and Mr. Dickens was more amused than annoyed at our unexpected reception.

Providence being an isolated sort of place (reminding the traveller of some of the Dutch cities in appearance and construction), we did not anticipate a large house here, and I was greatly surprised to find the tickets all sold; and at the Reading, Mr. Dickens was as delighted with his audience as he was with the receipts ($2,140).

Our next city was Worcester (Mass.), a most picturesque city, and one of the oldest in the States. Its inhabitants turned out in grand style for the Reading, which was given under peculiar circumstances; for in the basement of the City Hall (the hall in which the Reading was given being on the first floor), a Poultry Show was held, and as the birds connected the flaming gas lights necessary for their exhibition with the brightness of the morning sun, they kept up a constant crowing the whole evening, greatly disconcerting Mr. Dickens (until the exhibition closed at nine o'clock, when the birds were allowed to sleep), but evidently unheard by the audience, whose attention was as wrapt in Mr. Dickens and the Reading as if it had been given under the most auspicious of circumstances. We were curious to know how it would fare with Mr. McKean Buchanan (the tragedian), on the following evening, whose acquaintance we made before leaving, and who was announced to give a Shakespearian performance, but which report said had to be postponed, the birds being too much for the distinguished actor.

The business of this week having been accomplished, with its daily travelling in the coldest of weather and deep snow on the ground, it was with the greatest delight that we returned on Saturday, February 22nd, to our Boston home, at the Parker House Hotel, and the society of our Boston friends. That evening we dined with Mr. Fields, and a distinguished party was invited to join the company, amongst whom were some politicians of high standing. Since our departure from Washington the threatening storm in the political horizon had burst, and the impeachment of the President was all but certain. Everything in America has to give way to political matters, and I foresaw that in this excitement even the rage for Dickens in Boston was likely to abate for a time, for the sale of the tickets for the four Readings announced for the following week, although large, was not up to the standard of our previous Readings in Boston. This was fully accounted for by the friends of Mr. Fields, whom we met at dinner on the evening of our return to Boston, and who explained that the impeachment vote, which was to be taken at five in the afternoon of the following Monday, was all-absorbing to the public for the time being. It was our original intention to give eight Readings in all during this visit to Boston, four of which only were announced, and having in view the political excitement, and Mr. Dickens' state of health, we decided (on our return home to the hotel) not to give the last four, but to devote the week to rest and recreation, feeling assured that by that time the impeachment would have been a thing of the past (for no excitement lasts long in the States), and hoping that during the rest Mr. Dickens would have got rid of his catarrh. As we had still three weeks more travelling to do in smaller cities, this was most desirable at any cost. The effect of the Presidential impeachment made itself felt not only at our Readings on the first night of our return to Boston, but at every place of entertainment in the city. The three large theatres, although up to that time playing a tremendous business, were stricken with paralysis. We suffered the least of any of them, but our long line of persons waiting nightly at half-past seven on the chance of some unsold seats (or to deal with the speculators) was conspicuous by its absence, although had they come we could easily have accommodated them, for my friends the speculators had caught the political fever, and had held aloof for a time; consequently I was fairly well off for seats for the two first Readings of the week. When once the public became aware that the impeachment was to take place, and that March 9th was the date fixed for the discussion of it in Washington, they returned to their old habits and haunts; the theatres filled as of old, and our receipts for the remaining Readings of the week were up to their old standard (an average of three thousand dollars a Reading in Boston).

As there was no business to be done — a deputation only from New Haven to be received, when I on behalf of Mr. Dickens appointed another evening for that city in the middle of March; and Mr. Osgood being in the cities in the State of New York (Rochester, Buffalo, Syracuse, and Albany), superintending the sale of tickets for those places, I was left comparatively at my ease, with very little to do but to prepare for the walking match, which was to come off on the following Saturday, February 29th.

Mr. Dickens, according to his promise, had drawn up the articles of agreement, which had been sent to Boston to be printed, so as to be in readiness for signature by "the men" against the time Mr. Osgood and myself should return there; and he had arranged to give a state dinner party to commemorate the event.

The articles of agreement were as follows: —

The Great International Walking Match of February 29, 1868.

"*Articles of Agreement* entered into at Baltimore in the United States of America, this third day of February, in the year of our Lord one thousand eight hundred and sixty-eight, between George Dolby (British subject), *alias* the 'Man of Ross,' and James Ripley Osgood (American citizen), *alias* the 'Boston Bantam.'

"*Whereas* some bounce having arisen between the above men in reference to feats of pedestrianism and agility, they have agreed to settle their differences and prove who is the better man by means of a walking match for two hats a side and the glory of their respective countries; and whereas they agree that the said match shall come off, whatsoever the weather, on the Mill Dam Road, outside Boston, on Saturday, the 29th of the present month, and whereas they agree that the personal attendants on themselves during the whole walk, and also the umpires and starters and declarers of victory in the match shall be James T. Fields of Boston, known in sporting circles as Massachusetts Jemmy, and Charles Dickens, of "Falstaff's," Gad's Hill, whose surprising performances (without the least variation), on that truly national instrument, the American Catarrh, have won for him the well-merited title of the Gad's Hill Gasper. Now these are to be the articles of the match: —

"1. The men are to be started on the day appointed by Massachusetts Jemmy and the Gasper.

"2. Jemmy and the Gasper are, on some previous day, to walk out at the rate of not less than four miles an hour by the Gasper's watch for one hour and a half. At the expiration of that one hour and a half they are to carefully note the place at which they halt. On the match coming off they are to station themselves in the middle of the road at that precise point, and the men (keeping clear of them and of each other) are to turn round them, right shoulder inward, and walk back to the starting-point. The man declared by them to pass the starting-point first is to be the victor and the winner of the match.

"3. No jostling or fouling allowed.

"4. All cautions and orders issued to the men by the umpires, starters, and declarers of victory to be considered final and admitting of no appeal.

"5. A sporting narrative of the match to be written by the Gasper within one week after its coming off, and the same to be duly printed (at the expense of the subscribers to these articles) on a broadside. The said broadside to be framed and glazed, and one copy of the same to be carefully preserved by each of the subscribers to these articles.

"6. The men to show on the evening of the day of walking at six o'clock precisely at the Parker House, Boston, when and where a dinner will be given them by the Gasper. The Gasper to occupy the chair, faced by Massachusetts Jemmy. The latter promptly and formally to invite, as soon as may be after the date of these presents, the following guests to honour the said dinner with their presence, that is to say —

"Mistress Annie Fields, Mr. Charles Eliot Norton and Mrs. Norton, Professor James Russell Lowell and Mrs. Lowell, and Miss Lowell, Dr. Oliver Wendell Holmes and Mrs. Holmes, Mr. Howard Malcolm Ticknor and Mrs. Ticknor, Mr. Aldrich and Mrs. Aldrich, Mr. Schlesinger, and an obscure poet named Longfellow (if discoverable), and Miss Longfellow.

"*Now lastly.* In token of their accepting the trusts and offices by these articles conferred upon them,

Parker House, Boston.
The scene of the dinner after "The Great International Walking Match."

these articles are solemnly and formally signed by Massachusetts Jemmy and by the Gad's Hill Gasper, as well as by the men themselves.

"Signed by the *Man of Ross,* otherwise George Dolby.

"Signed by the *Boston Bantam,* otherwise James R. Osgood.

"Signed by *Massachusetts Jemmy,* otherwise James T. Fields.

"Signed by the *Gad's Hill Gasper,* otherwise Charles Dickens.

"*Witness* to the signatures, William S. Anthony."

In pursance of clause No. 2 Mr. Dickens *did* take Mr. Fields *over the ground,* and at such a pace that Fields (who was a good pedestrian) declared on his return *he* had "had enough of it," being surprised at Mr. Dickens's prowess in this respect. [1] As all Boston was talking of the match it was deemed expedient to keep time and place a profound secret, or "half Boston" would have turned out to witness the match if the weather and the state of the roads had permitted. The roads were covered with snow and sheets and blocks of ice, making it almost dangerous to walk at all. Neither Osgood nor myself had ever traversed the road before, and this made it the more difficult.

On the day of the match an early start was made, so as to elude the movements of the general public, who threatened to be on the look-out for us. Mr. Dickens's carriage and our men were in attendance to follow us; the carriage to carry our great coats and wraps and some creature comforts for the inner man. But as the match is so graphically and humorously described by Mr. Dickens in the "Sporting Narrative," I will reproduce it here.

"THE SPORTING NARRATIVE.

"*The Men,*

"The Boston Bantam (*alias* Bright Chanticleer), is a young bird, though too old to be caught with chaff. He comes of a thorough game breed, and has a clear though modest crow. He pulls down the scale at ten stone and a half and add a pound or two. His previous performances in the pedestrian line have not been numerous. He once achieved a neat little match against time in two left boots at Philadelphia; but this must be considered as a pedestrian eccentricity, and cannot be accepted by the rigid chronicler as high art.

"The old mower with the scythe and hour-glass has not yet laid his mawler heavily on the Bantam's frontispiece, but he has had a grip at the Bantam's top feathers, and in plucking out a handful was very near making him like the great Napoleon Buonaparte (with the exception of the victualling department), when the ancient one found himself too much occupied to carry out the idea, and had to give it up.

"The Man of Ross (*alias* old Alick Pope, alias All-our-praises-why-should-lords, &c.), is a thought and a half too fleshy, and if he accidentally sat down upon his baby would do it to the tune of fourteen stone. This popular codger is of the rubicund and jovial sort, and has long been known as a piscatorial pedestrian on the banks of the Wye. But Izaak Walton hadn't pace — look at his book and you'll find it slow — and when that article comes into question, the fishing rod may prove to some of his disciples a rod in pickle. Howbeit the Man of Ross is a lively ambler, and has a sweet stride of his own.

"*The Training,* "If vigorous attention to diet could have brought both men up to the post in tip-top feather, their condition would have left nothing to be desired. But both men might have had more daily practice in the poetry of motion. Their breathings were confined to an occasional Baltimore burst under the guidance of the Gasper, and to an amicable toddle between themselves at Washington.

"*The Course,* "Six miles and a half, good measure, from the first tree in the Mill Dam Road lies the little village (with no refreshments in it but five oranges and a bottle of blacking), of Newton Centre. Here Massachusetts Jemmy and the Gasper had established the turningpoint. The road comprehended every variety of inconvenience to test the mettle of the men, and nearly the whole of it was covered with snow.

"*The Start* was effected beautifully. The men taking their stand in exact line at the starting-post, the first tree aforesaid, received from the Gasper the warning, 'Are you ready?' and then the signal, 'One, two, three — go!' They got away exactly together, and at a spinning speed, waited on by Massachusetts Jemmy and the Gasper.

"*The Race.* "In the teeth of an intensely cold and bitter wind, before which the snow flew fast and furious across the road from right to left, the Bantam slightly led. But the Man responded to the challenge, and soon breasted him. For the first three miles each led by a yard or so alternately, but the walking was very even. On four miles being called by the Gasper, the men were side by side, and then ensued one of the best periods of the race, the same splitting pace being held by both through a heavy snow wreath and up a dragging hill. At this point it was anybody's game, a dollar on Rossius and two half-dollars on the member of the feathery tribe. When five miles were called the men were still shoulder to shoulder. At about six miles the Gasper put on a tremendous spurt to leave the men behind and establish himself at the turning-point at the entrance of the village. He afterwards declared he had received a mental knock-downer in taking his station and facing about to find Bright Chanticleer close in upon him, and Rossius steaming up like a locomotive. The Bantam rounded first; Rossius rounded wide; and from that moment the Bantam steadily shot ahead. Though both were breathed at the turn, the Bantam quickly got his bellows into obedient condition, and blew away like an orderly blacksmith in full work. The forcing pumps of Rossius likewise proved themselves tough and true, and warranted first rate, but he fell off in pace; whereas the Bantam pegged away with his little drum-sticks as if he saw his wives and a peck of barley waiting for him at the family perch. Continually gaining upon him of Ross, Chanticleer gradually drew ahead within a few yards of half a mile, finally doing the whole distance in two hours and forty-eight minutes. Ross had ceased to compete three miles short of the winning-post, but bravely walked it out, and came in seven minutes later.

"*Remarks,* "The difficulties under which this plucky match was walked can only be appreciated by those who were on the ground. To the excessive rigour of the icy blast and the depth and state of the snow, must be added the constant scattering of the latter into the air and into the eyes of the men, while heads of hair, beards, eyelashes, and eyebrows were frozen into icicles. To breathe at all in such a rarefied and disturbed atmosphere was not easy, but to breathe up to the required mark was genuine slogging, ding-dong hard labour. That both competitors were game to the backbone, doing what they did under such conditions, was evident to all; but to his gameness the courageous Bantam added unexpected endurance, and (like the sailor's watch that did three hours to the cathedral clock's one), unexpected powers of going when wound up. The knowing eye could not fail to detect considerable disparity between the lads, Chanticleer being, as Mrs. Cratchit said of Tiny Tim, 'very light to carry,' and Rossius promising fair to attain the rotundity of the anonymous cove in the epigram —

'And when he walks the streets the paviors cry,
  "God bless you, sir!" — and lay their rammers by."'

As will be seen by the narrative, I was badly beaten by Mr. Osgood, whom at the turning-point at the bottom of a steep hill, I allowed (acting under Mr. Dickens's instructions) to get too far away from me, never in the least supposing that he had staying power sufficient to carry him on for the rest of the journey. My supposition probably would have been confirmed had not Mrs. Fields arrived on the scene in her carriage, and turning round accompanied Osgood the rest of the walk, plying him the whole time with *bread soaked in brandy!* We all, with the exception of Osgood, of course, felt that she showed great favouritism in this respect, but she frankly admitted that she would have done the same by me, if she had met me coming in first, a confession that was made in so delightful a manner that we forgave her. The dinner was a great success, and as Mr. Dickens had received so many floral tributes at the hands of Mrs. Fields, he had made up his mind that the table should not be wanting in this respect, and had arranged to have a perfect flower-garden for its decoration. There were two immense crowns, having for their base the choicest exotics, and the loops composed of violets; and all round the table was a border of a choice creeper, with roses placed at intervals, a button-hole for each gentleman, and a bouquet of flowers for each lady, the whole presenting such a scene, of its kind, as had never been witnessed in Boston before. It was a source of great pleasure to numbers of people staying in the hotel, who were admitted to the exhibition before the hour for dinner had arrived. The usual form of speech-making on such an occasion was dispensed with, and only one toast proposed, which was "The health of Her Majesty the Queen of England;" but the conversation and fun supplied the place of speeches, and in parting for the night every one declared that there never before had been such a social gathering as this one.

The following week was a week of rest, so far as the Readings were concerned, but was a busy one in many other ways. "No Thoroughfare" had made a great success at the Adelphi Theatre, in London, and all the theatres in America were playing piratical versions of it; and although Mr. Dickens had, through Messrs. Ticknor and Fields, registered the play as their property (they being American citizens), still the managers defied the law, and continued playing the piece to overflowing houses. This was a source of annoyance to Mr. Dickens, less on account of the fees to which he considered himself entitled, than on account of the defiant manner in which his property was taken: notably in one case, in New York, when he proposed to a leading manager that he would be pleased to superintend the mounting of the piece in his theatre if he would accept his services, and would use his own book rather than a mutilated one. This offer was discourteously disregarded, and no notice whatever taken of Mr. Dickens's liberal offer.

With a view to the establishment of an International Copyright Act, some of the leading authors and publishers waited on Mr. Dickens in Boston, requesting him to attend a meeting, and to express his views on the matter, an invitation which Mr. Dickens declined, on the ground that he felt the case to be a hopeless one, as the Western men, in his opinion, were too strong for the legitimate publisher in the East. He gave his reasons why the passing of such an Act would be a matter of difficulty; as in his "experiences he never found any people willing to pay for a thing they could legally steal," and so he declined losing any time over the subject.

A dinner at Longfellow's on the Wednesday evening of the rest-week, and another dinner party given by Dickens, made the time pass pleasantly. The former was a "man's" dinner, and a most enjoyable one. The party consisted of Messrs. Longfellow, Dickens, Agassiz, Lowell, Oliver Wendell Holmes, Bayard Taylor, and myself; and the fun flew fast and furious.

The dinner given by Mr. Dickens was his last in Boston, as we had to leave for Rochester at the end of the week, not to return there until the end of that month, for the farewell Readings, when our time in Boston would be very limited, and would have to be devoted to the settlement of our affairs and farewells. On this occasion all ceremony was to be dispensed with, and as the catarrh showed signs of leaving the patient, Mr. Dickens was in the best of spirits, and his own joviality became so contagious that even the most dignified of the guests caught the infection and went in for fun. A favourite subject of conversation with Mr. Dickens was the art of speech-making, which he always said was one of the easiest and simplest things in the world.

I remember in England on one occasion, when Mr. Wilkie Collins joined us at supper after a Reading in a small country town, the conversation at supper turned on the subject of speech-making. Mr. Wilkie Collins remarked that he had invariably felt a difficulty when called upon for a speech either at a public meeting or after dinner, adding that for important occasions his habit was to make notes of what he had to say, and keep them before him for reference during the progress of the speech.

As is well known, Mr. Dickens was one of the happiest of speakers, and on all occasions without any notes to assist him in this most difficult of arts. Declaring that to make a speech was the easiest thing in the world, he said the only difficulty that existed was in introducing the subject to be dealt with. "Now suppose I am the president of a rowing club and Dolby is the honorary secretary. At our farewell dinner, or supper, for the season, I, as president, should propose his health in these words:"

Here he made a speech of the most flattering description, calling on the subject of it for a reply. As I did not feel equal to a response I asked Mr. Collins to try his skill first. He handed the responsibility over to Mr. Wills, who in his turn handed it back to Mr. Dickens, who then told us in a ludicrous speech what the honorary secretary ought to have said, though I am certain no ordinary honorary secretary would ever have dreamt of such a performance. Then I asked Mr. Dickens if he could explain to us his *modus operandi* of preparing an important speech, Mr. Wilkie Collins adding that it would be curious to know what (besides the speech) was passing in his mind during its delivery. He told us that, supposing the speech was to be delivered in the evening, his habit was to take a long walk in the morning, during which he would decide on the various heads to be dealt with. These being arranged in their proper order, he would in his "mind's eye," liken the whole subject to the tire of a cart wheel — he being the hub. From the hub to the tire he would run as many spokes as there were subjects to be treated, and during the progress of the speech he would deal with each spoke separately, elaborating them as he went round the wheel; and when all the spokes dropped out one by one, and nothing but the tire and space remained, he would know that he had accomplished his task, and that his speech was at an end.

Mr. Wills suggested that if he were in this position, the wheel would whiz round with such rapidity that he would see nothing but space to commence with, and that, without notes or memoranda, in space he would be left — a conclusion in which Mr. Wilkie Collins and I fully concurred.

It was my fortune on many occasions after this to accompany Mr. Dickens when he took the chair at public dinners or meetings, and remembering on all such occasions his plan of action, I have been amused to observe him dismiss the spoke from his mind by a quick action of the finger as if he were knocking it away. Even when listening to a speech he would (if interested) follow the speaker's words by an almost imperceptible action, as if taking down the speech in shorthand, that being, as he used to say, a habit contracted in the early part of his career; and many times when I have been writing a letter at his dictation, I have noticed him punctuate the sentences by the same movement.

Well, at the Boston dinner, Mr. Dickens proposed an illustration of his theory, Fields and himself were to nominate rival candidates to represent some imaginary borough at an English election, Mr. Dickens selecting me as his candidate, and Mr. Fields selecting Mr. John Bigelow (the ex-Minister Plenipotentiary). In his endeavour to establish my claims as a fit and proper person to represent the borough, Mr. Dickens instanced the fact that I had no hair on the top of my head, whereas the rival candidate being plentifully supplied with that article, could not be considered a desirable person to represent any borough in the House of Commons. After he had finished his speech, which was of the most ludicrous description. Fields commenced his, but was never allowed to finish it, for he was continually interrupted by Mr. Dickens in a variety of voices and cries, such as, "Down with the hairy aristocracy!" "Up with the chap with the shiny top!" &c., the whole resulting in such an uproar that poor Fields had no chance. The outbursts of laughter were so loud and continuous, and the side-splitting pain so great in consequence, that it was with sheer exhaustion that we all gave up and retired for the night.

[1] At the turning-point at Newton Centre, Fields was so much exhausted that he was in want of refreshments, but as the village supplied nothing but a *few oranges,* these were purchased, and the pedestrians sat down on a *doorstep* to enjoy them!

Chapter Nine - The Close of the American Tour, and the Return Home

A HEAVY snowstorm with a terrific gale of wind had been raging all the week, and as all the trains were some hours, and some of them a day, late in their arrival, we determined on starting a day earlier than originally arranged on our journey to the North-West, so as to avoid the chance of being delayed by being "snowed up;" and after a most unpleasant journey we arrived on Saturday evening, March 7th, in the city of Syracuse (breaking our journey at Albany). The circumstances under which Syracuse was visited were perhaps not the most favourable. A thaw had set in, rendering walking almost an impossibility, but a walk was taken later in the day to view the city, and the conclusion Mr. Dickens arrived at with regard to Syracuse was that it was a most out-of-the-way place, and looked as if it had "begun to be built yesterday, and was going to be imperfectly knocked together with a nail or two the day after to-morrow." There were no people to be seen in the streets, and it was a matter of surprise to us that Mr. Osgood had contrived to sell all the tickets for the Reading on the following night; but as this was Sunday it occurred to us that the population were all in church. The hotel was unbearable, and the bedrooms so bad that we were afraid to go to them at night. So we sat up playing cribbage and whist (double dummy) until, as Mr. Dickens wrote to Fields, "neither of us could bear to speak to the other any more." In the same letter he described his waking moments on the morning after his arrival: "The awakening to consciousness this morning on a lopsided bedstead, facing nowhere, in a room holding nothing but *sour* dust, was more terrible than the being afraid to go to bed at night." The bill of fare (the printed *carte de jour*) was a curiosity in itself, as was also the Irish waiter told off for our service. The bill of fare included such delicacies as "Fowl de poulet," "Paettie de Shay," "Celary," and a "Murange with cream." On my asking the Irish waiter what a "Paettie de Shay" was he said he would go and inquire, and came back with the startling intelligence that "it was the Frinch name the steward gave to the oyster patties!" The wine list was also curious, and included such vintages as "Mooseux," "Abasinthe," "Curacce," "Maraschine," "Annisse," and "Table Madeira." A bottle of the former had been tried on the evening of our arrival, to wash down some buffalo which had been prepared for our supper, and was described by Mr. Dickens at the time as a "tough old nightmare;" but as the wine displayed an utter absence of grape we resolved on leaving that in the future, and flew in desperation to the "Table Madeira" (which would have done discredit to good honest British wine of the ginger or cowslip species). Then we tried the "Margeaux," which, if we had persevered with it, would have terminated in colic. The only good feature in the wines was the price, for there was nothing under three dollars a bottle, and as the brandy ("Jersey lightning") was impossible, we had to fall back on our own flasks and small travelling stock for our stay in Syracuse.

The following morning Mr. Dickens's arrival in the city had become known, and the depression of the previous day and the badness of the hotel were forgotten in the geniality of the inhabitants of Syracuse, who all seemed desirous of contributing something to his pleasure and amusement, during the short time he had to pass there. Although there were no people to be seen in the streets on the Sunday after our arrival, there were plenty at the Reading at night, and a most delightful and appreciative audience too, taking all the points of the Reading and its delicate touches as well as had the audiences in the other cities. The receipts were quite on an average with the more pretentious places.

Our next city was Rochester, where the effects of the thaw had made itself felt, and threatened to give us a new sensation, for although most of the tickets for the Reading were sold, it was a question whether or not there would be any hall in which to read.

The sudden thaw had caused immense blocks of ice to float down the river, which having formed themselves into an enormous ridge, had refused to yield about the Gennessee Falls, and the town was threatened with inundation, a disaster that is no novelty in Rochester, the same thing having occurred a few years previously. At the time of our arrival, the city presented the appearance of a general move — piles of furniture being seen about in the streets, and boats about in various places for the safety of the inhabitants. In the basement of the hall where Mr. Dickens's Reading was to take place, there were already three feet of water, and but for the fortunate collapse of the ridge in the night, with a tremendous crash, the worst consequences would have ensued. We walked the following morning to the Falls of the Gennessee, and was greatly interested in their beauty. They were a good preparation for the grander sight in store for us, viz., Niagara, which we were to visit at the end of the week. The fear of the inundation had not deterred the public from attending the Reading to any great extent, although it had affected our receipts, which fell to $1,906, the lowest total during the American tour.

From Rochester we went to Buffalo, and in our progress through the State of New York no signs of Anglophobia had been seen, as my friend in Washington so much feared. Everything in Buffalo looked well for the usual success, and it was whilst we were seated at dinner congratulating ourselves that the Washington scare had come to nothing, that the waiter told me (he was a "darkie"), "Dar's free gen'leman want to see you downstars."

I asked him if they had sent up their cards, or if "he knew who they were." He guessed he didn't know them personally, but gave me to understand that he knew one of them was a sheriffs officer! I sent word down I would be with them immediately; and, leaving the dinner-table, went to my despatch-box, putting the travelling letter into my pocket, and went downstairs to see my visitors.

The waiter took me where they were standing in the public bar, discoursing freely and taking a drink with some of their friends, and several persons standing about eagerly wondering what their business could be.

On being presented to them by the "darkie," I inquired their business, and was informed by one of them that he was a sheriff's officer, in the service of the Internal Revenue Department, and that his business was "with Mr. Dickens, and nobody else." Here he politely introduced me to his two companions as his assistants. By this time a number of people had congregated, and had become interested in the interview.

The sheriff's officer wore a seal-skin cap, a thick muffler round his neck, and a thick pea jacket, while in his hand he carried a thick stick. Mr. Dickens, I said, was at dinner, and could not be disturbed then; but any business he had to transact with Mr. Dickens, could be as well transacted through me; and giving him my name as a proof of the relations that existed between Mr. Dickens and myself, I begged that he would state his business at once as I was in a hurry.

"Wall," he said, "I've come to tell you that Mr. Dickens can't read to-night."

I pretended not to understand his meaning, and replied, "You are quite mistaken, for Mr. Dickens's cold has nearly left him, and he is in excellent voice."

"I guess you don't understand who and what I am," he replied, "or what my power is."

Being a foreigner, I regretted I did not.

"Wall, then, to make the case clear to your British brain, I will explain," he proceeded. "I guess neither you nor Mr. Dickens have complied with the laws of this country in not getting a Mayor's license to read, and you haven't arranged with my department about the city tax."

I explained: "The Mayor, being a friend of Mr. Dickens and myself, has informed me that in Mr. Dickens's case no license is necessary, and with regard to the city tax, Mr. Dickens is not liable."

Turning to his assistants, he ordered them to serve me with notices prohibiting the Reading, and proceeding to leave the hotel himself, cautioned me that he was "going to place policemen at the entrance of the hall, to prevent the doors being opened." After he had gone a few paces I called him back, with a view, as he evidently thought, of making some arrangement with him, either in the form of a money compromise, or in free passes for himself and subordinates, which in reality, I afterwards ascertained, was what he wanted.

After much persuasion, and a great show of indignation, he came back only to repeat his threats, when I drew from my breast pocket my letter of authority from the head of his department. He read it, and having done so, simply re-marked, looking round at the assembled crowd, "Jerusalem, I'm beat;" and calling to his assistants to follow him, took himself off, amidst the jeers and laughter of the company. However, he was called back again to partake of a bottle of champagne with me, and further to accept an invitation to attend the Reading with his wife and family. He readily accepted the invitation, and came to me the following day with a request for similar treatment for that evening.

Besides being much struck with the change in Buffalo since he first visited it, Mr. Dickens was also much struck by the absence of female beauty from the Readings. In all the cities hitherto visited, the assemblage of pretty wom-en was remarkable, but on reaching the frontier this seemed to fade away, and a sort of German-Irish-Scotch-mixed-with-Indian face took its place. This was particularly noticeable in the streets, though we thought that when the evening came we should see a difference; but we had not a dozen pretty women in the hall (which was crammed to suffocation). Nor were their toi-lettes at all comparable with those of the American ladies in other cities. These deficiencies, however, were fully compensated for by the brightness of their perception, and their appreciation of Mr. Dickens and his Readings.

After Buffalo, we went on our two days' pleasure trip to Niagara, taking with us such of our staff as could be spared; and as the weather was fine, but severely cold, we had what the Americans call a good time.

The hotel on the Canadian (or as it is called there the English) side was not open, as the winter was so severe that but few persons visited Niagara. This was a disappointment to us, as from this hotel the best view of the Falls is to be obtained, so we had to stay at the Spencer House Hotel, close to the sta-tion, and some two miles from the Falls. Although the Falls were not visible at this distance, they made themselves audible all through the day and night, and felt also; the continual rumble and shaking of the hotel and window frames creating an impressive effect, and causing wonderment in the mind that all the houses in the neighbourhood did not collapse under its influence.

We not only did the Falls thoroughly (except going underneath them, as our men did), driving two miles up the country along the sides of the Rapids above the Horse Shoe Fall, and passing through a great cloud of spray, but journeyed downwards to the Whirlpool, which has, if anything, as great a fascination for the visitor as the Falls themselves — and on this occasion was well worth seeing, as the pool was filled with enormous blocks of ice and numberless trees that had been uprooted by the floods (up the country), and had been washed over the falls. Great was our excitement in watching these masses endeavouring to make their escape to the Niagara River, only to be driven back again by the never-ceasing eddies to the opposite side of the whirlpool from which they had started. A gentleman, introducing himself to us as the proprietor of the land through which we were passing, took great pains to explain to us all the attractive features in his neighbourhood, and amongst other curious incidents related to us that, before the Suspension Bridge over the Rapids below the Falls was placed there, he had frequently seen as many as six or seven dead bodies of British soldiers floating about in the Whirlpool for a fortnight at a time. The soldiers were in the habit of deserting from the Canadian to the American side on pieces of timber or leaves of tables, crossing over the Pool between the Falls and the Rapids. This Pool has the appearance of being as calm as a mill pond, but is in reality very dangerous and treacherous, from the almost imperceptible eddies (looking like dimples) always moving about on it. The unfortunate soldiers, not being aware of this, were sucked in and drowned, their bodies in many cases never being recovered; and if they were, were so mutilated by the action of the water that they were not recognizable.

On our second day at Niagara we were all anxiety to get back to the Falls, and to roam about the beautiful country, and in the woods on either side; and although the visitor to Niagara is disappointed by the first impression, after a very short time the Falls have such a fascination that it is difficult to keep one's gaze from them. As a farewell trip we drove to the spot we had reached the previous day, and on our return (the sun being at our backs), were rewarded by a scene of colour such as neither of us had ever witnessed before. This was described in a letter written to Mr. Macready by Mr. Dickens: "Everything in the magnificent valley — buildings, forest, high banks, air, water, everything — was *made of rainbow*. Turner's most imaginative drawing in his finest day has nothing in it so ethereal, so gorgeous in fancy, so celestial. We said to one another (Dolby and I), 'Let it for evermore remain so,' and shut our eyes and came away."

After this pleasure trip, we turned our backs on the West and journeyed towards home, much to Mr. Dickens's unfeigned delight; for although more than gratified with his reception everywhere, and the considerable amount of money he had made, his life in America was one of self-denial and misery to him, in consequence of his sufferings from the effects of his cold. A new cause for anxiety and of discomfort threatened him on our leaving Niagara, in the shape of the return of the old malady in his foot. This he ascribed to walking about at Niagara in the snow. Up to this time the illness was confined to the left foot, but symptoms now presented themselves of an attack in the right foot also, and caused him to be lame for the remainder of the time he was in America. Still he persevered with the task he had before him, and performed it without one word of complaint, all the time; seldom eating and drinking, and scarcely ever sleeping. All his thoughts were of home and of the loved ones there, and the five weeks to be got through before starting on our return seemed, in my anxiety for his safety, more than all the time we had already passed, and caused me also to long for the 22nd of April, when we were to set sail in the *Russia* for home.

Our journey westward commenced in a most unpleasant manner; for after leaving Rochester on our way to Albany, where two Readings were announced for the evenings of Thursday and Friday, the 19th and 20th March, we were informed that there were considerable doubts as to our being able to get through, as the sudden thaw had caused the river to overflow, and that the country for some three hundred miles was under water. We had fortunately taken the precaution, in the long journey we had before us, to allow an extra day for its accomplishment, and it was with more anxiety than would otherwise have been the case, that during the progress of our journey I was informed, privately, by the conductor of the train, that we should not be able to proceed farther than Utica. This official at the same time told me that there was but one hotel in the city, and that in all probability, as all the traffic going to the East would be stopped at Utica, there would be a difficulty in getting apartments for the night. He advised me to "make a bolt" for the hotel the moment we reached Utica. Arriving there I took the conductor's advice, and did "make a bolt," leaving Mr. Dickens in the drawing-room car in the train, and being the first at the hotel (whilst all the other passengers were wondering what to do with themselves), I succeeded in securing the only vacant sitting-room and bed-room in the hotel, returning to the station for Mr. Dickens and our men, but without in the least knowing where they, or even myself, were going to sleep for the night. Although we arrived early in the afternoon, every spare bed in the city had been engaged, and in consequence of the immense sudden influx of passengers there were grave doubts whether the commissariat would hold out.

The proprietor of the hotel had provided handsomely for our requirements, but had his doubts as to his powers in doing the same for our men, doubts that Mr. Dickens instantly set at rest in insisting that the men should have their dinner and supper with him. On this occasion he appeared in the same jovial and genial character he had played so often; and although neither the quarters nor the food were anything particular, still the desire to please, on the part of the proprietor and his servants, was so apparent, that the absence of a good *chef de cuisine* was not remarkable. Whilst waiting for dinner we took a stroll through the city to find the greater part of it under water, and looking, as Mr. Dickens said at the time, "as if the high and dry part of it could produce nothing particular to eat."

With the prospect of being called at any hour of the night to continue the journey in the event of the waters subsiding, the idea of going to bed seemed ridiculous, especially as Mr. Dickens seldom slept when he got there, so we resolved on playing cribbage and double dummy as long as we could, Mr. Dickens volunteering to brew a jug of gin punch. There was not a jug to be had, so the punch was brewed in a "bed-room pitcher" (as they call a wash-hand-jug in America), but was not the less appreciated for that. At midnight we were told that there was no chance of our being able to get through, and that we had better settle down for the night. Most of the passengers slept in the trains, whilst others slept on chairs about the hotel. At six the following morning we were aroused, and told to "get aboard and try it." Half an hour later, we learned that there was "no sort o' use" in getting aboard and trying it, but at eight o'clock it was decided to try it (all the bells in the city being rung to summon the passengers together), and away we went for this purpose, the time occupied on the journey (which is usually performed in less than three hours) being nearly ten hours.

On the way, we picked up and released the passengers from two trains, which had been in the water the previous day and night. These hapless travellers would have been without food but for the enterprise of one of their number, who had made a raft out of some floating timbers and rails, paddled up into the country to some farm-houses, and had bought all the eggs, milk, bread, and cheese he could find, "peddling" them amongst his companions at a handsome profit.

After this we released a cattle train, laden principally with sheep, which had been in the water for over a week. In their hunger the poor beasts had commenced to eat each other. The haggard and dismal expression on the faces of these sheep was almost *human,* and left an impression on the mind not easily forgotten. Having towed this train to a dry spot, where the cattle were turned into a field, we made another struggle for Albany, which we were more than desirous of reaching, for a Reading had to be given there that night, for which all the tickets were sold. This having been made known to one of the railway officials who was in charge of the train, he said to Mr. Dickens, "If you want to get along, I guess I'm the man as can get you along, and if I can't, why then it's impossible;" and turning out his gang of men, about a hundred strong, they preceded the train, each armed with a long pole to push away the immense blocks of ice and floating timber from the front of the locomotive. In this way we journeyed along through the inundated valley at the rate of about three miles an hour. As the ice and the timber was cleared away from the front of the train, it was not unfrequently drawn back again under the wheels, causing a jolting indescribably unpleasant in its effect. After travelling in this way some ten to twelve miles, we at last arrived at a part of the country where the influence of the river was not felt, and reached Albany at about five in the afternoon, just in time to make preparations for the Reading. Our men, although they had not been in bed the whole night, and, like ourselves, had not had any food since the previous day, worked away with a good will, and got the screen and little table fixed within an hour and a half. The arrangements on the platform and in the hall (the Tweddle Hall) were as perfect as if the whole day had been given to the work. Neither was Mr. Dickens apparently any the worse for the extra exertion and inconvenience he had undergone, but gave the "Carol" and "Trial" in his happiest mood, to the great delight of his crowded audience.

Instead of returning to Boston to spend the following Saturday and Sunday, a journey of over six hours, we determined on staying in Springfield, which was our next reading town, and by so doing saving some unnecessary travelling; and as Springfield is a pleasant city, with an excellent hotel (the Massasoit House), we had no reason to regret our change of plan; for three most agreeable days were passed here, days which were rendered the more pleasant by the receipt of an unusually large batch of "home" letters, full of congratulations on our triumphant progress through the States, and promising hearty and affectionate welcomes to us when we should arrive in our respective homes.

There was also a letter for Mr. Dickens of large proportions, which, I remarked, seemed to have but little interest for him, being laid on one side until such time as he had got through the letters, which evidently were of more moment. During the progress of dinner, which was served on our arrival at the hotel, Mr. Dickens bethought himself of the large letter, and, handing it to me, asked me to open it, on doing which I found it to contain a photograph of a pony of beautiful form, with a young gentleman (instead of a groom) standing at his head. On the pony were a couple of panniers, and it wanted but a child in each of them to make the picture complete.

Mr. Dickens being asked by myself the meaning of the picture, he replied, "Can't you see? look at it closely." This being done I recognized the portrait of one of my nephews (the son of Madame Sainton), but as this did not assist me in the elucidation of the subject, I remarked, "There's Charley Sainton, and there's a pony with panniers on him; but what the portraits mean, and what they are sent to *you* for, I cannot imagine." He then explained that, when the news of the birth of my boy arrived at Washington, he determined on marking the event in some manner, and could think of nothing better than to write to Wills and instruct him to purchase on his behalf the handsomest pony he could find, and to send him with his trappings complete, as a present, to my wife at Ross in Herefordshire, with "the Chief's love;" and thinking to interest me the more in the subject, had made arrangements for my nephew to have his portrait taken in the position in which he then was, rather than have a groom or stable-boy holding the pony.

Valuable as was the present, the pleasure in the receipt of it was greatly enhanced by the manner of its gift, and was a proof, amongst many others, of the affectionate friendship which existed between us. As was natural, under the circumstances, our conversation on that particular evening was more on home matters than anything else; and many were the plans made for the coming summer, to which he was looking forward with so much pleasure and interest.

Our operations in America were now confining themselves within narrow limits, and it was fortunate that it was so, for Mr. Dickens's health was becoming a graver source of anxiety every day. There was very little more travelling to be done before the "farewells" in Boston and New York, the only new cities to be visited being New Haven, on the evening following Springfield, New Bedford, and Portland.

After the New Haven Reading I had to leave him for the last time, to look after the New York "farewells," and the Press dinner about to be given to him at Delmonico's in that city, Mr. Osgood travelling with him to New Bedford and Portland.

The New Haven Reading had not suffered by the postponement, and a happily chosen speech previous to the commencement of it tended to put every one in a good humour, the audience being as pleased with the few words of explanation offered by Mr. Dickens as he was with their reception of it, and of the Reading which followed.

A return of the snowstorms and severe frost brought a return of the "true American" (as he used to call the catarrh), and also a return of the sleepless nights, with the additional trouble of the pain in the swollen foot, which rendered walking almost an impossibility.

Whilst in New York, I received a letter from him asking me to call on his doctor there (Dr. Fordyce Barker), and to get from him a prescription for a composing draught, in the hope of producing a night's rest; and on my return to him in Boston I was much shocked at the change that had taken place in the few days I had been away. At the same time, I had my fears that he would not be able to get through the farewell Readings in Boston.

The Fields were all and everything to him in his illness, and the affectionate attention of Mrs. Fields, who as usual had decorated his rooms with flowers, and the genial society of Fields, did much to make him forget his sufferings, and when night came he went to the little table as if nothing had been the matter with him. The exertion of getting himself up to reading pitch, and the fatigue and excitement of reading, resulted in great depression of spirits, which fortunately did not last long; but it necessitated a departure from the usual routine of our Reading life, for instead of the immediate change of costume usual on these occasions with the "rub down," it was necessary that he should lie down on the sofa in his dressing-room for twenty minutes or half an hour, in a state of the greatest exhaustion, before he could undergo the fatigue even of dressing, and taking during this time about a wineglassful of champagne to give action to his heart. These attacks of nervous depression being over, he would be himself again; and on returning to the hotel would partake of a little soup or strong beef-tea, and spend an hour or two in genial conversation with myself, and sometimes two or three friends, discussing the events of the day and the incidents of the Readings, before retiring to undergo the agonies of another sleepless night. I used to steal into his room at all hours of the night and early morning, to see if he were awake or in want of anything; always though to find him wide awake and as cheerful and jovial as circumstances would admit, never in the least complaining, and only reproaching me for not taking my night's rest. I did not express to him my own misgivings that he might break down at any moment. This caused him at times to think that I did not understand "that the power of coming up to the mark every night with spirits and spirit may co-exist with the nearest approach to sinking under it," but in reality I did.

Our men though, and those who were not as much with him as I was (even Fields), could scarcely be made to understand the real state of the case with regard to his health, as they only saw him at his best. The men would receive my account of the bad way in which the Chief was, with the remark, "It'll be all right at night, sir. The gov'nor's sure to come up smiling when you call time, and the more's wanted out of him, the more you gets." They were very watchful and devoted to him (as he was to them), and frequently by many little acts of attention showed their love and affection for him. George Allison (the gasman), in particular was described by Dickens as the "steadiest and most reliable man I ever employed."

The nearest approach to an actual collapse occurred at the third Reading of the Boston farewells, when up to four o'clock in the afternoon it became a matter of grave doubt whether he would be able to read or not. Longfellow, Fields, and several of his friends from Cambridge University urged him to give in, but he would not, and at night astonished not only himself, but his audience also at his extraordinary powers of recuperation when once he found himself face to face with his task. On this particular occasion, he said, he felt fresher and better after the Reading than he had done for three weeks previously. The severe attack of the afternoon seemed to be the turning-point of the "true American," and the greatest anxiety was now as to whether it had left a lasting injury to the lungs. In addition to this, the lameness, and the pain resulting from it, became more acute, rendering walking a great difficulty, and it was only with the help of my arm that he could be got to the little table and away from it after the Readings.

The news of Mr. Dickens's illness soon spread in Boston, and many were the inquiries at the hotel as to the state of his health. When it became known (late in the afternoon) that he would read, some ladies gained access to the hall and decorated the reading-table with the choicest of flowers and exotics — a compliment which he highly appreciated, and the more so as it was quite unexpected. Before commencing the Reading, he addressed the following words to his audience: "Ladies and gentlemen, before allowing Doctor Marigold to tell his story in his own peculiar way, I kiss the kind fair hands unknown which have so beautifully decorated my table this evening." These words, as graceful as the compliment paid him by the ladies, drew forth the most enthusiastic applause, which may have had the effect of causing Mr. Dickens to forget his own discomforts for the time being, and thereby contributing largely to the success of the Reading.

The state of his health at this time rendered it impossible for him to accept any invitations to attend meetings either of a public or private character, and a public demonstration in the form of a farewell banquet had to be declined — a disappointment not only to the organizers of it, but to Mr. Dickens himself; for he was anxious to meet his friends once more, that he might express to them in public his appreciation of the liberality and kindheartedness displayed towards him in Boston. This, however, under the circumstances, was not to be done.

Although disappointed in this respect, there was one pleasure which he had promised himself, in which he was determined not to be thwarted, and which, not being dependent on his personal presence, was the easier of accomplishment.

The difficulty which presented itself was as to the manner in which he could carry out his design. He was desirous of leaving behind him, in a substantial form, some trace of his second visit to America. It was not easy to decide on the course to be adopted. Anything in the form of ostentation was abhorrent to him. He would perform an act of charity or benevolence in the most liberal and ungrudging manner, without ever referring to it afterwards; indeed, he would avoid the subject as if ashamed of the good he had done.

To give a sum of money to some charitable institution did not accord with his views, as in his opinion very little permanent good to those for whom the money was subscribed ever came of this means, besides which it had a purse-proud and ostentatious appearance; and if he gave money to the Boston institutions in any appreciable amount, the same thing would have to be done in the other cities in the Union. Again, in the large cities of America there are not so many needy persons as in England.

Going into his bed-room on one of my midnight visits, I found him as usual wide awake and very cheerful. Desiring me to sit down, he had a matter on his mind which was causing him great anxiety, and then took me to his confidence.

Having visited one of the Blind Asylums in Boston during the early part of his visit there, and his sympathies being always with the afflicted, especially the dumb and the blind, he had been much struck (as he had been at home) with the limited area of literature placed at the disposal of these sufferers, the New Testament and Dr. Watts's hymns being in his experience the only books ever placed in their hands. For the former, no one had a greater reverence than himself, it being the book of all others he read the most, and "the one unfailing guide in life;" but with all his admiration and reverence for this book, it was always a mystery to him that the blind had no other books than these two placed in their hands, with which to while away the hours of their perpetual darkness.

So he gave me instructions to ascertain the cost of having one of his own books ("The Old Curiosity Shop") produced in raised letters for the use of the blind in each asylum in the union.

I was bound to secrecy in the matter, and was permitted only to take the kind doctor of the asylum into my confidence. This being done, and a calculation having been made of the cost (an appreciable sum of money), the order was given, and some months after we had left America the books were distributed.

So well did the doctor keep the secret, that the distribution of the books was the first intimation the public had of Mr. Dickens's kindness. Even Fields, who was in our confidence in most things, was unaware of the good that had been done until Mr. Dickens's return to England, when in the following July the latter wrote to him in the following words: "I am delighted to find you both so well pleased with the blind book scheme. I said nothing of it to you when we were together, though I had made up my mind, because I wanted to come upon you with that little burst from a distance. It seemed something like meeting again, when I remitted the money and thought of you talking of it."

The scheme having been so successfully carried out, no reference was ever made to it afterwards, either in public or private, which, to some extent, is to be regretted, as so noble an act, if made public, might have suggested to the minds of benevolently disposed persons (who are frequently at a loss to know in what way to bestow their charity), to do a similar act for the suffering blind in this country.

On Thursday, April 8th, the farewell Reading took place in Boston, the subjects being the "Christmas Carol" and the "Trial from Pickwick."

Notable as had been the first Reading in America some four months previously, the success of it was as nothing compared with this final one, not only as regards the company assembled — all the notabilities of Boston being assembled — but as regards the success of the Reading itself, and the effect produced on the audience.

The receipts, which were the largest of any Reading in America, amounted to $3,456.

On the termination of the "Carol" with the words "And so, as Tiny Tim observed, God bless us every one," the audience were no less affected than the reader himself; and when it was seen that Mr. Dickens had left the platform, the pent-up feelings of the people found vent in an overpowering outburst of enthusiasm, causing him to return to the platform to bow his acknowledgments. The "Trial from Pickwick" which followed was provocative of the most uproarious laughter, Mr. Dickens giving it, if possible, with more than his usual sense of humour. Then came a storm of applause, and Mr. Dickens once more went on to the platform, with the tears rolling down his cheeks, to say "Farewell," and not only were the tears visible in his eyes, but they communicated themselves to his voice, in delivering the following words:

"Ladies and Gentlemen, — My gracious and generous welcome in America, which can never be obliterated from my remembrance, began here. My departure begins here too: for I assure you that I have never until this moment really felt that I am going away. In this brief life of ours it is sad to do almost anything for the last time, and I cannot conceal from you, although my face will so soon be turned towards my native land, and to all that makes it dear, that it is a sad consideration with me that in a few moments from this time this brilliant hall and all that it contains will fade from my view for evermore. But it is my consolation that the spirit of the bright faces, the quick perception, the ready response, the generous and the cheering sounds that have made this place delightful to me, will remain; and you may rely upon it that that spirit will abide with me as long as I have sense and sentiment left.

"I do not say this with any limited reference to private friendships that have for years upon years made Boston a memorable and beloved spot for me, for such private references have no business in this public place. I say it purely in remembrance of, and in homage to, the great public heart before me.

142

"Ladies and Gentlemen, — I beg most earnestly, most gratefully, and most affectionately, to bid each and all farewell."

The effect produced by this little speech can be better understood than described, and perhaps the dead silence which for the moment ensued on its delivery was the best compliment which could be paid to it, nor was it until Mr. Dickens had left the platform that the public seemed to realize the fact that he, who had become so much a part of themselves, had really vanished for evermore from Boston eyes.

The privacy of the dressing-room was invaded by intimate friends, to whom it was difficult to refuse admission, so eager were they to have one more opportunity of saying one more parting word.

After some time we were left to ourselves, and allowed to retire to our hotel, and to make arrangements for our departure from Boston, to take our leave of the New York public and of America.

In Mr. Dickens' state of health it was necessary that he should observe the strictest privacy on returning to the Parker House, and our supper party on this occasion was confined to ourselves; for, in addition to the fatigue of the journey to New York, there was much to be gone through there besides the Readings, which of themselves were sufficient fatigue for one suffering as he was, without the additional anxiety of an ordeal in the shape of a public banquet, which had been arranged should be given to him by the press-men of America, under the presidency of Mr. Horace Greeley.

This banquet was to take place at Delmonico's, on Saturday, April 18th, and in its arrangements and results was one of the most brilliant of its kind ever held in the Empire City.

We were accompanied in our last journey from Boston by Mr. and Mrs. Fields, who remained with us until our departure from America, and although every precaution had been taken to make the journey as comfortable for an invalid as is possible in a railway car, it was with a feeling of the utmost satisfaction that we found ourselves once more under the hospitable roof of the Westminster Hotel in New York, with a clear day's rest before us, prior to the commencement of the New York farewells, on Monday the 13th.

The political trouble in the country had certainly affected our prospects for these farewells, and although the outlook was not a cheerful one at the commencement, the public was true to its favourite, and the average receipts were in no-wise short of those of previous Readings in New York. The enthusiasm had not in the least abated, and the only drawback to the enjoyment of the Readings was the evident pain from which Mr. Dickens was suffering in walking to and from the little table, whither he was led leaning on my arm.

Amidst all the turmoil and anxiety of the farewell Readings, the Press Dinner, and Mr. Dickens' state of health, a new excitement was in store for us, in the shape of a tax collector, and more sheriffs' officers.

Whilst seated at dinner, on the evening of the last Reading but one in New York, and the evening before the Press Dinner, I was summoned out of our room to see two gentlemen, who had called "on very urgent business."

James T. Fields   **Mrs. James T. Fields**

Having presented myself to them, they proceeded to explain their business, which was to the effect that either Mr. Dickens or myself had again broken the laws of the country, in not making a return of our income whilst in America. The two gentlemen were not desirous of putting Mr. Dickens to any inconvenience in the matter, personally; and if I would accept service of a summons for him as well as myself to appear before a judge on the following Thursday, to explain the reason of our not making a return, and if at the same time I would fill up the income-tax papers they had with them, showing what our incomes had been in the States, much "trouble" might be prevented.

I explained that, having the authority of the head of the Internal Revenue Department (and I quoted the authority), to the effect that neither Mr. Dickens nor myself (as foreigners) were liable, added to which the Act of Congress distinctly stated that persons travelling for the purpose of giving "occasional lectures" were not liable for income-tax, I did not see any reason why I should attend, or take any notice of the summons, especially as on the day for which it was appointed I was greatly in hopes that both Mr. Dickens and myself would be some three hundred miles out at sea in the *Russia.* Apart from that, I had not sufficient money in America to meet so heavy a demand, having sent all the money we had (with the exception of what we required for our personal uses), to Coutts's bank in England by the previous mail. My remonstrances seemed of little avail, for my visitors intimated to me that they should at once take steps to arrest that night's receipts, and the receipts of the last Reading.

I pleaded that, the tickets being all "sold out" for these Readings, the course they pursued was quite unnecessary, not to mention that any such action would certainly end in the bailiffs being first kicked out of the Steinway Hall, and then handed over to the police for safe custody.

This threatened mode of proceeding, and the more reasonable arguments I had made use of, seemed to satisfy my two friends for the moment, and on my promising to call on the collector on the following morning, they retired.

Punctually at ten the next morning, I was with the "collector," whose reception of me was of the most unbending description. Having previously made inquiries about this official, I had discovered he was the brother of an old friend of Dickens in Boston, during the time of Mr. Dickens's first visit to America in 1842. This brother having fallen out of the *clique* in Boston for reasons of his own (not that that made any difference to Mr. Dickens at the time of his second visit), the "collector" in New York being unaware that Mr. Dickens visited his friend as of old, thought to cause annoyance by making him suffer financially for the imaginary wrong he had inflicted on his brother in Boston!

There was also another reason. It had occurred to the official mind of Mr. Collector that if he, in his district, could pay into the coffers of the Treasury Department so large a sum as five per cent, (which was the income-tax then) on Mr. Dickens's receipts (nearly $12,000), his chances of retaining his appointment under the new Presidency — should Andrew Johnson be turned out — would be very great.

These two circumstances were sufficient of themselves to account for my reception at the hands of the collector, who perhaps under different conditions would have been a fairer specimen of an American official than he appeared then.

Giving me a chair, and placing his back against an anthracite coal fire, he opened the interview by saying:

"Well, Mr. Dolby, this is an unpleasant business you have let Mr. Dickens in for; what are *you* going to do about it?"

"Did your officers tell you the result of my interview with them last evening?" I replied.

"Certainly."

"Well then," I said, "the next question is, what are you going to do about it?"

"Let us understand one another, Mr. Dolby. Do you mean to make a return of the amount of money Mr. Dickens has received in this country, or do you not?"

"Sir! Here is a letter from the chief of your department" (handing him the letter), "assuring me that Mr. Dickens is not liable for any tax in this country, and on that authority I resist any claim that you, or any one similarly placed, may make on me or Mr. Dickens in respect of his Readings."

"In the first place," replied the collector, "I don't care a ___ for the opinion of the chief of my department, as you call him, any way; and I may tell you at once, that unless you come to some arrangement with me for the payment of this money before leaving this room, you must look out for trouble."

I asked him, "What do you mean by trouble?"

"Well, it's just this," said the collector. "You say Mr. Dickens' hasn't got any money in this country."

"Not enough to meet your demands, even if they were legitimate," said I; "and you ought to know, as does every one else, that Mr. Dickens would be the last man in the world to evade a just claim upon him. So if you can prove to me, betwixt this and Tuesday afternoon next, at four o'clock, that you have a claim, I will take measures to satisfy that claim before we leave the country on Wednesday next."

"Admitting that what you say is true, Mr. Dolby, viz., that you and Mr. Dickens have no more money in this country than you want, will you, if I give you an undertaking not to arrest you (as a hostage), on the *Russia* on Wednesday next, give me an order on Messrs. Ticknor and Fields for the payment of $10,000 in gold if I can prove that my claim on behalf of my Government is a fair, legal, and just one?"

"I refuse to give you an order on Messrs. Ticknor and Fields, or any one else; for I rest Mr. Dickens's exemption from this tax on a much higher official than yours."

"You mean to tell me, then, that you intend leaving America on Wednesday without paying this money?"

"I do."

"Then good morning, Mr. Dolby; and if you are arrested on Wednesday, you will have the satisfaction of knowing that you will not be the first manager who has been arrested on the steamer when leaving this country."

This interview being over, I left the collector to his duties, and wended my way back to the hotel to report the result of it, and to arrange with Mr. Dickens what it was best to do under the circumstances, and to do my best to get him round for the great event of the evening, viz., the Press Dinner.

On my return to the hotel, I found him worse in health than I anticipated, and but little disposed to discuss or undertake any fresh annoyance, the pain in his right foot supplying this to an unlimited extent. With a view to the evening's work, and also in the hope of being able to afford Mr. Dickens some relief from the pain he was suffering, the collector and his threats had to be put on one side for a time, the attendance of Dr. Fordyce Barker being absolutely necessary.

I found H. D. Palmer in Mr. Dickens's room, and gave him the account of my interview with the collector, and asked his advice, as a thoroughly practical American, and one well up in the laws of his country.

The advice Palmer gave me was to consult Mr. William Booth (the brother of Edwin Booth), a distinguished lawyer; and if necessary, to send him off to Washington that evening to report the collector to his superiors, and get them to telegraph to that official, censuring him for his excess of zeal.

Palmer's advice being adopted, Mr. Booth started for Washington, and I having nothing more to think about on that score, gave myself up to the course of treatment recommended by the doctor. He found Mr. Dickens suffering from an attack of erysipelas, which had caused the foot to swell to such an extent that all hope of getting a boot on was out of the question; and the only chance there was of Mr. Dickens being able to go to the dinner would be in the bandaging of the painful member, and hiding the bandages by a gout-stocking — if such an article could be found in New York — a doubt which at the time struck me as being far-fetched. However it did not turn out to be so, for I drove about the city for over two hours, calling at all the principal drug stores without getting what I wanted, being informed everywhere that "gout was unknown in New York," a circumstance on which New York is to be congratulated. By a happy chance, however, I heard of an English gentleman who was occasionally afflicted in this way, and making my wants known to him, he readily supplied my requirements; and but for this it would have been impossible for Mr. Dickens to attend the banquet so generously and thoughtfully given in his honour.

As Mr. Dickens was more than an hour late, and as his state of health was well known, grave disappointment prevailed at the prospect of the guest of the evening not being able to be present to partake of the hospitality of the New York press-men.

From five o'clock, the hour when the guests began to assemble, messengers were running from Delmonico's to the Westminster Hotel eager in their inquiries as to the possibility of Mr. Dickens being able to attend the banquet; and at half-past five the final bulletin was despatched, announcing that, thanks to the successful application of lotions and careful bandaging, Mr. Dickens would use his best endeavours to be present — an announcement received with tremendous cheers.

Precisely at six o'clock, Mr. Dickens and myself arrived at Delmonico's, and being received at the door of this establishment by Mr. Horace Greeley and the committee (the band playing "God save the Queen"), Mr. Dickens was conducted, leaning on the arm of Horace Greeley, into the banqueting-hall to his place at the table, and, although suffering the greatest of pain, was pleasurably impressed by the geniality of his welcome.

There were over two hundred gentlemen present on the occasion, and this assemblage of newspaper men was said to be the largest ever seen in America.

In addition to the speech of the president, speeches were made by representative men from all parts of the States, including Henry John Raymond, William H. Hurlburt, George William Curtis, Charles Eliot Norton, and many others. The brilliancy of the scene, and the good taste and delicacy of the speakers, caused Mr. Dickens to forget his own sufferings for the time, and in a speech characteristic alike for its earnestness and truthfulness he thanked the American people, through them, for their reception of him throughout his Reading tour.

Although this speech has been printed elsewhere, it is reproduced here as forming a part of one of the most brilliant tours ever undertaken in the United States of America by a single individual.

Replying to the toast of the evening, proposed by the president, and received with loud hurrahs and waving of handkerchiefs, which lasted for some moments, Mr. Dickens said:

"Gentlemen, — I cannot do better than take my cue from your distinguished president, and refer at once to his remarks in connection with the old natural association between you and me. When I received an invitation from a private association of working members of the press of New York, to dine with them to-day, I accepted that compliment in grateful remembrance of a calling that was once my own, and in loyal sympathy with the brotherhood which, in the spirit, I have never quitted. To the wholesome training of severe newspaper work, when I was a very young man, I constantly refer my first successes; and my sons will hereafter testify of their father, that he was always steadily proud of that ladder by which he rose. If it were otherwise I should have a very poor opinion of their father, which perhaps, upon the whole, I have not. Hence, gentlemen, under any circumstances this company would have been exceptionally interesting and gratifying to me; but whereas I supposed that, like the fairy's pavilion in the 'Arabian Nights,' it would be but a mere handful, and I find it turn out, like the same elastic pavilion, capable of comprehending a multitude; so much the more proud am I of the honour of being your guest; for you will readily believe that the more widely representative of the press in America my entertainers are, the more I must feel the good-will and the kindly sentiment towards me of that vast institution. Gentlemen, so much of my voice has lately been heard in the land, and I have for upwards of four hard winter months so contended against what I have been sometimes quite admiringly told was a true American catarrh — a possession which I have throughout highly appreciated, though I might have preferred to be naturalized by any other outward and visible signs. I say, gentlemen, so much of my voice has lately been heard, that I might have been contented with troubling you no further from my present standing-point, were it not a duty with which I henceforth charge myself, not only here, but on every suitable occasion whatsoever and wheresoever, to express my high and grateful sense of my second reception in America, and to bear my honest testimony to the national generosity and magnanimity; also to declare how astounded I have been by the amazing changes that I have seen around me on every side — changes moral, changes physical, changes in the amount of land subdued and peopled, changes in the rise of vast new cities, changes in the growth of older cities almost out of recognition, changes in the graces and amenities of life, changes in the press, without whose advancement no advancement can be made anywhere. Nor am I, believe me, so arrogant as to suppose that in five and twenty years there has been no change in me, and that I had nothing to learn, and no extreme impressions to correct, when I was here first; and, gentlemen, this brings me to a point on which I have, ever since I landed here last November, observed a strict silence, though tempted sometimes to break it, but in reference to which I will, with your good leave, take you into my confidence now. Even the press, being human, may be

148

sometimes mistaken or misinformed, and I rather think that I have, in one or two rare instances, known its information to be not perfectly accurate with reference to myself; indeed, I have now and again been more surprised by printed news that I have read of myself, than by any printed news that I have ever read in my present state of existence. Thus, the vigour and perseverance with which I have for some months past been collecting materials for, and hammering away at, a new book on America have much astonished me, seeing that all that time it has been perfectly well known to my publishers on both sides of the Atlantic, that I positively declared that no consideration on earth should induce me to write one; but what I have intended, what I have resolved upon (and this is the confidence I seek to place in you), is on my return to England, in my own person, to bear for the behoof of my countrymen, such testimony to the gigantic changes in this country as I have hinted at to-night; also to record that wherever I have been, in the smallest places equally with the largest, I have been received with unsurpassable politeness, delicacy, sweet temper, hospitality, consideration, and with unsurpassable respect for the privacy daily enforced upon me by the nature of my avocation here, and the state of my health. This testimony, so long as I live, and so long as my descendants have any legal right in my books, I shall cause to be re-published as an appendix to every copy of those two books of mine in which I have referred to America; and this I will do, or cause to be done, not in mere love and thankfulness, but because I regard it as an act of plain justice and honour.

Gentlemen, the transition from my own feelings towards, and interest in, America, to those of the mass of my countrymen seems to be a natural one. "I was asked in this very city, about last Christmas time, why an American was not at a disadvantage in England as a foreigner. The notion of an American being regarded in England as a foreigner at all, of his ever being thought of or spoken of in that character, was so uncommonly incongruous and absurd to me that my gravity was for the moment quite overpowered; as soon as it was restored, I said that for years and years past I hoped I had had as many American friends, and had received as many American visitors, as almost any Englishman living, and that my unvarying experience, fortified by others, was that it was enough in England to be an American to be received with the readiest respect and recognition anywhere. Hereupon, out of half a dozen people, suddenly spoke out two — one an American gentleman with a cultivated taste for art, who, finding himself on a certain Sunday outside the walls of a certain historical English castle famous for its pictures, was refused admission there, according to the strict rules of the establishment on that day; but who, on merely representing that he was an American gentleman on his travels, had, not to say the picture gallery, but the whole castle placed at his immediate disposal. The other was a lady, who, being in London and having a great desire to see the famous reading room of the British Museum, was assured by the English family with whom she stayed that it was unfortunately impossible, because the place was closed for a week, and she had only three days there; upon that lady's going to the Museum, as she assured me, alone to the gate, self-introduced as an American lady, the gate flew open, as it were, magically. I am unwillingly bound to add that she certainly was young and exceedingly pretty; still, the porter of that institution is of an obese habit, and according to the best of my observation of him, not very susceptible. Now, gentlemen, I refer to these trifles as a collateral assurance to you that the Englishman who so humbly strives, as I hope to do, to be in England as faithful to America as to England herself, has no previous conceptions to contend against. Points of difference there have been, points of difference there probably always will be, between the two great peoples; but broadcast in England is sown the sentiment that those two peoples are essentially one, and that it rests with them jointly to uphold the great Anglo-Saxon race, to which our president has referred, and all its great achievements before the world; and if I know anything of Englishmen— and they give me credit for knowing something— if I know anything of my countrymen, gentlemen, the English heart is stirred by the flutter of those Stars and Stripes as it is stirred by no other flag that flies, except its own. (The audience here gave three cheers.) If I know my countrymen, in any and every relation towards America, they begin, not as Sir Anthony Absolute recommended that lovers should begin, with 'a little aversion,' but with a great liking and a profound respect; and whatever the little sensitiveness of the moment, or the little official passion, or the little official policy now or then or here or there may be, take my word for it that the first enduring great popular consideration in England is a generous construction of justice. Finally, gentlemen, and I say this subject to your correction, I do believe that from the great majority of honest minds on both sides, there cannot be absent the conviction that it would be better for the globe to be riven by earthquake, fired by comet, overrun by an iceberg, and abandoned to the Arctic fox and bear, than that it should present the spectacle of these two great nations, each of which has in its own way and hour striven so hard and so successfully for freedom, ever again being arrayed, the one against the other. Gentlemen, I cannot thank your president enough, or you enough, for your kind reception of my health, and of my poor remarks; but, believe me, I do thank you with the utmost fervour of which my soul is capable."

The speech being concluded, the breathless silence which had prevailed during the delivery of it was broken in a loud burst of applause, the band again playing "God save the Queen," the vast assemblage standing up the while, and joining heartily in the chorus.

Mr. Dickens' state of health rendered it necessary that he should leave the banqueting-hall prior to the termination of the proceedings, and leaning on the arm of Horace Greeley, as on arriving, he was lustily cheered by his hosts — the press-men of America.

The following day was one of great anxiety for our little staff. The old illness had asserted itself again, and I was in close attendance on my Chief during the two nights preceding the ordeal of the farewell Reading. Fields and

Osgood were with us the whole time, and were unremitting in their attentions, as were many other kind friends; and thanks to the medical skill of Dr. Fordyce Barker, the patient was sufficiently well to give the "Christmas Carol" and the "Trial from Pickwick," for the last time in America, to an audience numbering over two thousand persons, yielding a return of $3,298, the second largest receipt in America, and this exclusive of the premiums obtained by the ticket speculators, which, on that occasion, as on all others, must have been enormous.

On the termination of the Reading, Mr. Dickens made a short speech, as follows:

"Ladies and Gentlemen, — The shadow of one word has impended over me this evening, and the time has come at length when the shadow must fall. It is but a very short one, but the weight of such things is not measured by their length, and two much shorter words express the round of our human existence.

"When I was reading 'David Copperfield' a few evenings since, I felt there was more than usual significance in the words of Peggotty, 'My future life lies over the sea;' and when I closed this book just now, I felt most keenly that I was shortly to establish such an *alibi* as would have satisfied even the elder Mr. Weller. The relations which have been set up between us, while they have involved for me something more than mere devotion to a task, have been by you sustained with the readiest sympathy and the kindest acknowledgment.

"These relations must now be broken for ever. Be assured, however, that you will not pass from my mind. I shall often realize you as I see you now, equally by my winter fireside, and in the green English summer weather. I shall never recall you as a mere public audience, but rather as a host of personal friends, and ever with the greatest gratitude, tenderness, and consideration. Ladies and gentlemen, I beg to bid you farewell. God bless you, and God bless the land in which I leave you."

This little speech, like all the *impromptu* ones delivered by Mr. Dickens on all occasions, was listened to with rapt attention, and after many recalls, and much shouting, cheering, and waving of handkerchiefs, Mr. Dickens retired from the platform, never any more to appear in public in America.

Since the departure of Mr. Booth for Washington, telegraphic communication was being vigorously kept up between that gentleman and myself, and in the course of the farewell Reading I received a telegram from him to the effect that matters had been satisfactorily arranged in Washington, and that he would return to New York on the following day. The telegram stated further that the department had telegraphed to the collector informing him he was in the wrong, and instructing him to desist from taking further action in the matter.

Calling on the collector the following morning, I found him more intent on causing annoyance than he had been during the previous week; and setting the higher authorities at defiance, expressed his determination of arresting me as hostage, unless I carried out the conditions he had imposed at our first interview. So, regarding his threats as empty ones, I bade him "good-bye," and left him to carry them out if he felt so disposed.

Our last day in New York was a busy one, and was passed in making preparations for our departure on the following day, and such calls as are incidental to the duties involved by a long stay in any large city; and in the reception of visitors calling to bid their adieux to the great man who had afforded the Americans so much pleasure by his works and his presence amongst them.

Our rooms presented the appearance of a railway parcels office and a flower market combined, the larger cases containing presents of wine (for the voyage!) of the choicest description, boxes of cigars, pictures, some very large books, and photographs, the whole forming such an incongruous mass that it was with difficulty we could move about our apartments. Regretting as we did having to leave so many kind friends, it was with a sense of painful relief that we anticipated the morrow when we should say "farewell," and in that one word cut the chord that was from hour to hour the cause of such painful suspense.

In order to avoid as much as possible the crowd at the wharf of the Cunard Company on the departure of the *Russia,* an old friend of Mr. Dickens's (who was to be one of our fellow-passengers) had placed his private tug at our disposal to convey us, and such of our personal friends who were to accompany us on board, to the ship, which had steamed down the bay, and was lying at her moorings, off Staten Island, awaiting mails and passengers.

Although this plan had been kept as secret as possible, it became known to many persons that such was Mr. Dickens's intention, and a large crowd had collected outside the Westminster Hotel to witness his departure.

On emerging from the hotel, he was greeted by a loud cheer, and on entering his carriage, bouquets thrown from the windows of the hotel fell at his feet, the scene resembling more the going-off of a wedding party, than the departure of an individual attired in a costume equal to the exigencies of a sea voyage.

At the foot of Spring Street, the tug with its owner (Mr. W. D. Morgan), and several invited friends were awaiting us, and after a pleasant sail of half an hour we were alongside the *Russia.*

The Cunard Company, with characteristic liberality, had prepared a special lunch for Mr. Dickens and his guests. The saloon tables were laden with floral tributes to the Chief, with the cards of the donors attached to them; nor were these delicate attentions confined to the saloon, but his state-room (the chief steward's on deck) was also florally decorated.

In the midst of the lunch, when every one was in the enjoyment of the good things provided by the company, an officer reported to the captain that the police boat was making for the *Russia,* an announcement that did not tend to my enjoyment, for the thought occurred to our party that the collector meant business, and had put his threats into execution. For the moment I regarded myself in the light of a hostage, as did also our friends. In a very short time, however, all fears in this respect were terminated by the appearance in the saloon of Mr. Commissioner Kennedy (the chief of police), an intimate friend of my own, and Mr. Thurlow Weed, an old friend of Mr. Dickens's.

These gentlemen had called on Mr. Dickens and myself at our hotel, to bid us "good-bye," and finding we had left there, steamed down the bay after us. The weather was bitterly cold, and the snow was still lying about the country. The keen air had sharpened the appetites of our new guests, and my friend Mr. Kennedy's mind was more firmly fixed on the hot soup, and the lunch, than on any matter of official duty at that moment.

A stroll on deck and a cigar after the lunch, and I had an opportunity of placing before him my anxieties in respect of the collector.

He had heard *something* about it, and had come to the *Russia* prepared to protect Mr. Dickens and myself, if necessary, from any insult that might be offered us.

Calling to his own steamer, in a manner so as not to attract attention from our friends, he brought four of his own private detectives on board.

Introducing me to them, he explained that I was apprehensive of some trouble when the passenger tender arrived, and gave instructions to his officers that I was to be carefully guarded, and if any one molested me in any way, the delinquent was to be instantly arrested, and brought before him at his headquarters in Mulberry Street.

As there was still a good hour before the passengers and the mails were due, my protectors were taken care of in the officers' mess-room, and we were left to ourselves and the enjoyment of our friends' society.

The officers of the law in the States having authority to arrest any one, whether on civil or criminal charges, wear a small brooch or badge, which is affixed to the collar of the waistcoat, on the left breast, and being hidden by the lappel of the coat, is only exhibited when in the cause of duty, in the service of a warrant, &c.

When the time came for the arrival of the passenger tender my four protectors moved about, as I did, never leaving me for an instant. There was an enormous crowd in the passenger-boat, which was composed of all sorts and conditions of men, amongst them several personal friends, including M. du Chaillu (the African traveller), Mr. George W. Childs, of Philadelphia, who was the bearer of a magnificent basket of flowers from Mrs. Childs, and, much to Mr. Dickens's delight and amazement, Mr. Anthony Trollope, who on the day of our departure had arrived out in the *Scotia* just in time to get on board the mail tender going to the *Russia.* His advent to America had not been heralded, and the surprise at seeing him was only equalled by the cordiality of the meeting of the two friends.

Having occasion to go below to my state-room, I was stopped at the head of the companion by two rough-looking men, in seal-skin caps, who, walking up to me, proceeded to unbutton their coats and to show their badge of office; and whilst fumbling in their pockets, in the evident search of a document of some kind, my four friends imitated their action by doing as they had done, and, displaying *their* badge of office, remarked, "Too late, we've got him!" Seeing the police badges, which it is to be presumed take precedence in matters of arrest, and also seeing the police boat alongside, the civil officers seemed satisfied that I could not leave the country; and the first bell, to warn those who are going ashore to leave the ship, being rung, the collector's officials beat a hasty retreat, with no more harm done than a hearty laugh at their expense.

The collector, as we afterwards heard, was very irate to find I had got away, and some weeks afterwards served Messrs. Ticknor and Fields with some process in the hope of arresting any monies they might have in hand belonging to Mr. Dickens, through the sale of his books in America. This coming to the knowledge of Mr. Dickens, instructions were sent to Mr. Booth from England to attend to the matter, and being so attended to, ended in the defeat of the collector.

Such of our personal friends as could spare the time were invited by Mr. Kennedy to follow the *Russia,* in his boat down the bay. Those who could not, had to return to the shore in the company's tender, which was the first to get off; but before this was possible much time had to be expended in the shaking of hands and the little speeches attendant on such an occasion.

The departure of Charles Dickens from New York on this 22nd April, 1868, is thus described by the "New York Tribune" of the 23rd April: —

"It was a lovely day — a clear blue sky overhead — as he stood resting on the rail, chatting with his friends, and writing an autograph for that one, the genial face all aglow with delight, it was seemingly hard to say the word 'Farewell,' yet the tug-boat screamed the note of warning, and those who must return to the city went down the side.

"All left save Mr. Fields. 'Boz' held the hand of the publisher within his own. There was an unmistakable look in both faces. The lame foot came down from the rail, and the friends were locked in each other's arms.

"Mr. Fields then hastened down the side, not daring to look behind. The lines were 'cast off.'

"A cheer was given for Mr. Dolby, when Mr. Dickens patted him approvingly upon the shoulder, saying, 'Good boy.' Another cheer for Mr. Dickens, and the tug steamed away.

"'Good-bye, Boz.'

"'Good-bye,' from Mr. Fields, who stood the central figure of a group of three, Messrs. Du Chaillu and Childs upon each side. Then 'Boz' put his hat upon his cane, and waved it, and the answer came 'Goodbye,' and 'God bless you every one.'"

The police boat, and several private tugs and steam launches, in which were many ladies, followed us for some distance down the bay, and the evening rapidly closing in, the *Russia* was saluted by the miniature cannon on these craft, and then, turning round, sped their way to the city, leaving our noble ship to steam her way to England.

Charles Dickens and George Dolby

A caricature from an American paper on the eve of their departure for England.

We had not been at sea three days before there was an evident improvement in the state of Mr. Dickens's health. During this time he had to keep his room, but on the fourth day he was enabled to get a boot on his right foot and to take some exercise. The sea air brought a return of appetite, and with this came a return of health.

The voyage was a very rough one, but what did that matter? We were making one of the "fastest passages on record" at that time, and in a little over eight days from the time of leaving New York we were outside Queenstown Harbour, at four o'clock in the morning, waiting for the tender from the shore to relieve us of our mails, and to bring us letters from our homes; and well within the ninth day we were comfortably housed in the Adelphi Hotel, Liverpool, partaking of dinner at eight o'clock in the evening of May 1st.

When all collected together, on the deck of the Russia, our baggage looked enormous, and I had gloomy forebodings of what I should have to undergo to get it all through the Custom House in Liverpool, in anything like a reasonable time. These forebodings were not of long duration, and were allayed by the courtesy of the Surveyor of Customs at that port, who kindly volunteered to land us, and our men, with the effects in the mail boat. By this means we avoided the delay and inconvenience of a Custom House search, and saved some hours in arriving at our hotel.

After so long and rough a voyage, we deemed it inexpedient to travel to London the same night by the mail train, and so, remaining quietly in Liverpool, we continued our journey the following day. Reaching the Euston Square Station at about three in the afternoon, we parted from one another as if we had arrived there from one of our ordinary English journeys.

By arrangement, there were no friends to meet us at the station to give us welcome after our travels, and it was something almost ludicrous to see Mr. Dickens walk out of the station, bag in hand, on his way to the Charing Cross Station and Gad's Hill, where of course his arrival had been made known by telegraph to his family.

The men had their instructions to take his portion of the baggage to the office, and to report there on a given day at the end of the following week, for the purposes of a settlement of their accounts, on which day I was to be there also for the same object. So with a hearty shake of the hand, we parted— he for his home in Kent, and I for my home in Herefordshire.

We had undergone so much in the way of demonstrations and ovations in America that, certainly for a time, Mr. Dickens was desirous of avoiding anything of the kind, feeling in want of rest and retirement after the fatigues and excitement of our campaign, and for this reason his arrival home was conducted in the manner described.

It came to the knowledge of Miss Hogarth and Miss Dickens, that had the Chief arrived at his own station of Higham, the villagers had intended to take the horse out of his carriage, and to drag him to his own house. So, in order to avoid this, he arranged to have his carriage meet him at Gravesend, and to drive from there. The villagers, not to be done out of their anticipated pleasure, turned out on foot, and in their market carts and gigs; and escorting Mr. Dickens on the road, kept on giving him shouts of welcome, the houses along the road being decorated with flags. His own servants wanted to ring the alarm bell in the little belfry at the top of the house, but that idea was speedily crushed. The following day being Sunday, the bells of his own church rang out a peal after the morning service in honour of his return.

Meeting Mr. Dickens on the following Thursday named, I was surprised to find all traces of his late fatigues and ill-health had disappeared, and, to quote the words of his own medical man, he was looking "seven years younger." The sea air, and the four days' rest at Gad's Hill, favoured by beautiful weather, had brightened him so that he looked as if he had never had a day's illness in his life.

Already he had entered thoroughly into the work of the office, and it became doubly necessary that he should do so, for during the last three weeks of our stay in America a correspondent had informed Mr. Dickens of an accident which had befallen Mr. Wills whilst hunting, from which he was then suffering, and was greatly in want of rest in consequence, thus throwing all the work of "All the Year Round" on Mr. Dickens.

The closing of the American accounts revealed a state of affairs to Mr. Dickens, far in excess of his anticipations; for beyond knowing from time to time the amounts I had remitted to his credit at Messrs. Coutts's, he had taken no particular notice of the details, as on leaving England for America he had determined on not troubling himself with these affairs until his return.

The original scheme embraced eighty Readings in all, of which seventy-six were actually given.

Taking one city with another, the receipts averaged $3,000 each Reading, but as small places such as Rochester, New Bedford, and many others of the same class did not exceed $2,000 a night, the receipts in New York and Boston (where the largest sum was taken), far exceeded the $3,000 mentioned above. The total receipts were $228,000, and the expenses were $39,000, including hotels, travelling expenses, rent of halls, &c., and, in addition, a commission of 5% to Messrs. Ticknor and Fields on the gross receipts in Boston. The advertising expenses were very trifling — a preliminary advertisement announcing the sale of tickets being all that was necessary.

The hotels for Mr. Dickens, myself, and occasionally Mr. Osgood, and our staff of three men averaged $60 a day. Supposing gold to have been at par, it will be seen from the figures named that the profits of the enterprise would have been nearly £38,000; but as Mr. Dickens had no faith in American securities at that time, he preferred to convert the currency we received into gold, paying the difference 39½ per cent., and an additional ¼ percent, for banker's commission.

After paying all these charges, my commission, the preliminary expenses (£614), and taking into account the money Mr. Dickens had drawn for his own personal uses, the profit on the enterprise amounted to nearly £19,000.

One remarkable circumstance in connection with the taking of so much money, and all in paper (greenbacks), is worthy of mention which is, that on the entire amount taken, I had only two notes of $2 each, and one note of $20 that were forged — a compliment alike to Mr. Dickens and to the honesty of the heterogeneous material of which the mass of ticket purchasers was composed. The first were taken in Philadelphia, and the latter in Washington.

Book Three - *The Final Farewell Tour in the United Kingdom* (1868-1870).

Chapter Ten - *Eight Thousand Pounds for a Hundred Readings*

BEFORE leaving for America, Mr. Dickens had resolved on giving a series of farewell Readings on his return to England; and Messrs. Chappell, anticipating the American success, had already entered into negotiations with Mr. Dickens, prior to his departure.

Liberal as the terms had been for the two previous English tours, the proposal forwarded by Messrs. Chappell to America, before even the Readings had begun there, exceeded in liberality the terms they had already paid.

The proposal was that Mr. Dickens should give seventy-five farewell Readings in London and the provinces, for which he was to receive the sum of six thousand pounds, and in addition "all expenses whatever." This proposal, however, did not meet with Mr. Dickens's approval; for having fully determined never to read in England again after this series, he was under the impression that the country would stand a greater number of Readings than seventy-five, and that by giving one hundred of these instead of seventy-five, Messrs. Chappell's profits would be the greater by twenty-five per cent.

This idea having been transmitted by mail from Halifax, a prompt reply reached Boston before the termination of the first series of Readings there; to the effect that Messrs. Chappell agreed to pay the sum of eight thousand pounds (and all expenses) for one hundred Readings — a proposition assented to by Mr. Dickens by return of post.

It will be seen that this proposal was not the result of any excitement from the success in America, as at the time it was made no one could have said what the result of the campaign might be. Neither was Mr. Dickens actuated by any selfish or mercenary motives in making an alteration in the original proposition. No one cared less for the actual possession of money than he did.

Having made up his mind to abandon the Reading life for ever (certainly so far as England was concerned), that he might devote the rest of his time to his literary pursuits, he was desirous of freedom from monetary cares, that he might the easier provide for the increased expenditure consequent on the requirements of his sons (three of whom he had still to provide for); and although the strain on his constitution in the Reading life had become severe, he bore this uncomplainingly that he might the better do his duty to his family.

The Readings so far had been of the greatest assistance to him in this respect, and the temptation to add another £8,000 to the eighteen or nineteen thousand he had made in America was very great; and in his mind all personal considerations and inconveniences had to be put on one side in the fulfilment of the object he had in view.

The lovely weather we encountered on our return to England, and the rest and repose of the sea voyage, had caused all the bad symptoms in his health to disappear, and a week after his return no traces of his American sufferings were discernible — those best acquainted with him declaring that he looked better than ever.

Great as the temptations were to devote the remaining time, between the return to England and the commencement of the new engagement, entirely to rest and pleasure (as many would have done after so complete a success), Mr. Dickens, always eager for work of one kind or another, returned to the ordinary routine of his London life, as if he had never left it. Even had he been disposed to retire on his laurels for a time, the state of affairs disclosed at the office would have prevented him from so doing. The accident to Mr. Wills in the hunting field had resulted in concussion of the brain; and the doctors having ordered him away for complete rest, it was necessary that Mr. Dickens should take entire charge of "All the Year Round;" this requiring a supervision, not only of the literary department, but of the financial department also; and as this latter was entirely foreign to his previous experiences, the amount of labour it involved in the mastery of its details was an extra source of worry and annoyance to him.

A change of sub-editorship necessitated a change in the construction of the journal, and, having decided on this, he resolved to establish a new series, and discontinue the Christmas numbers, which he fancied were becoming monotonous to the public — so many other journals having imitated them. Then he set to work with a will to make the journal as attractive as possible in other respects, by writing more for it himself, than he had been able to do whilst in America. A new series of the "Uncommercial Traveller" being the result.

"No Thoroughfare" was still pursuing its successful career at the Adelphi Theatre, and, being translated into French, was produced in Paris (at the Vaudeville Theatre) early in June, meeting with a success equal to that in London. For the purpose of superintending the rehearsals, and *assisting* at the first representation, Mr. Dickens went to Paris, returning highly delighted with the success of the play in the French capital.

Some weeks before this, we were busy with the details of the Final Series of Readings, arranged to commence in London on Monday, October 5th, at St. James's Hall; and already the necessity for a Reading novelty had taken possession of Mr. Dickens's mind, with a view to a success sufficiently large to secure a handsome profit to Messrs. Chappell and Co., for their increased liberality.

The great difficulty in this case was to find a subject which would not only be attractive, but which would create a sensation, and it was only after great consideration that the murder of Nancy by Bill Sikes, in "Oliver Twist," was decided on for the purpose. The subject itself was so terrible that his friends besought him to abandon the idea; this, however, he would not listen to, and, requesting those whose advice he valued to withhold any opinion on the matter until the Reading had been finally prepared, the subject was allowed to drop for the time being.

In the midst of so much business, he had arranged to give a series of parties at Gad's Hill, and during the summer there was not a week when he did not entertain those friends whose society afforded him so much pleasure. The early days of the week were devoted to business purposes; Mr. Dickens, on these days, taking up his residence at the office in London, returning to "Gad's" with his guests, as a rule, on Friday, and remaining there until the following Monday, when all returned to London together in a saloon carriage.

Having been the recipient of so much good feeling and hospitality in America from old and valued friends, it is not to be wondered at that he should have been desirous of marking his high appreciation of these favours, whenever opportunities presented themselves in the arrival of these friends in his own country; and, as the intercourse between Longfellow and himself had been almost daily in our visits to Boston, it was but natural that his advent to England should be made the subject of special rejoicings at Gad's Hill.

The poet was accompanied by his daughter, his brother-in-law (Mr. Appleton), and Mr. and Mrs. Charles Eliot Norton; these, with Mr. Forster, Mr. Charles Kent, and myself, formed the "house party" at one of the earliest of the social gatherings in July.

The visit of Longfellow was a very brief one, and could not have been but gratifying to him in the cordiality of his reception at "Gad's;" and, although he had been there on previous occasions, the charm of the beautiful summer weather we were then enjoying added greatly to the pleasure of this visit.

Two post carriages, with postillions in the "old red jacket of the old red royal Dover Road," were turned out, and the antiquities of Rochester and its castle having been visited, we drove to Blue Bell Hill (a favourite spot with Mr. Dickens); and when the time came for our return to London, the holiday had passed all too quickly.

These excursions, taking frequently the whole day, were as much a source of pleasure to the Chief as to his friends, and seemed always to possess a novel charm for him.

Ever mindful of the comfort and convenience of his guests, and knowing how much the happiness of the day depends on these, Mr. Dickens had a plan of his own in the conduct of these arrangements; and instead of entailing the labour, consequent on the carrying of the lunch-baskets to some picturesque and secluded spot, on certain individuals of the party, he arranged that everyone should carry his own lunch, and nobody else's. For this purpose he had a quantity of small baskets, in which were packed all the necessaries for the midday meal; and as nothing — not even the pepper, salt, mustard, and cork-screws — was ever forgotten, the petty worries and annoyances so common at picnics were avoided by his forethought.

Besides his public and editorial duties, another matter pressed heavily on him at this time. During his absence in America, he had the misfortune to lose an old and valued friend, and a very eccentric one too. This gentleman had originally been a clergyman of the Church of England, but disapproving of many of the doctrines he had to preach, and being a man of large means, he left the Church, and in his retirement devoted his life to antiquarian research, and the writing of some papers explaining his religious opinions. At his decease, he bequeathed a considerable sum of money, and his papers, to Mr. Dickens, with the desire that he should edit them for publication. This was no inconsiderable task, and involved immense labour.

Calling on him one day, I found him nearly distracted by the conglomeration of ideas he had to deal with, of which he could make neither head nor tail.

Under the circumstances I suggested to him that it might not be easy to find a suitable title — a difficulty he had already anticipated. The only one that had occurred to his mind, viz., that of "Religious Hiccoughs," being neither respectful to the subject, nor grateful to the memory of his friend, the matter was still in abeyance when I left him, and remained so for some months afterwards.

The book appeared in the following year, under a title it is not necessary to mention, as, since its publication, it has been buried in obscurity.

Between the intervals of pleasure and work, the summer of 1868 passed all too quickly; and in my almost daily intercourse with him I was the recipient of many tokens of his love and affection for me, amongst others the fulfilment of a desire he had expressed to stand as sponsor to my boy, the news of whose birth reached us at Washington.

The christening took place at Marylebone Church, on Thursday, July 2nd, the occasion being marked on his part by the presentation of a *service of plate suitable to the requirements of a baby,* which consisted of a massive silver bowl, plate, fork, and spoon.

Before returning to our reading life, he had to encounter a grave sorrow in the parting from his youngest son, Edward Bulwer Lytton Dickens (nick-named Plorn), who had elected to join his brother, Alfred Tennyson Dickens, already settled in Australia as a successful sheep farmer.

"Plorn" was the favourite of his father, and his departure caused him great uneasiness and pain. He sailed on the 26th September, in the sailing ship *Somerset* (Captain Miller), and in Mr. Dickens's anxiety for the comfort of his son, I was enabled (through the instrumentality of a valued friend of my own, whose son had already made a voyage with Captain Miller) to bring the captain and Mr. Dickens together.

My friend, Mr. Stephen Holland, of Porchester Terrace, arranged that the meeting should take place at a dinner party given by him at the Westminster Club, with the view to securing for "Plorn" the like good offices on board that the captain had rendered to Mr. Holland's son George, during his voyage.

Mr. Dickens, who had been very humorous during dinner, described later in the evening a visit he had that morning paid to the Post Office in St. Martin's-le-Grand. So pleased was he with all he had seen that he proposed to go again, asking Mr. Holland to accompany him.

The conversation turning on the subject of the handing over of the telegraph to the Government, Dickens expatiated on the importance of such a course, remarking that we should soon be able to send a telegram for 3d., and that he "could not imagine anything more calculated to advance education than this facility of conveying ideas."

"Should we not rather use the word *information* than *education?*" suggested Mr. Holland; "for we have no doubt all seen the servant girl racking her brain and consulting a dictionary over the composition of a three-page letter, the writing of which would surely be more in self-teaching than putting a few words on paper in the form of a telegram."

The conversation changed, and, becoming general after this, Dickens was evidently in deep thought, and after a short time called out —

"Holland, you are wrong! Your servant-girl *might* get some one to write the letter for her, but she would have to write the telegram herself."

Our host admitted the fact, but was evidently more amused than convinced thereby.

If Dickens were alive now he would be greatly shocked to find that his prophecy is still unrealized, even to the extent of a reduction in the cost of sending a telegram to 6d., let alone 3d.

It was a hard struggle with the Chief to get over the separation from his son; but it was one that had to be borne, and in referring to it at the time, he remarked to me that he was grateful in his sorrow that he had the means and influence to start his son so well in the world.

We were now approaching the commencement of the Reading tour, and this of itself came as a relief to his mind. His health being apparently restored, he looked forward to the approaching campaign with pleasure, and the great interest he took in all the details made him forget his sorrow to a considerable extent.

For these farewell Readings, the advertisement which he persuaded Messrs. Chappell to issue, and which he reproduced in his own journal, is so characteristic of him that a reference to it will not be out of place here, certainly so far as its integrity is concerned:

"It is scarcely necessary to add that any announcement made in connection with these farewell Readings will be strictly adhered to and considered final; and that on no consideration whatever will Mr. Dickens be induced to appoint an extra night in any place in which he shall have been announced to read for the last time."

The emphatic terms in which the foregoing paragraph is couched, added to the fact that the public regarded every announcement in connection with Mr. Dickens's name as authentic, had the desired effect; so much so that, before the titles of the Readings had been announced, there was a run on the ticket department of Messrs. Chappell's establishment, to secure the best seats.

When informed as to the progress of matters, Mr. Dickens became the more convinced of the necessity for the powerful novelty in the form of a Reading in order to keep up the receipts; and as nothing more sensational in this respect presented itself to him than the "Sikes and Nancy" murder, he would listen to no remonstrance in respect of it; at the same time being impressed himself with the dangers by which the subject was beset. So much so, that when he had arranged the incident for Reading purposes, and had begun to "get it up," he had his own misgivings as to whether the impression would not be so horrible as to prevent persons from coming to the Readings a second time.

He paid me the compliment to read the story to me, and I confess to having done all in my power to dissuade him from continuing with it. My reasons for this had reference not so much to the inappropriateness of the subject for Reading purposes — because I knew well that the sensational character of it would be a great attraction — as to the effect which the extra exertion might have on his constitution and the state of his health, which had now begun again to show signs of failing and to assume the old American form; for whether from close application to work during the summer months, or from excessive exercise in the pedestrian line at Gad's Hill, the pains had begun to return in his foot, this time in the right, instead of the left one.

Not wishing to take the responsibility of deciding in this matter myself, I proposed that he should refer the book to Messrs. Chappell, they having the largest vested interest in the matter. This proposal being accepted, the book was sent to them, and in due course was returned with a suggestion that a select party of representative friends, whose opinion could be relied on, should be invited for a private reading of the work in St. James's Hall, on a date when we should be in London for one of our regular Readings.

This arrangement seemed to please all parties, and so the matter was left; Saturday evening, November 14th, being the date selected. Mr. Dickens had ample time to prepare it for presentation to our friends.

The commencement of our last engagement with the Chappells was all that could be desired, with the old success staring us in the face, and up to a certain point with no dark clouds before us, save and except a probability of a return of the ill-health. This, however, was not to last long, for we had not been at work a fortnight when I received a communication from a personal friend of my own in Darlington, announcing to me the death of Frederick Dickens, the last surviving brother of my Chief. He had been staying with some friends in this place, and as no one had any idea that he had been ill, the suddenness of the news, apart from the melancholy nature of it, had a serious effect on Mr. Dickens.

At his request I went to Darlington, there to find, to my satisfaction and his own, that in the last moments his brother had been carefully tended by the friends with whom he had been staying.

This knowledge, however, did not tend to relieve his distress of mind at the loss of his only brother; and, coming as it did so shortly on the separation from "Plorn," of whom he was always speaking in the most affectionate terms, as his youngest and favourite child, it was with the greatest difficulty that he could get up the required spirit to go through the evening's work.

But, as in America, the sight of the hall in which he had to read, and a quarter of an hour at the "little table" before dressing, and the opening of the doors, banished all this depression, and he forgot himself and his own sufferings in the excitement of his duty.

Chapter Eleven - The Last Tour in Scotland and Ireland

AFTER a very few Readings had been given, we found ourselves going on in the same way and leading the same life we had led so often before, and it was at times difficult to imagine we had ever had any cessation of it. But for the fear of a recurrence of Mr. Dickens's illness, and the precautions it was necessary to take to prevent such a misfortune, the life would have been a most pleasant one. There was always this anxiety though, and it was with a great feeling of hopefulness and relief that, in order not to run the risk of bad business during the time of a general election — then about to take place — we decided on suspending operations during the month of November — certainly so far as the provinces were concerned — and confining our efforts entirely to London.

This gave Mr. Dickens plenty of time to prepare the "Sikes and Nancy" murder Reading, which it had been decided should be subjected to a private trial in St. James's Hall, on Saturday evening, the 14th of November.

Our provincial Readings for the time closed in Liverpool and Manchester at the end of October, and although the country was in a state of the most tremendous turmoil on account of the elections, our receipts did not fall off in the least.

On one of our "off" nights in this week both Mr. Dickens and myself had accepted invitations to dine with friends in Liverpool; but Mr. Dickens, being too unwell to carry out his part of the engagement, I had to go without him, leaving him at the Adelphi Hotel alone, to amuse himself the best way he could.

Before my departure, he begged of me to call at a bookseller's and to send to him a book with which to pass away the time until my return. I was embarrassed to know the sort of book he would prefer, and was met with the reply, "Oh, *you* know! anything you like." This not satisfying me, I pressed for more precise instructions on the point, getting only the same reply as before, with the suggestion that something of Sir Walter Scott's or *his own* would answer the purpose. As this did not assist me very much, I decided on getting for him one of his own books, and knowing "The Old Curiosity Shop" to be a favourite with him, I purchased that. Taking it to him myself, he was delighted that I had done this, for he had not *read the book for years!* On hearing this I was naturally curious to see the effect of his own work on him when I should return to the hotel, and was greatly amused to find him laughing immoderately at certain incidents in the book, as if he had never seen it before. I was as much amused at this as he was with his book, and lest I might think he was vain of his own work, he explained to me — he was not laughing at his own creations, so much as at the recollection of the circumstances under which certain passages and incidents were written.

The return to the Reading life, with a resumption of the long railway journeys by express train, brought back all the painful feelings of America; and that these might be got rid of as much as possible, it was decided to re-arrange the tour, as far as it was possible, so as to do our travelling on "off" days, and then only by slow trains.

The "Sikes and Nancy" Reading trial came off, as arranged, in the great St. James's Hall, and instead of the invitations being restricted to a limited circle of close and intimate friends, it was considered advisable to extend the circle by inviting persons whose judgment could be relied on, and, amongst these, leading members of the press.

The arrangements made were those of a public Reading, and everything was done as if the trial had been one of these. The audience consisted of some hundred to a hundred and fifty persons, and was composed of all classes of people representing art. The utmost attention was paid to every word, look, and gesture during the recital of the horrible incident, spoken as it was with an intensity which gave a reality to the whole scene.

It being generally known amongst those present that Mr. Dickens himself had his own doubts and fears as to the advisability of pourtraying so dreadful a subject on the platform, it was a matter of no surprise to him to find considerable hesitation on the part of his friends in expressing an opinion with regard to it. This hesitation was due to two or three reasons, the principal one being the great additional labour it required to give due effect to the subject.

The Reading being concluded, Mr. Dickens descended into the body of the hall to discuss the merits or demerits of the Reading, during which time the reading table and screens had been whisked away, as if by magic, discovering to the gaze of those assembled a long table, on the level of the platform, arranged for an oyster supper. A large staff of men were in readiness to open oysters and champagne. His own words in a letter to a friend will best describe the scene:

"Directly I had done, there was disclosed one of the prettiest banquets you can imagine; and when all the people came up, and the gay dresses of the ladies were lighted up by those powerful lights of mine, the scene was exquisitely pretty, the hall being newly decorated, and very elegantly, and the whole looking like a great bed of flowers and diamonds."

So completely awe-stricken were the miniature audience by the Reading, that it required some such accessory as this to set them talking.

One visitor, a celebrated critic, expressed an opinion as to the danger of giving the Reading before a mixed audience, *as he had an irresistible desire to scream.* A celebrated physician, concurring in this, declared that if "only one woman cries out when you murder the girl, there will be a contagion of hysteria all over the place."

Some of the ladies described it as "awful;" whilst one, a celebrated actress, and a good judge of what is likely to be successful, on being asked whether it should be done in public or not, said: "Why, of course do it! The public have been looking out for a sensation these last fifty years, and now they have got it."

Charles Dickens's Reading of "Sikes and Nancy."
Two studies from a contemporary magazine.

These and similar opinions caused Mr. Dickens still to waver in his determination; but having been at the pains of getting it up, it was certainly worth a trial; and as Messrs. Chappell were not indisposed towards this, it was arranged that the first public Reading should take place at the commencement of the New Year, and simultaneously with this that it should be tried in Dublin — these two Readings to settle the fate of it for ever. It is almost to be regretted that these two Readings of the murder were received with acclamation, for otherwise Mr. Dickens would have been saved an enormity of labour and extra fatigue which he was ill prepared to endure, and which, in my opinion, and in the opinion of those who knew him the best, did more to hasten his end and to aggravate his sufferings than he himself would admit.

The general election being over, and Mr. Dickens being much benefited by his rest, he started off again for heavy work, the intention being to run off the remaining Readings of our engagement without any rest or cessation, with the exception of a fortnight at Christmas. The first of these Readings took place in Brighton, in which town Messrs. Chappell accepted a certainty by way of engagement, from the firm of Messrs. Lyon and Hall, who paid the sum of £650, and all expenses, for four Readings — this being the largest amount ever paid to any individual reader; and it is satisfactory to be able to record the fact that the spirit which actuated so liberal a venture was handsomely responded to by the public.

The "Times," "Daily Telegraph," and "Morning Post," taking advantage of the ordinary Reading at St. James's Hall, on Tuesday, November 17th (the one following the private Reading), had written elaborate articles on the subject of the "Sikes and Nancy" Reading, and through these the curiosity of the provincial public was already awakened; and I found on my arrival in Edinburgh, whither we had travelled on Saturday, December 5th, a desire on the part of the public that this Reading should be included in the series which we were about to commence there and in Glasgow. Finding that such a desire could not be gratified, the personal feeling of the Edinburgh public towards Mr. Dickens (or, as he expresses it, "the affectionate regard of the people") was of such a kind that but few days sufficed to fill the stall place for all the Readings announced; and, contrary to our previous Edinburgh experiences, the first of these Readings was as largely attended as the holding capacity of the Music Hall would allow.

Sunday, never a joyous or pleasant time in Scotland, was pleasantly passed in a walk up Arthur's Seat. This did much to calm Mr. Dickens's nerves after the shaking of the journey by the "Flying Scotchman" the previous day, from which he suffered greatly on our arrival in Edinburgh. The Staplehurst accident was always in his mind, and, since his return from America, seemed to recur to him with increased horror. On this particular journey, we amused ourselves by calculating the number of shocks the nerves received in journeying so long a distance by express train as from London to Edinburgh; and, according to Mr. Dickens's mode of calculation, he estimated this at thirty thousand 1 Should this calculation be correct, it is no matter of surprise that any one in Mr. Dickens' state of health should suffer greatly by such a journey.

Scottish audiences are as uproarious in the reception of their favourites as they are cold to those who have not made their mark amongst them. The greeting accorded to Mr. Dickens on this occasion was worth a journey to America and back to receive, putting the Chief in the best of spirits for his work, which he went through with enjoyment to himself no less than the pleasure he afforded to his audience; amongst whom were such old friends as Peter Fraser, Ballantyne (the Scottish bard), John Blackwood, and Mr. Russel (editor of the "Scotsman"). These last were invited to a dinner party given by Mr. Dickens in their honour on the following Saturday.

Messrs. Peter Fraser, Ballantyne, and John Blackwood being the only survivors of the time when Mr. Dickens in his early career had received so much kindness and hospitality in Edinburgh at the hands of Lord Jeffrey, and other Scottish friends (and who had done so much to make the city so pleasant to him), it was but natural that the evening should be spent in recollections of the old associates.

Peter Fraser sang, as he only could sing, the songs that Lord Jeffrey most delighted in; and Ballantyne recited the older poems, bringing back to our host the recollections of five and twenty years previously. In this way a most enjoyable evening was spent, and it was not until the early hours of the Sabbath that these gentlemen left us.

This being the first visit to Edinburgh and Glasgow since Mr. Dickens's return from America, we were fully prepared to find that the receipts were far in excess of those of any previous visits to these places; for public curiosity to see and hear the popular author would alone account for such a result; but apart from this, it was the greatest gratification to Mr. Dickens to find with what attention and delight the old Readings were listened to and applauded.

These were not the only matters which gratified him so much, for the old private and personal feeling towards him were commensurate with the increase in the treasury department, and not a day passed but some fresh proof of this sentiment presented itself, either in the form of invitations to banquets which he would not accept, or of presents of various kinds, reminding us of our experiences twelve months previously in Boston, and other places in the United States. Under these circumstances, it was not without regret that we parted with our Scottish friends on Saturday, December 18th, to give one more Reading in St. James's Hall on the following Tuesday, previous to our short Christmas vacation.

Up to the moment of the train leaving Edinburgh, there were fresh evidences of the good feeling towards the Chief, a large concourse of friends assembling at the station to wish him a merry Christmas, and a speedy return to Scotland for the farewell Readings. In the hope of making this night-journey a pleasant one, Mr. Mason, the general manager of the North British Railway, had telegraphed to London for one of the royal saloon carriages of the Great Northern Railway, which was improvised for the occasion into a comfortable sleeping apartment, the bedding and furniture being supplied from Mr. Mason's own house. So this wintry night's journey was comfortably performed; and as the weather was almost unbearably bad, we had good cause for gratitude to Mr. Mason for his kind thought and attention, which Mr. Dickens was never tired of recalling.

Christmas week is not considered favourable to large receipts at places of public amusement in London, and it was thought a bold venture to announce a Reading in St. James's Hall, to take place only three days before the great festival; but the popularity the Readings had acquired was of such a character as would have emboldened less astute caterers than Messrs. Chappell in announcing a Reading of the "Christmas Carol" at that time. The result justified the experiment to such an extent as to lead every one connected with us to the belief that "we couldn't do wrong in announcing a Reading at any time."

The appropriateness to the season of the subject selected for reading, suggested that the table should be decorated with holly, a proceeding which met with Mr. Dickens's warm approval and appreciation, and, slight as was this small token of respect to the occasion, it had the effect of affording the audience a pleasure which greatly assisted Mr. Dickens in his labours. After three months of incessant travel he required some such stimulus, trifling as it was, to brace him up to the task of entertaining so large an audience by his own unaided efforts. Then it was refreshing to think that Christmas would be with us in three days, and then he would be able to take a holiday of ten days in the enjoyment of the festive season and the society of his family and friends at Gad's Hill, where there was always a goodly gathering.

My own domestic arrangements at Ross precluded me from accepting an invitation to join the family party; and as I was desirous of being represented at the dinner table on Christmas Day, I bargained to supply the turkey for that particular occasion. Being sensible of the responsibility I had incurred in this respect (as I felt it a privilege to be allowed to provide the author of the "Christmas Carol" with such an important accessory to his dinner-table), I caused immense pains to be taken for the production of the finest turkey the neighbourhood of Ross, or even the whole county of Hereford, could afford.

A magnificent bird, weighing some thirty pounds, was procured, packed in a large hamper, with a quantity of other good things, and despatched in ample time to reach Gad's Hill on Christmas Eve, leaving Ross, indeed, on the day of the Christmas Reading in London, a circumstance which was solemnly communicated to Mr. Dickens and the ladies of his family.

The day following the Reading Mr. Dickens went to Gad's Hill, and I joined my family at Ross, easy in my mind as to the safe delivery of the turkey; but the next afternoon I was startled by the receipt of a letter from Mr. Dickens, written like this:

**WHERE
IS
THAT
TURKEY?
IT
HAS
NOT
ARRIVED
!!!!!!!!!!!**

At the same time I received several telegrams from other friends, saying that promised hampers (of which there were about a dozen) had not come to hand.

Knowing that the courteous station-master at Ross had taken great pains in the transmission of my parcels, especially the one for Dickens (of whom he was an ardent admirer), I drove at once to the station to ascertain, if possible, the fate of my property.

On my way there I met the station-master, breathless, hurrying with an official telegram in his hand, desiring him to inform me that all my parcels had been transferred to a horse-box, with a lot of others, at Gloucester; and that by accident this vehicle had caught fire *en route,* and had been detained at Reading until it had cooled down sufficiently for the amount of damage to be ascertained.

Of course the disappointment this entailed was not to be repaired by a money payment; for the value of the whole of my consignment was as nothing compared with my distress of mind at the thought of *Mr. Dickens going without his turkey on Christmas Day;* and as we were then late in the afternoon of Christmas Eve, the only hope of his having one was to telegraph to him the state of the case, and get the Great Western authorities to do the same. After the first annoyance of this mishap Mr. Dickens used to refer to the matter frequently, and speak of it with gratitude, as our misfortune proved a blessing to the poorer inhabitants of Reading, who were enabled to purchase the charred remains of turkeys and joints of beef at sixpence a-piece, the price at which the railway company sold the contents of the horse-box.

With the commencement of the New Year (1869) we seemed to begin, as it were, a new career, for we had got through but little more than one-fourth of the number of Readings Mr. Dickens had arranged with Messrs. Chappell to give on the final Farewell Reading Tour. There were still seventy-eight more Readings to be given, and these would keep us fully occupied until the end of May, under the most favourable circumstances. The pressure of time under which these would have to be given, and the chances of interruptions which might arise from ill-health, or any other unforeseen cause, were sources of the greatest anxiety to us, and it was only by the strictest observance of a system, and by taking the utmost precautions against accidents of any kind, that we could see our way to accomplishing the task we had before us.

Taking the chances of a travelling life, such as we were in the habit of leading, and with our experiences in this respect, we felt — or thought we did — pretty secure; but there was one point on which we did not feel safe, and that was the uncertain state of health in which Mr. Dickens then was, and had been since his return from America. The pain in the foot was always recurring at inconvenient and unexpected moments, and occasionally his old enemy, the American catarrh, would assert itself; and, although he always spoke of himself as well in other respects, it was evident that these two ailments were telling greatly against him.

This being the case, I was more than ever opposed to his continuing with the "Sikes and Nancy" Reading, which, in my knowledge of him, and of *it,* I always regarded as one of the greatest dangers we had to contend against.

As I knew that any further opposition to his ideas about this on my part would only make him the more determined to overcome the difficulty, I ceased talking on the subject, preferring to wait until the Reading had been given in public, when, if it should be coldly received, his own perception of the popular judgment would induce him to abandon it. Nothing but that could affect his resolve, for his idea in preparing it for reading purposes was solely to increase our coffers and to make the remainder of the tour as great a financial success as possible.

When produced in St. James's Hall on Tuesday evening, January 5th (1869), the effect of the "Sikes and Nancy" Reading was all that Mr. Dickens had anticipated from a financial point of view, and from an *artistic* point of view he had no reason to be disappointed; but in the vigour and the earnestness with which it was delivered, it was painfully apparent to his most intimate friends, and those who knew his state of health the best, that a too -frequent repetition of it would seriously and permanently affect his constitution. The terrible force with which the actual perpetration of this most foul murder was described was of such a kind as to render Mr. Dickens utterly prostrate for some moments after its delivery, and it was not until he had vanished from the platform that the public had sufficiently recovered their sense of composure to appreciate the circumstance that all the horrors to which they had been listening were but a story and not a reality.

The reception accorded to this Reading by the press was such as to create a demand for it in future Readings in London and the provinces, a fact which caused him to continue working away at it to make it as perfect for representation as were all the other Readings. The horrible perfection to which he brought it, and its novelty, acted as a charm to him and made him the more determined to go on with it come what might, and all remonstrance to the contrary was unheeded by him, notwithstanding in his own mind he knew with what danger to his constitution he was beset, and that by continuing with this additional labour he was running risks against which he was cautioned by his medical advisers and his friends.

On the morning following the first reading of "Sikes and Nancy" I called at the office, and was not surprised to find my Chief in a state of great prostration after the efforts of the previous night; but as my object in calling on him was more with a view to a friendly chat, and to make arrangements for a journey to Ireland, which we were about to take that same evening, I did not specially allude to the Reading of the previous evening, except to congratulate him on the success of it, so far as its effect on the public was concerned, and the reception it had met with from the press.

There was no immediate necessity for me to do more than this, for we should have plenty of time on our Irish journey to discuss the future of the "Murder" as a stock Reading. Moreover the Readings were already announced in the various towns on our list, for some weeks in advance, and could not be altered.

My reticence on this subject made him the more determined to discuss the matter in its fullest extent there and then, and having done this in its entirety we decided on leaving the point to Messrs. Chappell to decide — the only condition of this arrangement being that, as we were going to Cheltenham on the 23rd of the month, and as Macready lived there and was too feeble to undertake a journey to London to be present at one of the Readings, the "Murder" should be given there for his especial behoof.

I looked forward with great pleasure to the Irish journey, as I felt that the change of scene would do Mr. Dickens much good, and that in the social intercourse with his Irish friends, in private life, much of the fatigue from which he was suffering would pass away.

We had but two places to visit, viz., Dublin and Belfast, therefore the fatigue of travelling would not be very great; and as I had arranged to take these journeys by easy stages, and we had a fortnight before us, we left Euston Square with comparatively light hearts for Chester, where I had arranged we should break the journey.

The reports from Dublin, sent by our agents, were of the most exhilarating character, but they came far short of the real state of the case. There were three Readings in Dublin and two in Belfast. For the former city all the reserved seats were sold in advance, and without encroaching unfairly on the liberties of the public in the second and third places, I and my agent in Dublin were at our wits' ends to know how to meet the pressing demands on our space.

At the first of the Dublin Readings this difficulty we contrived to overcome, but for the second and third Readings the pressure was so great that it required a strong body of police — mounted and on foot — kindly placed at my disposal by Colonel Lake, to control the traffic in the neighbourhood of the Rotunda. All money payments at the doors (except in the shilling places) were refused, and only those with tickets allowed to enter the building, the doors of which were strongly guarded by police in plain clothes. By this plan everything passed off quietly, and no one but the officials and the disappointed ones were inconvenienced by the undue pressure.

At the third Reading, for which the demand was even greater than for the previous two, I decided, on consultation with Mr. Dickens, to place chairs in the reserved seats, wherever it was possible to do so without danger to the public, and nearly two hundred of these were disposed of at the agent's shop within the short space of two hours.

It was impossible for Mr. Dickens to begin at the advertised time, so taxed were the resources of our staff, although increased for the occasion, and he was compelled to stand at the reading-table for nearly a quarter of an hour. His presence there had the effect of putting his public in good humour, and when at last silence was restored, and he was about to commence, a well-known author made his appearance in the silent room, and, proceeding to look for his seat, was greeted with the salute from a stentorian voice, "Sit down, Mr. ____"

The Dublin public, always appreciative of a joke, and knowing the gentleman to be an intimate friend of Mr. Dickens's, burst into hearty laughter, which, extending itself to the platform, caused another delay in the commencement of the proceedings.

Everything went well until close upon the termination of the second Reading, when an alarm of fire was caused by a downpour of smoke into the Hall. The hall-keeper, being fortunately at my side, accounted for this by the lighting of a fire in one of the upper rooms in the building in a grate which had been disused for some time — the down draught causing the smoke.

Before any harm could come of this I was on the platform telling Mr. Dickens the cause of the smoke, and he in a humorous speech imparted the information to the public, who, resuming their seats, settled down for the rest of the Reading as if no casualty had arisen.

We had to leave for Belfast the following day, and so a supper-party of intimate friends was extemporized at the Shelborne Hotel. At this Dickens was in one of his merriest moods, all traces of ill-health having for the time left him.

On occasions such as this he' would entertain his guests with stories of the most interesting kind, and as they generally took a theatrical turn, it is painful now to remember the energy with which he illustrated the scene he was depicting, whether of a serious or ludicrous kind. In either case he was thoroughly in earnest, and it was difficult to believe that he had gone through so much on the platform, and that his never-flagging spirit came to his rescue when he felt bound to amuse his friends in the social circle.

The successes of Dublin repeated themselves in Belfast, where it was proposed that a great banquet should be given him by the Mayor and Corporation. Much as Mr. Dickens appreciated the compliment, this project had to be abandoned, and our visit was purely one of business.

We left Belfast by the midday limited mail on Saturday, January 16th, in order to catch the mail boat from Kingstown the same evening. An accident occurred which but for a most watchful Providence might have resulted in most serious consequences. This train consists of but two carriages for passengers, with the necessary travelling post-office carriages and guards' vans. As we did not wish any society but that of our own party, I had secured a coupe (made to contain only five persons) for our special use on this journey, but as these compartments are but little known in this country now, it may be as well to explain that they are composed almost entirely of plate glass.

Whilst running along at a rapid speed, about forty miles from Belfast, we received a severe jolt which threw us all forward in the carriage. Looking out we observed an enormous piece of iron flying along a side line, tearing up the ground and carrying some telegraph posts along with it. The breaks were suddenly applied, a lumbering sound was heard on the roof of the carriage, and the plate-glass windows were bespattered with stones, gravel, and mud.

Possibly having the recollection of the dreadful Staplehurst accident in his mind, Mr. Dickens threw himself to the bottom of the carriage, and we all followed his example.

The train was speedily brought to a stand-still, and on our dismounting and taking a view of the situation, we found that the great tire of the driving-wheel had broken, and that the piece of iron we had seen travelling with such destructive force and carrying the telegraph posts with it was a portion of the tire, and that the noise on the roof of the carriage was caused by another enormous piece of iron falling on it. Had this piece of iron struck the glass instead of the framework of the carriage, it would have been impossible for us to escape, and in all probability there would have been a repetition of the Staplehurst catastrophe.

The promptitude with which the driver brought his train to a stand prevented the engine leaving the metals. It was a lonely spot in which to spend an hour awaiting the arrival of another engine to take us on to Dublin, but we were all grateful to think that no one personally was the worse for the circumstance, and that the only damage was done to the engine, into the machinery of which huge pieces of metal had been driven, mixed with ballast.

Our spirits flagged for a time after we started again, and it was with great relief that we found ourselves safe on the Holyhead boat making our way once more for home; though it was unfortunate that the remembrance of so pleasant a visit to Ireland (the recollection of which was so inspiriting) should have been marred by such a mishap.

Chapter Twelve - The Beginning of the End

I WAS not able to perform the whole journey from Dublin to London with Mr. Dickens and his companions, having been suddenly called to Ross by the severe illness of a near relative; and so I left the party in the dead of the night at Stafford. It was not without considerable uneasiness that I did so, for the recollection of the escape we had in the Belfast train had inspired Mr. Dickens with the old dread of railway travelling.

Finding my relative much improved in health, I remained in Ross but a few hours, leaving on Sunday evening, in order to reach Gloucester by road to catch the night mail, that I might report myself early on the following morning at the office. Having an important fortnight before us, in which Readings were announced for St. James's Hall, Birmingham, Cheltenham, Clifton, Torquay, and Bath, I was fearful that a shock to Mr. Dickens's system might bring back the ailment to his foot, and that these Readings would have to be postponed, in which event the loss to every one concerned would have been enormous.

I found that, although somewhat refreshed after a day and a night's rest, it was only his strength of will and determination which prevented a catastrophe such as the one I feared; and it was with mingled feelings that I was enabled to report to my principals, the Messrs. Chappell, that matters looked well for a prosperous fortnight.

One item in our programme for the coming week was the prospect of Mr. Dickens meeting his old friend Macready in Cheltenham, when the special Reading of the "Murder" was to be given for the old tragedian's delectation on the following Saturday afternoon.

The programme on this occasion consisted of three Readings, viz.: "Boots at the Holly Tree Inn," the Murder in "Oliver Twist," and the "Trial from Pickwick" — a selection which could not fail to interest the veteran actor, whose love of children would cause him to appreciate the mimic elopement of Master Harry Walmers, Junior, with "the adorable Norah," whose tragic susceptibilities would not fail to be aroused by the horror of the murder scene, and whose sense of the comic — for Macready had a sense of the comic — would be appealed to by the humorous whimsicalities of the "Trial."

The effect produced on Macready by the "Murder" Reading has already been described by other hands than mine; but as I was present when he entered the dressing-room after the performance, and consequently an eyewitness of what took place, I think I might be allowed to describe the episode.

Mr. Dickens having sufficiently recovered his composure after the excitement of the Reading, sent me into the stalls to bring Macready to him.

Macready (who was very infirm) was as much excited and affected by the Reading as if he had given it himself; and leaning on my arm as he entered the room, glared speechlessly at Dickens, who, seeing his condition, desired me to give him a glass of champagne, which, however, he declined. I forced the wine on him, and taking the glass from me with a scowl (as if I had done him a personal injury), he said he would drink it later on.

Turning to Dickens, who had by this time placed him on a sofa, he said, in the manner peculiar to himself and with great hesitation, "You remember my best days, my dear boy? No! that's not it. Well, to make a long story short, all I have to say is — Two Macbeths!"

Although a compliment to the Chief, the peculiar way in which this remark was delivered— with a scowl at me — so tickled Dickens that he burst out laughing; and reminding Macready that he had yet another Reading to give, he prevailed on the old man to take the wine, and I ushered him back to his seat in the front row of the stalls.

On the way he seemed to remember that Dickens and myself were to be his guests that evening at dinner, and once away from the dressing-room, which he had entered with so much apparent trepidation, his manner suddenly changed, and he was all geniality.

The party at dinner consisted of Macready, Mrs. Macready, their son, Dickens, and myself. Dickens was all life and vivacity, and when he found his old friend relapsing into feebleness and forgetfulness, was equal to the occasion, and refreshed his memory by some question about the olden days, which

175

caused Macready's face to change from its usual stolidity to an expression of quite vivacious humour.

He had an idea that, as he had retired to Cheltenham, all his old associates had forgotten him, and that he was unheeded by the world.

In one of these intervals of stolid silence, Dickens remarked —

"By-the-by, Mac, who do you think I met in the Strand the other day?"

Of course, Macready had no idea.

"Smith," said Dickens.

"What Smith?" demanded Macready, with energy.

"Don't you remember Smith who was your harlequin?"

"Good gracious!" shouted Macready, "does he remember *me?* Well, I *am* surprised!"

"Yes," said Dickens; "and, what's more, I told him I should see you to-day, and he desired to be respectfully remembered to you."

"I am much obliged to him," was Macready's reception of the message, "and when you see him again, you tell him what I say."

The fact of Smith remembering Macready, put the latter in such a good humour that he insisted on having another bottle of the "old straw Madeira" (a quantity of which had been given him in America, at the time of the Macready-Forrest riots) brought into the room. This being done, he cheered up and proceeded to tell us anecdotes of his managerial days, more especially in connection with his pantomime productions. In the recital of these he seemed to have changed his nature, and, as Dickens remarked afterwards, it was difficult to imagine that Macready had ever been a tragedian at all, in fact that he was ever anything but a low-comedian.

This little incident, told here, can scarcely produce much effect, but the *vis comica* employed by Macready, and the manner in which Dickens contrived to enliven his friend by his brief visit — and especially the way these stories were extracted from him — formed a pantomimic treat not easily to be forgotten.

Mr. Dickens being under promise to me to spend the following day (Sunday) at my house at Ross — only twenty-five miles distant from Cheltenham — we had to leave Macready early in the evening, in order to get there in reasonable time; otherwise the manner in which we were entertained would have resulted in a much later sitting than was possible under the circumstances.

It was a wet, gloomy evening when we left Cheltenham, but the recollection of the time we had passed with Macready caused us much merriment on our short journey, and made it seem but a few moments. I felt it to be a great compliment to entertain my Chief under my own roof, and my household were naturally anxious that he should be received in a manner befitting the occasion. For this there was no necessity, as from the moment he entered the house it seemed to contain more than its wonted share of sunshine— if such a thing were possible.

The following day he went about the place with me, taking as much interest in everything as if he had been at "Gad's" — nothing escaping his attention and observation. My son (to whom he had stood sponsor in the early part of the previous year), the pony he had caused to be presented to my little girl (whilst we were in America), and the dog "Chops," who recognized his old master, gave him a reception which pleased him immensely.

About the house were relics of our American campaign, in the shape of pictures and other *objets d'art*. In my small library was the row of his own books, which he had presented to me after our first tour. The selection of books he scanned carefully, with a critical eye, and whilst I was engaged writing some letters at the library table, I was greatly amused to watch him in this operation, and more so to see him passing his fingers over the tops of his own works. When I asked why he did this, he explained in a jocular manner that he was merely anxious to ascertain by this means if *any* of them had been cut — an easy method of learning if any of them had been read!

He had heard much of the beauties of the scenery in and about Ross, and expressed a wish to be taken for a walk along the prettiest road in the neighbourhood. I chose the one which is supposed by old travellers to be the "prettiest in England," viz., from Ross to Monmouth, about eleven miles.

Sending on a carriage to Monmouth to drive us back in time for dinner, we started on this afternoon walk, in the course of which an amusing incident occurred.

Monmouth is approached by a descent of about two and half miles, through a very pretty wood.

Walking down this hill at the rate of about four miles an hour, we met three young men. One of them was so overcome by the apparition of Charles Dickens, whom he at once recognized, that he fell back into the wood, pulling his companions with him, and shouted, "Make way! Blow me if that ain't Charles Dickens!" This was done with such a theatrical air, that it caused the Chief to laugh uproariously. Calling the youth back, he asked him for the honour of shaking him by the hand, and at the same time begged him to accept the assurance that the surmise which had "blown" him was quite correct.

We continued our walk to Monmouth, highly amused at the incident, Dickens wondering what the young man would have done, if with his knowledge of celebrities he had lived in the olden times, and under the same circumstances had encountered "Dick Turpin."

The next week's work was one of comparative ease and pleasure, the journeys being short and the towns (with the exception of Bath) great favourites with Mr. Dickens.

The day after our departure from Ross was the day for the Clifton Reading, and as we had nothing to do until the following Wednesday (when the Torquay Reading was to be given), I took advantage of the day's cessation from labour to leave Clifton by an early train in the morning, in order to give Mr. Dickens as much time as possible in Torquay.

177

As he had never been there since the town had assumed its present beautiful proportions, I anticipated great pleasure in the enjoyment I felt certain he would experience from his visit. These anticipations were fully borne out.

Our apartments were secured at the Imperial Hotel, commanding a magnificent view of the Bay; and although we were then only at the end of the month of January, vegetation was as far advanced as it is in the Midland and Northern parts of England early in May.

After dinner, on the evening of our arrival, we went out to take stock of the building in which he was to read, and as a pantomime was being performed there, by a very fair company, he had an opportunity of judging of the acoustics of the hall or theatre, though it was neither the one nor the other, but a most ungainly-looking place. With the prospect of the next night's Reading before him, this had a somewhat depressing effect on his mind; but as we were so accustomed to patching up halls acoustically bad (as this one was), he relied on our invariable success in this particular, and the feeling of depression soon passed away, and he gave himself up to the humours of the pantomine.

The demand for tickets was enormous, and as the Readings selected ("Doctor Marigold" and the "Trial from Pickwick") caused him but little exertion, and were in fact a delight to him, the visit to Torquay looked more like a pleasure trip than a matter of business. As for the public, they came in such numbers as to make the Torquay Reading memorable as one of the most brilliant of the final Farewell Reading Tour, The receipts amounted to nearly £270, an amount unprecedented in the history of entertainments in the town.

As Clifton, the following night, was equally brilliant, and the public there (as usual) equally responsive, we had but one dread before us, and that was lest Bath should prove a damper on our spirits, to destroy the happiness and brilliancy of our Western trip. To a certain extent it did, for we arrived there in a pouring rain, and when it rains in Bath you have about the gloomiest city in the world.

Returning from a visit to the ticket agents, I found Dickens standing at the hotel window viewing the miserable streets. Assuming a comical attitude, and approaching me in a melodramatic manner, he said in a hoarse whisper:

"Dolby, I have a new idea about this mouldy old roosting-place.

"Depend upon it," he continued, "this place was built by a cemetery-full of old people, who, making a successful rise against death, have carried the place by assault, and, bringing their gravestones with them, have contrived to build the city, in which they are trying to look alive. But" (shaking his head) "it's a miserable failure."

My report from the ticket agents was *not* up to our usual standard of excellence, although it was considered "good for Bath." The agent explained the cause of what Dickens called the "mouldiness of the let." It seemed that one section of society wanted one particular Reading, another section another, and so on. All of these objections, however, being "boiled down" (to use an

Americanism), amounted to but one practical reason, which was that Bath could not *afford* to pay the prices of admission charged, notwithstanding that they were the same as those charged in other places in that part of the country.

The result of the two Bath Readings was, however, more satisfactory than the indications foreboded; and after all, we felt we had passed one of the happiest fortnights of this Reading life.

This feeling was enhanced in the Chief's heart by the receipt of news of his son Sidney (an officer in Her Majesty's navy, on the South American Station). This was brought to him by Sidney's old captain, who, being in Bath, came to see Mr. Dickens at the morning Reading, and conveyed to him the pleasing intelligence that his son had been appointed first lieutenant on board a new ship on his station.

There had been no time for this news to reach him through the official channels, and, coming as it did, it was the more welcome, and was the means of sending Dickens home in good spirits and improved in health to prepare for the following week's work. This, however, was not a very arduous one, as there were only three Readings to be given in it, one at St. James's Hall, one at Nottingham, and one at Leicester.

The "Murder" Reading had now firmly established itself amongst the other Readings, and when given was always provocative of the same dangerous symptoms in Mr. Dickens' system. It was a hobby of his, and the public were attracted by it, coming in crowds to be horrified; which in itself was a compliment to the reader, making him the more resolved to go on with it, all other considerations being put aside. In my opinion, and the opinion of others, it was a dangerous course to pursue; and as our Readings were never announced more than a fortnight in advance, it would have been very easy to strike this Reading out altogether (or at all events to keep it for certain large towns); and the public in their desire to hear Mr. Dickens read for the *last time,* would have come forward in the same numbers for an old favourite as readily as they would for this "atrocious novelty."

That the frequency with which he persisted in giving this Reading was affecting him seriously, nobody could judge better than myself, living and travelling with him as I was, day after day and week after week. His own good-nature, affectionate disposition, and sense of justice, prevented a display of irritability when he was remonstrated with on this subject, and rather than cause him pain I refrained as much as possible from approaching it (except so far as the exigencies of the business demanded); and as I could not shake his determination, I watched with great trepidation the course of events.

I had not to wait long, for only a fortnight after our return from the West, our first Reading break-down occurred.

A Reading was announced to take place in St. James's Hall on Tuesday, February 16th, and the day afterwards we had to leave for Scotland, for our farewell Readings there. Calling on Mr. Dickens, as was my habit, on the morning of the London Reading, I found him in bed in great agony, owing to a return of the ailment in his foot. In close attendance on him were his friend and medical adviser, Mr. Frank Carr Beard, and the eminent surgeon, Sir Henry Thompson. This was the worst attack he had yet experienced, not excepting the American experiences of the same kind, and was not alleviated by the distress of mind from which the patient was suffering in the thought that he might not be able to appear that evening. This matter the doctors very soon settled by their prohibition of any such proceeding, or even an attempt at it. Mr. Dickens remonstrated that his non-appearance would cause unheard-of inconvenience to hundreds of persons, and great loss to Messrs. Chappell, as, at that time of the day, it would not be possible to apprise those who had purchased tickets that the Reading could not take place. But so serious was his condition that the doctors declared that even with a strong will such as Mr. Dickens possessed, it would be physically impossible for him to undergo the fatigue and pain of standing at the table for a couple of hours, to say nothing of the mental exertion necessary for giving proper effect to the Reading. A certificate in accordance with the circumstances of the case was duly signed by Sir Henry Thompson and Mr. Frank Carr Beard, and it was not until after two o'clock in the afternoon that we were really in a position to give notice that the Reading could not take place on that evening.

The respect for Mr. Dickens was so widespread, that nothing but the greatest good humour prevailed, and expressions of sympathy for him in his illness were general, the public accepting the situation with the utmost kindness and consideration.

After assisting at the returning of the money, and dismissal of the public at St. James's Hall, I had to start immediately for Glasgow, for the purpose of postponing the whole of the Readings in Scotland, indefinitely — or such of them as were announced in Glasgow and Edinburgh for that week.

Leaving London by the night mail, I had the hope that Mr. Dickens's extraordinary recuperative powers would come to his aid, and that he would be able to give, at least, the Readings announced for the week following, in which case the disappointment of the public would be concentrated in but three Readings at most.

My appearance at the office of our ticket agents in Glasgow on that particular morning was most unexpected, it being supposed that I was with Mr. Dickens in London, and that I should not turn up until the following day. The object of my visit was very speedily explained, but not so easily effected, for the state of affairs in the ticket-office disclosed an unprecedented demand for tickets, even for Glasgow, where our business had always been enormous. Fortunately we had two clear days before us in Glasgow, and three clear days in Edinburgh, in which to advertise the postponement, and inform the public their monies would be returned.

By this arrangement all chances of pressure were lessened; and as, on reaching Edinburgh, I found a telegram awaiting me, containing the comforting news that the swelling and pain in the foot were abating, and that Mr. Dickens's general health being good, he would be able to leave London in three or four days at the most, I was enabled to announce in the morning papers that his illness was only a temporary one, and that he would appear and give the Readings the following week.

As these advertisements reduced the pressure at the doors, they in the same proportion increased it at the ticket-offices; but the effect on the whole was good, and the public getting over their first disappointment, were satisfied by the arrangement. Telegrams of an assuring character continued to be received from London during the week, the final one announcing that Mr. Dickens, accompanied by Mr. Arthur Chappell, would leave King's Cross on the following morning for Edinburgh. Meeting them at the railway station, I found Mr. Dickens very lame, but in excellent spirits. It was evident, though, that his recent attack had affected him seriously, and there were traces of the acute suffering he had undergone; although by his vivacity of manner he tried to disguise the fact that he was any the worse for it, and assumed that, beyond the temporary inconvenience, there was not much the matter.

Whilst regretting the trouble his illness had occasioned me, and the disappointment to the public, he was highly gratified at the way matters had been conducted, and greatly flattered at the prospect of the brilliant week before him.

Mr. Arthur Chappell spent the following day with us, which was partially given up to a long drive in the environs of Edinburgh (of which Mr. Dickens was very fond), Roslyn Chapel being visited on the way, in order to give our horses a rest.

Mr. Chappell had no sooner left us than the foot again became troublesome, showing symptoms of so dangerous a character that it became necessary to send for Mr. Syme, the celebrated surgeon of Edinburgh, who rejected the idea of Sir Henry Thompson, that gout was the cause of the trouble.

Mr. Syme attributed it entirely to cold, due to getting wet feet in long walks in the snow in America, and again in England. Moreover, he thought the fatigue of the Readings had as much to do with it as anything else — an opinion in which I fully concurred.

The difficulty, Mr. Syme thought, might be overcome by perfect rest, and this he recommended strongly; but how that was to be obtained, in face of the work cut out for Mr. Dickens, he did not say, and as none of us were in a position to prescribe for this evil, all that could be done was to take as much care as possible, in the hope of bringing about a cure.

The excitement of the public in these last Scotch Readings knew no bounds, and if the prices of admission had been doubled there would have been no difficulty in obtaining them. As the fame of the "Murder" Reading had reached Edinburgh, the desire to hear it was so great that not a place was to be obtained in either the first or second seats, and a few minutes after the opening of the gallery doors that portion of the house was full to overflowing.

The great interest taken in this, and the dead silence which prevailed during the delivery of it, had the effect of making Mr. Dickens more vehement, if possible, than on any previous occasion. He worked himself up to a pitch of excitement which rendered him so utterly prostrate, that when he went to his retiring-room (which he reached with difficulty), he was forced to lie on the sofa for some moments, before he could regain strength sufficient to utter a word.

It took him but a short time, though, to recover, and after a glass of champagne he would go on the platform again for the final Reading, as blithe and gay as if he were just commencing his evening's work.

These shocks to the nerves were not as easily repelled | as for the moment they appeared to be, but invariably recurred later on in the evening, either in the form of great hilarity or a desire to be once more on the platform, or in a craving to do the work over again. After the Edinburgh Reading, Dickens's friends in Edinburgh who had the *entrée* to his dressing-room, having regard to the state of his health, and perhaps being a little overcome and alarmed at what he used jokingly to call his "murderous instincts," contented themselves with calling in to thank him for the pleasure he had afforded them; and, wishing him an affectionate goodnight, declined all invitations to supper, so that we were left to eat this meal by ourselves. During supper he asked me for how many Readings in advance we were advertised.

I replied, "You are advertised up to and including York on the nth of next month."

"That's all right," he said; "let us fix the Readings for the remainder of the tour."

I went to my writing-case and produced my tour list, he at the same time producing his.

We went on with our supper, making notes the while (on our respective lists) of the Readings he had chosen for the various towns; and when we had got through about sixteen of these (a month's work), and seeing that the "Murder" was taking precedence of everything else, I ventured to remark —

"Look carefully through the towns you have given me, and see if you note anything peculiar about them."

"No," he replied. "What is it?"

"Well," I said, "out of four Readings a week you have put down three 'Murders.'"

"What of that?"

"Simply this," I said; "the success of this farewell tour is assured in every way, so far as human probability is concerned. It therefore does not make a bit of difference which of the works you read, for (from what I have seen) the money is safe any way. I am saying this in the interest of your health, and I feel certain that if either Tom or Arthur Chappell were here, he would endorse every word I have said, and would agree with me that the 'Carol,' 'Copperfield,' 'Nicholas Nickleby,' or 'Marigold,' will produce all the money we can take, and you will be saved the pain of tearing yourself to pieces every night for three nights a week, and to suffer unheard-of tortures afterwards, as you have to do. Reserve the 'Murder' for certain of the large towns, just to keep your hand in; and if you do this you will be all the better in health, and we shall be none the worse in pocket. Even if we are, I am sure the Chappells will not regret it, but would do anything and everything to save you unnecessary fatigue."

"Have you finished?" he said, angrily.

"I have said all I feel on that matter," was my reply.

Bounding up from his chair, and throwing his knife and fork on his plate (which he smashed to atoms), he exclaimed —

"Dolby! your infernal caution will be your ruin one of these days!"

"Perhaps so, sir," I said. "In this case, though, I hope you will do me the justice to say it is exercised in your interest."

I left the table, and proceeded to put my tour list in my writing-case. Turning round, I saw he was crying (my eyes were not so clear as they might be), and, coming towards me, he embraced me affectionately, sobbing the while:

"Forgive me, Dolby! I really didn't mean it; and I know you are right. We will talk the matter over calmly in the morning."

In all my experiences with the Chief, this was the only time I ever heard him address angry words to any one, and these probably would not have been uttered had the conversation taken place under different circumstances and apart from the influence of the excitement of the evening's work. But the storm had passed, and there was an end of it.

The next day was an "off" day, and we passed the greater portion of it indoors. The weather was too wild to permit of his going out; and even if it had been otherwise he could not have taken walking exercise, for his foot was swathed in what he used to call "a big work of art." He was always open to conviction, and did not disdain to defer to the judgment of another in whom he had faith, even though his own mind had been made up on any particular point; and in the frankness of his disposition he admitted that perhaps there was a little too much "Murder" in our future arrangements, and that it would be better in certain places to moderate his instincts in that respect.

In this way we made such alterations in the distribution of the Readings as greatly to reduce the chances of another break-down. But the bad weather we encountered throughout our Scottish tour had an evil effect again on Mr. Dickens's health, and I lived in fear and trembling that he would not be able to get through the week. This he contrived to accomplish, but not without great personal suffering, such as few men could have endured.

Mr. Syme was consulted again before we left Edinburgh for Glasgow; but he had no remedy to offer except complete rest, which, alas! was impossible.

Gratified as we were by the enormous receipts both in Glasgow and Edinburgh, we were not sorry when the time for our departure from the latter place arrived, and were glad to get into the train on Saturday evening, February 27th, on our way to London, where Mr. Dickens could go to his own comfortable quarters and have the advantage of better nursing than it was possible to get in an hotel.

This was a necessity now, for on the following Tuesday the "Murder" had to be repeated at St. James's Hall for the second time; and on Saturday in the same week had to be given for the first time in the Free Trade Hall, Manchester, the size of which under ordinary circumstances made a Reading a great anxiety; but in this instance the anxiety became far greater, as, for the full appreciation of the Reading, no less than the comfort of the reader, great attention on the part of the audience was necessary, whilst the strictest silence had to be observed.

These elements were never wanting in Manchester; but it was impossible to tell when an accident might occur, such as a person screaming in fright, dropping a stick or umbrella; any interruption of this kind would be the means of taking the attention off the reader, and his work in so large a hall as this would be nearly double in the endeavour to get it back again. Fortunately no such interruption ever did occur, but during the forty minutes which this "Murder" Reading occupied I had a nervous dread of some mishap.

The second Reading in London was even more successful than the first, the reputation of the "Murder" causing the great St. James's Hall to be filled in every part. On our way to Manchester we stopped in Wolverhampton, where Mr. Dickens read "Doctor Marigold" and "Mr. Bob Sawyer's Party" — the pathos of the one and the fun of the other acting as a great relief after the horrors of the "Murder."

Our next town was Hull, where Mr. Dickens was announced to read two nights, and then came a day's rest, with a Reading at York to follow; after this our programme was to return to London, where he could take a rest until the following Tuesday, when another of our fortnightly Readings was announced for St. James's Hall. All this looked well as a means of getting what Mr. Syme prescribed, but Fate was against us.

We had passed an enjoyable and quiet Sunday at the Queen's Hotel, Manchester, and as by a wonderful circumstance it did not rain, we drove to Alderley Edge, the fresh air reviving the Chief wonderfully. The journey to Hull being an easy one, we did not hurry ourselves to get there on the Monday morning, but sent the men on with the things, we following by a midday train.

When I returned to the hotel after transacting the necessary business, I found Mr. Dickens in a paroxysm of grief, for in my absence the news had reached him of the death of his old and valued friend, Emerson Tennent. This had so thoroughly unnerved him that, for the time, it became a question whether the Hull and York Readings would not have to be given up. Manfully he fought against his feelings, and resolved to get through as best he could, and what this meant I knew full well by this time; it meant self-sacrifice and acute suffering, in this instance not only bodily suffering, but acute mental agony.

The letter containing the news of his friend's death also contained a request that he would attend the funeral on the following Friday, the 12th. It is pretty generally known with what horror he attended a funeral, and what a feeling of disgust he entertained for the dismal pomp of that ceremony. The relations that had existed between himself and Sir James Emerson Tennent had been of such a character that he could not with grace refuse to be present on this sad occasion. The difficulty of getting to London from York after the Reading in the latter place seemed at first to be insuperable, inasmuch as the Reading would not be over before ten o'clock, and the train for London left York at 9.45 p.m. Half an hour would be necessary for a change of dress, and it would take another ten minutes to drive to the station, by which time the Great Northern express would be some forty odd miles on its way.

He was determined to do his duty by Messrs. Chappell, for they had lost enough by the abandonment of the London, Edinburgh, and Glasgow Readings three weeks before, and it would be unfair to the York public to disappoint them. There was only one way of getting over the difficulty, and that was more self-sacrifice. As a means of meeting the case, he arranged to take twenty minutes out of the time allotted to the Readings (there were three announced for this evening, "Boots at the Holly Tree Inn," the Murder in "Oliver Twist," and "Mrs. Gamp"), and this time was to be gained by sacrificing the rest he needed after the "Murder." So by means of a printed notice, circulated in the room, the audience were informed that, owing to a circumstance of a painful character, within the general knowledge, Mr. Dickens had been suddenly called to London; but not wishing to disappoint the people of York, he had determined on giving the Readings announced, dispensing with the time he usually took to himself for rest between each Reading.

I had arranged with the courteous manager of the Great Northern Railway at York to let me have a saloon carriage with comfortable sofas, and, if necessary, to keep the train for me three or four minutes.

In the presence of the Archbishop of York and all the notabilities of the city, Mr. Dickens was in his place precisely at eight o'clock, and without curtailing one sentence, or neglecting a customary look or gesture, he went through this task as if he were under no pressure whatever, merely retiring after each Reading for his usual glass of champagne and a new book, and appearing again apparently as fresh as on ordinary occasions. And so we arrived together at the railway station, two minutes before the advertised starting time of the train.

I had sent his servant (Scott) to the station with our change of clothes, and our saloon carriage presented a mixed appearance of a miniature dressing and dining room. Scott had made all preparations for his master's usual rub down after his Reading, and the landlord of the hotel had arranged an excellent supper for us. Punctually at g.45 p.m. the train steamed out of the station, and we proceeded to divest ourselves of our evening dress, and assumed that of the traveller of the period. The supper was disposed of with infinite relish, and after a cigar we settled down for the night, Mr. Dickens sleeping the whole way to London — not awaking until we were close to King's Cross, and then looking as fresh as if he had done an ordinary journey in the course of his daily life.

"The more you want out of master, the more you'll find in him," was the remark of our gasman to me one day in America, and here was an instance of the truth of his remark.

I dined with him on the day of the funeral, and was shocked to observe to what extent he was unnerved and pulled down by the fatigues of the previous night, and the feelings of sorrow incident to such an occasion.

"Of course I made an ass of myself," he said, "and did the wrong thing, as I *invariably* do at a funeral."

He proceeded to explain that, arriving at the house of his late friend, he was met in the hall by an elderly gentleman, who extended his hand. Presuming this to be a friend of Sir James's, whom he had met somewhere but had forgotten, he shook the gentleman by the hand, saying at the same time —

"We meet on a sad occasion."

"Yes, indeed," was the reply. "Poor dear Sir James."

(This with a long-drawn sigh.)

Dickens passed on to the dining-room where several other friends were congregated, and where for a time he quite forgot his friend in the hall; but presently he was reminded of that affecting meeting by the entrance of the elderly gentleman carrying before him a trayful of hats adorned with long mourning bands, and so high was the pile as to almost hide him from view.

The elderly gentleman's position in society was now made manifest. He was the undertaker's man, and wanted Dickens's hat for the purpose of funereal decoration; hence his object in holding out his hand. Mr. Dickens was greatly amused (the seriousness of the occasion notwithstanding) when he discovered the mistake he had made.

Our farewell Readings in the large towns were fast closing in, and we had now only Birmingham, Liverpool, and Manchester, to dispose of (in this class), a prospect which was very encouraging, as the discontinuance of long railway journeys gave hope of some rest and repose to Mr. Dickens, of which he stood in sore need.

Against this was the extra exertion necessary to give due effect to the Readings in the large halls in these towns, but as this had already been done under less favourable circumstances, we were justified in the supposition that with less travelling the ailment to the foot, which continued to make itself felt, would speedily disappear, and that Mr. Dickens would again be able to resume his walking exercise, the want of which he felt sorely.

Our progress through the country, whether in large towns or small, was a continued round of successes, every hall being crammed to its fullest capacity.

In Birmingham and Manchester the halls (besides being suitable for the Readings) were large enough for all reasonable wants (in Birmingham on one night Mr. Dickens read to nearly 2,500 persons); but in Liverpool there was no room that would meet our requirements, unless we fell back on our old friend, the small concert room in St. George's Hall, and raised our prices. As it was contrary to our principles to do this, I decided on taking the Thea-

tre Royal for our four farewell Readings there. These were to be supplemented by a public banquet given to Mr. Dickens in the great St. George's Hall, on
the evening after the closing Reading in Liverpool, viz., Saturday, April 10th.

The theatre, which had fallen into disuse for some time, was in a distress-
ingly dirty state, but a fortnight's rubbing, scrubbing, and sweeping, with a
liberal allowance of red baize and carpets in the passage-ways and in the
stalls, converted it into a perfect reading-house; and as Mr. Dickens preferred
a theatre to any other class of building, and his audiences were both numerous and sympathetic, the Liverpool farewells were not less brilliantly successful than others I have had occasion to describe.

At one time we were afraid that the excitement in connection with the public banquet would detract from the success of the Readings, by drawing the
money in another direction, but as a matter of fact the total receipts of the
four Readings exceeded £1,000.

The great St. George's Hall in Liverpool was the only one in the town capable of dining six hundred persons together, and for this reason it was selected. A more unsuitable place for such a purpose could not well have been chosen. The arrangement of the tables prevented a word of the speeches being
heard, and as in addition to the guest of the evening such men as Lords Dufferin and Houghton, Anthony Trollope, Hepworth Dixon, Mark Lemon, Mons.
Esquiros (of the *Revue des Deux Mondes*), George Sala, and others were set
down to speak — this department of the entertainment was entitled to some
consideration.

Mr. Dickens took much trouble in the matter, and suggested a plan whereby the difficulty might be got over. But it was found now that the committee,
for some inscrutable reasons of their own, could not submit to any alteration
of their plans, at least not to such as Mr. Dickens had proposed; that, in short,
things must remain as they were to the possible detriment of the whole affair.

In such a vast hall, and in the presence of such beautiful decorations as had
been devised, it would not have done to resort to the carpet and baize trick
as we should have done in a small country town, "for one night only."

This idea being proposed to the honorary secretary (Mr. Clarke Aspinall),
he sent at once to the guardship (the *Donegal*) lying in the river for the loan
of such of the ship's flags as might be necessary to correct the acoustic de-
fects of the hall. The captain, with a ready courtesy, not only granted this request, but sent a boat's crew of man-of-wars men to hang and drape the flags
in the places assigned for them by Mr. Dickens, who personally superintended the whole matter.

The leading men of Liverpool and the whole surrounding district were
present, Manchester paying Mr. Dickens the compliment of sending its
Mayor.

With the exception perhaps that the proceedings were too long, the banquet was a great success. The Mayor of Liverpool was nominally the chairman of the evening, but being in ill-health, and not a great speaker, he hand-

ed the toast of the evening over to Lord Dufferin (at that time Chancellor of the Duchy of Lancaster). Speeches were made by Mr. Philip H. Rathbone, who proposed "Her Majesty's Ministers," which was replied to by Lord Dufferin. Lord Houghton spoke for "The Houses of Parliament;" Lord Dufferin, in an elegant and eloquent speech, proposed the toast of the evening, viz., the health of Charles Dickens; to which Mr. Dickens replied, taking some exception to a remark of Lord Houghton's, as to his (Dickens's), objection to entering Parliament. Mr. J. A. Picton proposed "Modern Literature;" Mr. Anthony Trollope replying for "Light Literature," and Mr. Hepworth Dixon replying "as regarded Literature of a more serious nature." Mr. George Augustus Sala was entrusted with the toast of "The Distinguished Visitors;" M. Alphonso Esquiros replying thereto as a representative of "French Literature." Mr. Andrew Halliday responded to the toast of "The Drama;" after which Lord Houghton proposed "The Newspaper Press," to which Mr. George Sala and Mr. M. J. Whitty (the proprietor of the "Liverpool Daily Post"), responded. Mr. Charles Dickens proposed "The Ladies," after which Mr. Dickens proposed "The Mayor and Corporation," to which the Mayor responded. The proceedings, which had been of a highly complimentary character to Mr. Dickens, terminated here; everything having been done by the Mayor and Corporation of Liverpool to make the farewell visit of Dickens to the town a pleasant memory to him and to those who took part in it.

Banquet to Dickens in St. George's Hall, Liverpool, April 10, 1869: Charles Dickens Speaking.
From a contemporary print.

Here was the last of the large towns disposed of, and as Liverpool was a great favourite with Mr. Dickens, it was with a certain feeling of depression that we quitted it on the following day for London, where we were due for a Reading in St. James's Hall.

We were rather a large party on this journey, and a very jolly one. Many of our London friends who had attended the banquet returned with us in our saloon carriage, and those whom business or pleasure detained in Liverpool came to the station to see us off.

Mr. Dickens walked to the station, and the good feeling of the people of Liverpool showed itself heartily in the street; for during his progress to the station, he was repeatedly stopped by persons of the working classes wanting to shake hands with him, and all of them eager to thank him for the pleasure his books had afforded them. This, however, was not a new experience to him in the large manufacturing towns.

Another gratifying and complimentary evidence of the power of his Readings, and the pleasure they afforded persons of intellect, presented itself in the shape of a numerously-signed circular letter from the actors and actresses of the principal London theatres, begging him to give a morning Reading in St. James's Hall; their curiosity having been excited about the famous "Murder" scene. Although he disliked a morning Reading, this request, coming as it did from the members of a profession for which he had so much sympathy, was entirely pleasing to Mr. Dickens. Wishing to make such an arrangement as might meet the convenience of the greatest number, he agreed with Messrs. Chappell to give three of these morning Readings, when the provincial Readings should have been disposed of.

They were planned for the early part of the following May, and were to be as follows: — Saturday, May 1st: "Boots at the Holly Tree Inn," and "Sikes and Nancy" (from "Oliver Twist"); Saturday, May 8th: "The Christmas Carol;" Saturday, May 22nd: "Sikes and Nancy," and the "Trial from Pickwick." But these Readings unfortunately were never given.

After the St. James's Hall Reading of Tuesday, April 13th, our next towns were Leeds, Blackburn, Bolton, Preston, and Warrington — none of them genial or agreeable in climate for a person in such a state of health as Mr. Dickens then was, whose sufferings from fatigue of mind and body gave him such exquisite pain as to bring a return of the sleepless nights he had experienced in America.

Watching his sufferings, and sympathising deeply, I arranged in the hotels at which we stayed to have a bed-room adjoining his, generally with a door communicating between the rooms, that I might quietly drop in on him during the night (as in America) to see how he was getting on, and again, as in the States, nearly always finding him wide awake, but invariably cheerful. At daybreak he could read, but up to that time he used to describe his weariness, except for my visits, as unendurable.

Being in Leeds at this time, and having two vacant days before going to the Lancashire manufacturing towns, we decided to escape from the smoke and gloom in which we had been living; and as Chester, with its old walls and picturesque streets, promised a pleasant change, we went there for the Saturday and Sunday.

The change of air affected Mr. Dickens beneficially, and in my nocturnal visits to him I had the satisfaction of knowing that he was gaining rest.

But he had one very bad night here, and this was the subject of conversation between us at breakfast on the following morning. His mind was more disturbed by it than his manner would lead any one (not knowing him well) to suppose.

The days were getting longer, and the weather was beautifully fine and warm for the season, a happy combination of circumstances that made me suggest a drive into the country as far as Mold (a small and picturesque Welsh market-town about fourteen miles from Chester).

A carriage was turned out immediately after Mr. Dickens had finished his breakfast, and we started for this place; the conversation again turning on the miserable night he had spent. Knowing his recent sensitiveness on all matters concerning his health, I refrained from making any suggestions as to our future course; although at the same time I had an instinctive feeling that the travelling career was at an end, if not the Reading career also.

Although greatly revived by the invigorating air, and the sight of the spring blossoms, as we travelled through the country, Mr. Dickens was thoughtful, and at times greatly depressed, and the old geniality had disappeared.

Staying a couple of hours in Mold, to give our horses a rest, we passed the time in a leisurely stroll towards the Welsh mountains, when Mr. Dickens consulted me as to the best course to pursue in the face of what I had seen of his condition the previous night.

In this consultation he impressed on me that he did not wish the conversation to have any particular reference to himself, but rather to the interests of Messrs. Chappell, whose losses would be very great if we relinquished any more of the Readings in order that he might have rest.

Having given me this chance, I was not slow to take advantage of it, assuring him (as the representative of Messrs. Chappell), that I felt sure they would do all and everything in their power to adapt their arrangements to the altered condition of his health.

Added to this, I suggested that we should go to London that evening to consult Mr. Beard on the crisis which seemed impending, and that as I had gone to Glasgow to return the money there, I should hasten back to the Lancashire towns and do the same thing in the places arranged for in the following week.

It was then impossible to get back to Chester in time to catch the only train there was to London that (Sunday) afternoon, so this plan had to be given up.

After further talk on the subject, Mr. Dickens determined to write a letter to Mr. Beard, detailing his symptoms, the moment he should get back to the hotel in Chester, and await the result of his reply; at the same time carefully watching the effect on himself of the two following Readings.

190

To this plan I was entirely opposed, but with my knowledge of his pluck and determination, I felt it to be useless to attempt to argue the point with him, and so, unwillingly, I had to fall in with his views.

On our way back to Chester all conversation suddenly ceased between us, and he fell asleep in the soft balmy air, just as I had seen him do a fortnight previously, during a drive we had taken in Liverpool, on the day prior to the commencement of the farewell Readings there.

He wrote by that evening's post to Mr. Beard, then dismissed the matter from his mind, and his old spirits returned.

The two following days, with a Reading each evening, were days of great anxiety to us both.

He begged me not to communicate to Messrs. Chappell the circumstances of the Chester attack, until he had received a reply from Mr. Beard. Mr, Beard's letter came by return of post, and although Mr. Dickens did not communicate its contents to me, I felt certain they were not of a satisfactory character.

Though moody and dull the whole day, he fought manfully through the Reading in Blackburn that evening, and gave it with his accustomed verve and vigour.

Early the following morning we left Blackburn for Blackpool, where (having no Reading that evening), we had arranged to pass a quiet day.

This was rather a sudden determination on our part, but we deemed it preferable to remaining in the smoky and oppressive atmosphere of Blackburn, or of Preston, our next town.

I telegraphed to the Imperial Hotel for apartments, which on our arrival there we found most comfortable, and the fresh breeze blowing from the sea was most invigorating, and beneficial to Mr. Dickens, who revived in a wonderful manner. He gave me much hope that he would be enabled to get through the two remaining Readings of the week, in Preston and Warrington.

From here he wrote again to Mr. Beard, telling him of the advantage he was deriving from the change, but complaining of a certain sense of deadness on the left side, also of the difficulty of taking hold of any object with the left hand.

With the return of appetite came a return of spirits, and as he had enjoyed two good nights' sleep we went to Preston on Thursday, the 22nd April, about midday, in the full conviction that the Chester attack (whatever it might have been), had passed away; and in this belief I refrained from communicating on the subject with Messrs. Chappell.

Preston (described by one of the most astute and successful theatrical managers in London, as the "rock on which many a dramatic ship has been wrecked"), was if possible more dirty and melancholy than usual, its depressing effect being the greater after the invigorating walk we had taken together, in a gale of wind, before leaving Blackpool, when we were both nearly blown away.

We were, however, cheered by the news that every ticket for the Reading that evening in the Guildhall had been disposed of, the proceeds amounting to nearly £200. This information I received when I got to the Bull Hotel, where the local ticket agent was awaiting my arrival.

In my anxiety to give Mr. Dickens the welcome tidings, I hastened to our sitting-room, there to find him standing in the front of the fire with a telegram in his hand, which, without a word, he handed over to me. It was from Mr. Beard, announcing that the letter from Blackpool had decided him on coming to Preston at once; that he was then on his way, and would arrive in Preston at about half-past three in the afternoon.

We passed the time until then in superintending the erection of the reading-screen, and, having done that, went to the station to meet Mr. Beard's train, which, in the perversity of things, was an hour late. Notwithstanding it was now considerably past our dinner hour, Mr. Dickens insisted on waiting his friend's arrival.

He came at length, and we walked to the Bull Hotel together, calling in by the way at the Guildhall to show Mr. Beard the platform with the "fit-up" as arranged for the evening's Reading, little thinking it was to be the last time he would see it in a country town.

So anxious were both Mr. Dickens and Mr. Beard to get at the real state of the case as regarded Dickens's health, that the dinner was postponed until the consultation had taken place.

This lasted over half an hour, during which time Mr. Dickens underwent a strict examination at the hands of his medical man. At the end of that time they joined me in the sitting-room, where I was waiting.

"Shall I ring for dinner?" I asked.

"Wait until Beard has said what he has to say, and then do as you think best," was the Chief's reply; and I turned to Mr. Beard.

"All I have to say is this," answered the doctor; "if you insist on Dickens taking the platform to-night, I will not guarantee but that he goes through life dragging a foot after him."

Big tears were now rolling down Dickens's face, and, crossing the room to me, he threw himself on my neck saying —

"My poor boy! I am so sorry for all the trouble I am giving you! With all the tickets sold, and so late in the day, too! How will you manage with these people?"

Then turning to Beard, he said, "Let me try it to-night. It will save so much trouble."

"As you like," replied the doctor. "I have told Dolby what I think. If you insist on Reading to-night I shall have only to stand by and watch the results."

"But how will Dolby get through?"

"Never mind me, I'll get through somehow; if you and Beard will only leave the town at once," I said. "Go anywhere you like — to the Adelphi at Liverpool, for instance — and I will join you some time to-night."

To remain in Preston was, under the circumstances, quite out of the question; for some ill-disposed person seeing him there, at the railway station, for instance, on the following morning after a "dismissal," might set some false report going, and put a wrong construction on his non-appearance. This suggestion being agreed to, on their part, I left them to get away as best they could, and I went my way to do the best I could.

In catering for the public amusement, the difficulty of obtaining a large paying audience is well known, and it falls to the lot of few managers to dismiss their public at two hours' notice, with every ticket sold.

It being now after five in the afternoon, and the doors being announced to open at seven, it became a matter of serious consideration with me, how to prevent persons living at a distance from coming to the Guildhall only to be disappointed; and, if they should all come, how to get sufficient money in sovereigns, half-sovereigns, half-crowns, and shillings, to return to them in exchange for their tickets.

Our local agent had paid all the money he had received into the bank, and at that hour the banks were closed.

The landlord of the Bull Hotel (Mr. Townsend), who had formerly been station-master at Preston, gave me with the utmost kindness all the money he had in the hotel; and borrowing all he could from the gentlemen in the commercial room, we contrived between us to make up about £120, which, being converted into change, made me feel easy on that score.

The next thing to do was, if possible, to prevent people from coming into the town, and here Mr. Townsend was of the greatest service to me, going to the railway station and telegraphing to all the places within a radius of fifteen or twenty miles, to the effect that Mr. Dickens had been suddenly taken ill and could not appear; at the same time the disappointed ones were informed that their money would be returned to them on the presentation of their tickets, on any subsequent day.

The next to be considered were the townspeople, and those living in the immediate neighbourhood. These were attended to by the Mayor, who, hearing of my difficulty, had kindly and promptly come forward with an offer of help.

Summoning to him the Chief Constable, he caused a number of mounted police to be despatched along the roads leading into Preston, and every carriage or cab coming in that direction was stopped, and its occupants apprised of what had happened.

The Mayor personally assisted me in the distribution of the money to such persons as came to the hall, and this was done in a very efficient manner, by the simplest of means.

A long table covered with green baize was arranged across the principal staircase leading up to the hall, behind which stood the Mayor and myself. The principal door was kept closed, and a policeman stationed there directed all comers to a side entrance, through which they reached the room where the Mayor and myself were.

The total amount of money returned did not exceed £20, and instead of the anticipated confusion and grumbling, nothing was heard but words expressive of deep sympathy for Mr. Dickens in his illness. There was, however, a little trouble with one or two ill-conditioned persons, who had seen Mr. Dickens at Blackpool in the morning, running after his hat, which had been blown from his head, in the course of our walk to the railway station, in the teeth of a gale of wind. These individuals caused County Court summonses to be served on Mr. Dickens, for compensation and disappointment, on the ground that they had seen him on the sands at Blackpool "kicking his hat about as if he had been a boy." The only result of their action was that they had to apologize for their want of courtesy.

I was greatly relieved when I had got rid of this Preston business, and was now all anxiety to get to Liverpool to join the Chief, as arranged, at the Adelphi Hotel, which we looked upon as our headquarters in the North of England.

As our movements were so well known here, great surprise was expressed at my sudden appearance at the hotel at about midnight, and some eagerness also, a report having reached Liverpool that Mr. Dickens had broken down in Preston, and had suddenly left for London Nothing had been seen of him at the Adelphi Hotel, and my embarrassment was great in consequence, to know what had become of him and of Mr. Beard.

As it was impossible to get any information at that late hour of the night, I could only wait until the following morning, comforted by the thought that, wherever he was, he had the advantage of Mr. Beard's care and attention. I went to bed thoroughly worn out with fatigue and anxiety, knowing that I should have to go through at Warrington, on the following day, all that I had just undergone at Preston.

The news of Mr. Dickens's illness, which through the medium of the Preston newspapers, had reached Warrington before I got there, materially assisted me in making my arrangements; and, as no difficulties presented themselves here, I was enabled to leave by the night train for London, to make my report to Messrs. Chappell, and to go in search of Mr. Dickens.

I found him at the office apparently well, but much dejected, by reason of a consultation between Sir Thomas Watson and Mr. Frank Beard, on the previous day. These gentlemen had recognized the gravity of the case, and had declared that the attack in Chester evidenced a disposition to paralysis. Sir Thomas Watson confirming the opinion expressed by Mr. Beard, when he refused to listen to Mr. Dickens's appeal at Preston — to allow him to go through that night's Reading. They both said peremptorily, that there must be no Readings in London for the present, and that all travelling in connection with Readings must be suspended, at once and for ever. I append a copy of the medical certificate.

"The undersigned certify that Mr. Charles Dickens has been seriously unwell, through great exhaustion and fatigue of body and mind, consequent upon his public Readings and long and frequent railway journeys. In our judgment, Mr. Dickens will not be able with safety to himself to resume his Readings for several months to come.

"Thos. Watson, M.D.
"F. Carr Beard."

This was a sad blow to Mr. Dickens, but the decision of the doctors was final, and had to be respected. Apart from the disappointment to himself, in being deprived of a labour in which he took so much delight, he was inconsolable in his sorrow at the thought of the inevitable losses that would accrue to Messrs. Chappell, whose treatment of him in all matters connected with the business had been liberal and disinterested in the extreme.

The moment the doctors had decided in this wise, Mr. Dickens took occasion to write to the firm a letter expressive of his grief at the turn matters had taken; but his mind was set at rest in this particular by the receipt of a reply from the head of the firm (Mr. Thomas Chappell), who, in a characteristic letter, couched in the most generous terms, begged Mr. Dickens to dismiss from his mind all thoughts of any inconvenience to which the firm might have been put by his illness, and expressed an earnest wish for his speedy and complete recovery.

This handsome letter sent Mr. Dickens to his beautiful home, at Gad's Hill, in a comparatively easy frame of mind; but the feeling of regret still remained, and in his retirement he did not cease to long for a return to the Reading life.

Some months afterwards, all suspicion of the impending disease had so completely vanished, that Sir Thomas Watson gave it as his opinion that Mr. Dickens might venture on twelve farewell Readings, in London only. At the same time, he strictly forbade all travelling in connection with them.

This announcement was received by Mr. Dickens with the utmost delight, and did more, I think, to promote his recovery to health than anything else could have done — except perhaps the peace and tranquility of Gad's Hill, and the affectionate care and attention bestowed upon him there by his family and friends.

Chapter Thirteen American Visitors at "Gad's" — The Last Readings and Farewell to the Public

THE actual state of Dickens's health was so very little known outside the circle of his immediate friends, that his rapid recovery and resumption of his ordinary mode of life, gave rise to the belief in the public mind that the medical men had exaggerated the dangers of his case. Those, on the contrary, who were constantly with him, and who had had opportunities of observing his symptoms, felt that the restrictions placed on his activity were perfectly jus-tifiable.

No one was more thoroughly assured of this than Mr. Dickens himself, as was shown by a letter he wrote to Sir Thomas Watson on the subject, in which he expressed his "implicit reliance on the professional skill and ad-vice" of the distinguished physician.

In looking back to the letters he addressed to members of his family and personal friends, and calling to mind, as I do, his own words to me, I cannot but be certain that he was fully aware of the terrible malady by which he was threatened; but the permission of Sir Thomas Watson (given some five or six weeks after the Preston break-down), for twelve London Readings, to take place early in the coming year, inspired him with new hope, and did much to promote what we all hoped would be his perfect recovery.

Nor was this all to him, for with these Readings in prospect, he felt and hoped that he would be able to make a handsome return to Messrs. Chappell for the disappointment and losses they had sustained by the unavoidable stoppage of the former series.

Had Mr. Dickens's health not given way, it was his earnest desire to make a voyage to Australia. This, indeed, was a frequent topic of conversation be-tween us; but I was bound to secrecy in the matter, for it was obviously un-desirable that any inkling of his wishes in this respect should get into the press, either here or abroad. Had the papers got wind of the project, an amount of pressure would have been brought to bear upon him that must have compelled an immediate decision one way or the other, and this, in the then undecided state of his health, could not but have resulted in serious in-convenience to him.

The tidings that had reached him of his sons' good progress in Australia, afforded him the keenest pleasure, and he had a strong paternal yearning to see them in their new and far away home. Apart from this, there was the pos-sibility of finding in Australia a new subject for a book. Without doubt, but for the reasons given, this voyage would have been made; in which event there is little reason to doubt that a series of Readings in the colony would have resulted in the addition of another fortune to his already ample means.

This idea of a visit to Australia was not a new one with him, for some six or seven years previously, when travelling with my predecessor (Mr. Arthur Smith), he had received a proposal from a well-known firm in the colony to go out there and give a series of Readings during eight months, for which he was to receive the sum of £10,000 and all expenses paid.

At that time there were many weighty considerations which made him hes-itate; — the separation from his family at a period when he could ill be spared, and the difficulty of finding a suitable person to conduct "All the Year Round" in his absence, being amongst the chief.

There were not such strong objections now on either of these accounts. He had placed his family in positions which rendered them largely independent. As regarded "All the Year Round," the unfortunate accident that had happened to his partner and sub-editor (Mr. Wills), in the previous year, inca-pacitated that gentleman from the full discharge of his duties, and rendered some sort of change advisable in the administration of the paper.

It seemed best to appoint a responsible person, who would be capable of taking the sole charge, conducting it of course on the lines laid down by Mr. Dickens himself; Mr. Dickens to furnish an article now and again, which could readily be sent from a distance.

The American experiences had taught him that a speculator was not neces-sary in a foreign country, and he had determined, if the journey were under-taken at all, to do it entirely on his own account.

His regret at the enforced abandonment of this trip was very great; but he found some consolation in the thought that he was at any rate free to return to his literary labours; and he now began to cast about for a subject for a new book. The sub-editorship and general management of "All the Year Round," he gave into the hands of his eldest son Charles, who was well qualified for the work.

As often as he was in town, I was his constant companion, and many a pleasant little dinner we discussed together, at the "Blue Posts," in Cork Street, and elsewhere; and many a happy night we spent at the establish-ment, or at a theatre. But all this while I noted with pain the change that was coming over him. I missed the old vivacity and elasticity of spirit, which were always wanting, except when specially called into requisition.

Early in May, that he might be near his medical men for a while, and might at the same time avail himself of invitations from innumerable friends, he secured apartments at the St. James's Hotel, in Piccadilly, for himself, his daughter, and his sister-in-law. He had another object in so doing, since our valued friends, Mr. and Mrs. Fields, of Boston, and Mr. and Mrs. Childs, of Philadelphia, were on their way to England in the *Russia;* and he particularly wished to be in London to meet and show them as much attention as possi-ble, in return for the many kindnesses he had received at their hands in America.

This, in the most literal sense of the phrase, was a labour of love with him; and as he never did anything by halves, the programme he drew up for their entertainment was Brobdignagian in its proportions. I may describe it briefly by saying that it would have taken many months to accomplish, and was ut-terly out of proportion to the time his friends could have had at their dispos-al.

Besides visits to Gad's Hill, excursions were arranged to all sorts of places in and around London, not excluding visits to the slums for those gentlemen of the party who might be disposed to make them. As these pilgrimages to "Horrible London" were chiefly nocturnal, they were made under the care and guidance of experienced detectives from Scotland Yard.

One night in particular, we found the value of an escort of this kind, when we visited the opium dens in the neighbourhood of Ratcliffe Highway, finishing up the evening in a place of resort for sailors of every nationality, known as "Tiger Bay."

This was a curious experience for our American friends, for if there be many such "institutions" in the United States, they are kept well out of the public gaze.

The advent of Mr. Dickens's American visitors at this particular time, made a bright episode in his life; and assisted more effectually than anything else could have done to make him forget all that he had undergone the previous month or two.

He seemed never to tire of arranging some new pleasure party; but the chief item in the programme for his friends' amusement was the visit of the whole of the party to Gad's Hill.

To the American guests were added on this occasion a fair sprinkling of English friends, of whom I was fortunate enough to be one.

The house was full to overflowing, and I, with some others, had to be accommodated at the "Falstaff," opposite the gates of the house.

In addition to Mr. Dickens's family there were present at this memorable gathering: Mr. and Mrs. Fields, of Boston; Miss Mabel Lowell, daughter of the American ambassador; Mr. and Mrs. Childs, of Philadelphia; Mr. Sol Etynge, the American artist, who was engaged in illustrating a new edition of "Pickwick," then about to be published by Messrs. Fields and Osgood, in Boston; Doctor Fordyce Barker (Mr. Dickens's medical man in New York); Mr. Frederic Ouvry (Mr. Dickens's solicitor), and myself.

This visit to "Gad's" was excellently timed, taking place as it did in the month of June (1869), when the country was looking its very best — the trees and hedgerows resplendent with blossom, and the fields a mass of colour; the nightingales, too, were in full song, and I remember how they astonished and delighted the Americans.

My business engagements prevented me from travelling to Gad's Hill with the party on the first day of their visit; but joining them on the following day, I was met at the Higham Station by Mr. Dickens, who drove there in the basket carriage, accompanied by the big dogs.

I was most pleasurably surprised at seeing him, and more than this, for all traces of his illness had disappeared. In his light suit of clothes and round hat, carried jauntily on the side of his head, he looked the picture of health. He was very much sunburnt, and although I had only parted from him a few days previously, the change in him was so great that I hardly believed I saw before me the man who had looked so haggard and worn but five or six weeks ago.

During our short drive, I expressed the surprise and pleasure it gave me to see so great an improvement in him, but he took my congratulations as a matter of course, telling me that three or four days at the most in the beautiful air of his country home always sufficed to put him in health again.

We got to the house just before luncheon time. All the guests were in the pretty enclosure known as the croquet ground, and it was a happiness worthy of a much longer journey to find one's self in the midst of so much that was gay, bright, and picturesque. Croquet and bowls, two games comparatively unknown in America (there being but very few grass lawns in that country), were both in full swing.

The luncheon gong sounded, the signal for a general adjournment to the house. A very jolly party we were, and a large one too, for several neighbours, in addition to some officers from Chatham, who had dropped in in the course of the morning, had remained for the midday meal.

As usual at this meal, the plans for the remainder of the day were discussed, and it was arranged that such of the party as were disposed for a walk should accompany Mr. Dickens through Cobham Park; others elected to drive into Rochester, there to take up Mr. Sol Etynge, who had gone to make some original sketches for the edition of "Pickwick" on which he was engaged, and to take a ramble amongst the interesting antiquities of the city. These, under the circumstances, had an additional charm, as being the scenes of so many episodes in the works of our host.

Time was never allowed to hang heavily on the hands of the visitors to "Gad's," and there was no reason why it should; for, independently of the unceasing efforts of the host and the resources at his command, when stress of weather kept us indoors, there was, when the season favoured, so much to be seen and done in the neighbourhood.

As for Dickens himself, the weather very seldom kept him from the pedestrian exercises, of which he was so fond; and many a misty walk we took to the marshes at Cooling, that we might get a realistic notion of the dreariness and loneliness of the scenes in "Great Expectations," made famous by "Pip" and the convict. On such occasions as these we not unfrequently returned wetted to the skin by a drenching rain.

One of the most delightful days of this visit was occupied by a drive from Gad's Hill to Canterbury, a distance of twenty-nine miles, over the old Dover Road, through Rochester, Chatham, Sittingbourne, and Faversham.

We were to make an early start, so as to give plenty of time for luncheon, in a beautiful spot already chosen, and allow for a ramble afterwards.

Two post carriages were turned out with postillions, in the red jackets of the old Royal Dover Road, buckskin breeches, and top-boots into the bargain.

The preparations for this new pilgrimage to Canterbury were of the most lavish description, and I can see now the hampers and wine baskets blocking the steps of the house before they were packed in the carriages.

Every one was in the best of spirits, the weather was all that could be desired, and the ladies did honour to it by the brightness of their costumes. We were all glad, too, that the restoration of the Chief's health enabled him to enjoy as much pleasure himself as he was giving to his friends.

We started sharp to time, and travelled merrily over the road, with hop gardens on either side, until we reached Rochester, our horses making such a clatter in this slumbrous old city that all the shopkeepers in the main street turned out to see us pass.

Mr. Dickens rode in the foremost carriage, and having occasion to pull up at the shop of one of the tradesmen in the main street of Rochester, a small crowd collected round the carriages. It seemed to be pretty generally known amongst them that Dickens was of the party, and we got a good deal of fun out of the mistake made by a man in the crowd, who pointed up at Mr. James T. Fields, and called out, "That's Dickens!" Poor Fields was in great confusion, especially when Mr. Dickens, to complete the deception, handed up a small parcel to him, with the request, "Here you are, Dickens, take charge of this for me."

Away we went again through Rochester, and, skirting Chatham, were soon again in the open country on the road to Sittingbourne, where a relay of horses was awaiting us.

A short rest in the brick-making town was quite sufficient for us, and we sped on to that haven of rest where it had been arranged that we should lunch. A more suitable spot could not have been found. It lay in the deep shades of a wood, with a rippling stream running through.

The breakfast hour had been an early one, and the long drive had given an excellent edge to our appetites. We turned too with a ready will to unload the carriages, and carry the baskets into the wood. Everybody did something, and the cloth was speedily laid. An hour was the time allowed for luncheon, and out of this we had to let the postillions get their meal when we had finished. Dickens would not let us start again until every vestige of our visit to the wood in the shape of lobster shells and other *débris,* had been removed.

We drove into Canterbury in the early afternoon, just as the bells of the Cathedral were ringing for afternoon service. Entering the quiet city under the old gate at the end of the High Street, it seemed as though its inhabitants were indulging in an afternoon's nap after a midday dinner. But our entry and the clatter of our horses' hoofs roused them as it had done the people of Rochester, and they came running to their windows and out into the streets to learn what so much noise might mean.

We turned into the bye-street in which the Fountain Hotel is situated, where the carriages and horses were to be put up while we explored the city.

We went first to the Cathedral, where service was just commencing. There was a very small congregation, and we were all disappointed at the careless, halfhearted manner in which the service was performed. The seeming indifference of the officiating clergy jarred most acutely on Dickens's feelings, for he, who did all things so thoroughly, could not conceive how (as he afterwards said), any persons accepting an office, or a trust so important as the proper rendering of our beautiful Cathedral Service, could go through their duties in this mechanical and slip-shod fashion. He returned to this subject on several subsequent occasions. As the service had tended rather to depress than to elevate our spirits, we were all glad to get out into the fresh air of the cloisters, on its termination.

Being in Canterbury Cathedral, Mr. Dickens considered it necessary to show his friends the many objects of interest to be found there; and after he had politely but speedily got rid of a tedious verger who wanted to lead the way, he played the part of cicerone himself, in the most genial and learned style in the world.

Under his pleasant and instructive guidance, the afternoon passed only too quickly, and we stayed so long in the grand old Cathedral that we had but little time to spare for a ramble through the sleepy streets. Some of the Americans were rather disappointed at this, for, knowing the accuracy of Dickens's descriptions, they had shown an extreme curiosity to see and examine for themselves the very house where David Copperfield went to school.

There are, however, many houses in Canterbury which would answer to Dickens's description of "Doctor Strong's"; and in reply to one of the party who had asked him to point out the particular house, he said, laughingly, that "there were several that would do." We took tea at the hotel, and then at about six o'clock started on our homeward journey, Canterbury having by this time quite got over the effects of its day-sleep. The people were enjoying their stroll in the cool of the evening, and the streets presented a much more animated appearance than they had done on our arrival.

In the interval between drowsiness and wakefulness, Canterbury had evidently summoned sufficient energy to make inquiries about our party; and learning that no less a person than Charles Dickens was responsible for having disturbed their slumbers earlier in the day, the good people at once forgave us all, and were quite hearty in their salutations as we left the town.

There was never a more delightful ride on a summer's evening than the one we took then. The day was fast closing in, and as there was no reason for loitering on the road, we sped along at a rattling pace.

The journey from Gad's Hill to Canterbury had taken nearly five hours, including the time allowed for luncheon and loitering. The journey home was made in less than three, and we forgot our fatigue in the enjoyment of supper. It seems to me, as I look back over the years that have intervened, that I enjoyed a great privilege, no less than a rare pleasure, in being in the company of my dear old Chief when he took this his last visit to Canterbury, in the streets of which he had so often wandered in his earlier days.

The next day, the red-jacketed postillions were ordered out again, and we commenced with a visit to Chatham, which in an aesthetic point of view is not an interesting place. The streets are very narrow and most consumedly dirty. But if the town itself be disagreeable, the society is very much the reverse. Mr. Dickens had many friends among the naval and military officers and their families, .whom duty compels to exist in that objectionable place, and of these, none whom he valued more than the general commanding the district at the time — General Freeman Murray.

In compliment to Mr. Dickens and his American friends, the general had organized an early reception at his house, in the grounds of which he had provided us with a military band.

The general conducted us through some of the barracks, and we visited several of the officers in their quarters, returning to Gad's Hill for luncheon. General Murray, who made one of the party, afterwards had his drag out, and gave us a most enjoyable drive. He brought us home through Cobham Park, where, disdaining the roadways, he made short cuts across the level turf, dodging in and out under the magnificent trees, which made it rather lively for the general's outside passengers. But the general is an excellent whip, and nobody was killed.

There was a grand dinner-party in the evening with a reception afterwards, which many friends in the neighbourhood attended. The furniture had been removed from the drawing-room during dinner for a dance, and it was not until the morning light peeped in at the windows that the guests separated.

This was the last party given at "Gad's" on so extensive a scale, although there were several smaller ones during the happy summer of 1869. Most of these were given in honour of American friends, whose kindness to him in their own country he seemed never able to repay to his own full satisfaction.

On occasions like these he would sacrifice himself entirely to their pleasure; and with his happy gift of divining the tastes and sympathies of each one of his guests, he would collect such English friends around them whom he felt would complete a harmonious party.

Later on, I was present at a gathering of this kind, which was promoted in honour of Mr. W. H. Palmer, of Niblo's Theatre, New York.

The friendship which existed between Mr. Dickens and Mr. Charles Fechter, the tragedian, is well known; and he was endeavouring at this time to procure for Fechter a season's engagement at Niblo's.

At Mr. Dickens's request, I undertook the preliminary negotiations, and we were both gratified by the success with which our efforts were rewarded.

After much correspondence, and the usual troubles incident to such undertakings, Mr. Palmer came to England to close the matter. Mr. Dickens himself drew up the agreement.

The signing of this document was made the occasion of another "international" gathering at Gad's Hill, where, on a particular day, the parties to it were to meet and affix their signatures, in the presence of witnesses specially chosen by Mr. Dickens.

The party was composed of representative actors and dramatic critics of the time, the late Mr. Benjamin Webster being the selected representative of the English Theatre.

It was a merry gathering, and as no lady visitors were in the house at the time, Bohemianism held undisputed sway. On this, as on other occasions, every hour of our visit was mapped out, and there was not a dull moment in the day.

The weather unfortunately was miserably wet, so that we were dependent for our amusements on the internal resources of the establishment.

The business on which we had met was first disposed of, and success to the enterprise having been proposed by Mr. Dickens, and drunk in a glass of old Madeira, we adjourned to the billiard-room, where a match had been arranged between Mr. Benjamin Webster and Mr. Palmer. Mr. Dickens acted as marker.

The disparity between the players appeared to be very great, for the American was in the prime of life, whereas the Englishman was far advanced in years and very feeble. Dickens, however, who knew Mr. Webster's "form," opened the betting by backing him to win. Fechter backed his new manager, and the rest of the company held aloof from the market for a time. It must be said that the bets were of a very trifling description, for Dickens always set his face against gambling.

The game was closely contested, but Webster carried it off. Notwithstanding his great age and infirmity, it was most entertaining to see with what unerring certainty he made his strokes, although before each one it took him some moments to make his bridge. Dickens was delighted at his old friend's success, but to me he said — "Bless you! that's nothing. Ben, as a young man, was in the habit of tossing in the streets with piemen for pies, and invariably won! He'll show us after dinner some of the tricks he used to do in those days, and I think he'll rather astonish you."

Webster did give us an exhibition after dinner, which was very ingenious and amusing, Dickens using all his endeavours to baffle the skill of the operator.

His interest in all that appertained to the theatrical world never left him, and one of the latest acts of his life was to correct an agreement for Miss Glynn (Mrs. Dallas), who had received offers to visit Australia, through the agency of the late Mr. E. P. Kingston, Artemus Ward's manager. Mr. Dickens took immense pains to revise the agreement, making in it such alterations and amendments as would protect her interests in the Colonies, and doing it all in an eminently practical and business-like manner.

All too rapidly, the happiest of summers passed away, and with it departed the friends whom he had taken so much pleasure in entertaining. When they were gone, the Chief was more free to follow his own pursuits; with intervals of visiting. He had long been under a promise to pay a visit to his friend Earl Russell, at Pembroke Lodge, and he went there now. As he was only to remain one night, he did not take a servant. Knowing Lord Russell's very temperate habits, he had ordered a bottle of Ballard's celebrated punch to be packed in his portmanteau, intending (as Lord and Lady Russell always retired early), to mix his own grog when he went to his room.

While talking with his host and hostess in the drawing-room before dinner, Lord Russell's valet entered and asked Mr. Dickens for the key of his portmanteau, so that he might have his things in readiness for him when he should need to dress for dinner. Remembering the punch, he thanked the valet, and said he "would put out his things himself."

The conversation continued, and when the dressing-bell rang, Mr. Dickens went to his room, where he was amazed to find his dressing-table arranged from the contents of his travelling-bag (which had not been locked), and his bottle of punch placed on the mantle-shelf, with a tumbler, wine-glass, and corkscrew placed beside it. At this spectacle he was troubled in spirit.

At about half-past ten, the early hour observed by Lord Russell's household, he rose to wish his host and hostess "good-night," when Lady Russell, with a laugh, in which her husband joined her, said, "Don't be in a hurry, the *tray* will be here in a minute."

At this moment the servant came in with a tray, on which were all the materials for the manufacture of punch; "just the same," said Dickens, "as it always was at Gad's Hill."

The incident amused him a good deal, and gave him one more story to tell against himself.

As always happened in his intervals of work, we were much together at this time. We still kept up our Thursday luncheons, and in the afternoon of these days we generally made an excursion somewhere, finishing up with a dinner at one or other of his favourite taverns, a proceeding which pleasantly refreshed our memory of bygone days. The houses he liked best were "The Cock" and "Cheshire Cheese" in Fleet Street, the "Blue Posts" in Cork Street, Clunns Hotel in Covent Garden Market, or the "Albion" opposite Drury Lane Theatre. After dinner, if there were no special attraction at any other theatre, we would call in at the "Princess's," where Fechter was playing his farewell engagement, or step across to the office for a glass of his "celebrated gin punch," and a cigar, before separating for the night; which, by the way, we never did without making an appointment for some future day.

It was his rule never to say "good-bye" to his intimates. To me, when we had settled our next meeting, it was always a cordial "Good-day."

Towards the end of July, the idea for a new book had taken possession of him — the unfinished "Edwin Drood" — and in our rambles at this time I could see that it was much in his thoughts.

In the early pages of this work, he utilized the scene we had witnessed at the opium den in Ratcliffe Highway, which we visited with Fields, Sol Etynge, and his American friends in the early summer.

The price agreed to be paid to him for this book, he confided to me, was the largest sum given for any work from his or any other hands. It was to be £7,500 for the copyright, and a half share of the profits after a sale of twenty-five thousand copies. In addition to this he was to receive £1,000 for the advance sheets sent to America.

Gigantic as these figures seemed to me at the time, it would appear that the publishers had not made their bargain rashly (indeed I never heard of a publisher who did make a bargain rashly), inasmuch as the total sales of the work during the author's lifetime exceeded fifty thousand copies; though the book was little more than half finished, and only about one-third of it in the press.

The composition of this work gave him a great deal of trouble and anxiety. I asked him one day how he liked returning to the writing of a serial story, and he replied at once that he "missed the pressure" of former days; which I took to mean that as his circumstances were comfortable now, the work was irksome.

There is, to me at all events, a suggestion of pathos in one of the conditions between Dickens and his publisher in regard to the sum to be paid for "Edwin Drood." It could, I think, only have been suggested by himself, and proceeded from his nervous fear that a return of the Chester illness might prevent him from carrying the work to a conclusion. The condition was to the effect that in the event either of Mr. Dickens's death, or of his inability from any other cause, to complete the work he had undertaken, it should be referred to the arbitration of such persons as he then appointed, to decide what amount of money ought to be returned out of his estate to his publishers, as just and proper compensation for the loss sustained by them.

Not only was the composition of this book a severe labour to him, but he was sorely puzzled for a long while to find a title that pleased him. This, however, being at length decided on, he gave a little dinner of three, a sort of christening party, at which we drank but one toast, "Success to the 'Mystery of Edwin Drood.'" This was proposed by myself, and was humorously responded to by the parent author.

With "Edwin Drood" to complete, and "All the Year Round" to edit; with the preparation necessary for the twelve farewell Readings in London, and for an Inaugural Address, which, in his capacity of President of the Midland Institute, he was under promise to deliver at Birmingham, his hands and brain were again fully occupied — too fully indeed for one who had escaped, by a miracle, as it were, a terrible and most dangerous illness. Indeed, his time was so fully absorbed by the matters I have mentioned, to say nothing of his extensive private correspondence, that it became absolutely necessary for him to decline all hospitable invitations, and to settle down again to his systematic mode of life. The monotony of this was varied only by weekly visits to Gad's Hill, with a friend or two for company; visits which seldom lasted longer than from Saturday to Monday, except perhaps when some friends from abroad were passing through London on their way home.

The Birmingham Inaugural Address was delivered on Monday, September 27th, and the Town Hall was crammed; inconveniently so, in fact, as far as Mr. Dickens's comfort was concerned. Education for the People was the subject of the address, and the applications for tickets were so numerous that the committee had no alternative but to give up a portion of the platform. This was an arrangement which Dickens always strongly objected to. He hated talking to people who were sitting behind him, for in his case at all events they were certain to lose much, if, while hearing his voice, they could not at the same time watch the varied play of his features.

This objection he desired me to state one day in a letter he asked me to write in answer to the request of a committee, that a distinguished nobleman should take the chair at one of the Readings. I said that notwithstanding Mr. Dickens's "appreciation of the compliment proposed to be paid to him, he regretted being compelled to decline it, as it was a rule he made on such occasions, never to allow any gentleman on the platform (except himself), certainly not in view of the audience."

As I found that the arrangements of the committee of the Midland Institute (when I waited on them on our arrival in Birmingham), were as unalterable as certain famous laws, the Chief accepted the situation with a good grace, and made a most effective speech on this favourite subject of his, promising to return the following year to distribute the prizes to the students.

Having occasion to make some purchases before leaving Birmingham, we went to Elkington's for this purpose. While we were being escorted over the factory, Mr. Dickens's quick eye detected some dilapidated tea-urns, whose appearance struck him as familiar. On inquiry he learned that they were old friends, from one of the refreshment-rooms on the London and North Western Railway. Dickens overhauled them with much interest; and observing the shocking bad state of the insides, he derived a melancholy gratification in thinking how true was his satire in the "Boy at Mugby," upon the manner in which "refreshmenting" at railway stations was then conducted. To quote Mr. Dickens's words at the time, these urns had been "for goodness knows how many years the cause of poisoning the passengers with a beverage produced under the active agency of hot water, and a mixture of decomposed lead, copper, and a few other deadly poisons."

This remark was made to Messrs. Elkington's manager who, being well up in his Dickens, had a lively recollection of the "Boy at Mugby," and was greatly pleased at having first hand from him so pertinent a criticism on a trade in which he was remotely interested.

Mr. and Mrs. Fields returned to London from their continental trip, early in this October, and during their brief sojourn were constant visitors at "Gad's." Dickens, Fields, and myself were a good deal together in play hours; and in our peregrinations about town we discovered that Fields, whilst on the Continent, had developed the collector's mania for bric-a-brac and old furniture. Mr. Dickens, who quite entered into his friend's humour in this matter, would spend whole afternoons with him in Wardour Street, Hanway Street, and New Oxford Street; and, but for his frequent intervention, Fields would have bought at fabulous prices old chairs and old furniture enough of all descriptions to fill the hold of an Atlantic steamer. With a view to cure him of the mania, Mr. Dickens wrote him a letter one day describing a chair we had both seen in a shop in Great Queen Street. "There is a chair (without a bottom), at a shop near the office, which I think would suit you. It cannot stand of itself, but will *almost* seat somebody, if you put it in a corner, and prop one leg up with two wedges, and cut another leg off. The proprietor asks £20, but says he admires literature and would take £18. He is of *republican* principles, and I think would take £17 19s. from a cousin; shall I secure this prize? It is very old and wormy, and it is related, without proof, that on one occasion Washington declined to sit down on it."

Being in America two years after the death of Mr. Dickens, Fields gave me a copy of this letter, with permission to reproduce it. He himself, I believe, published it in an American paper.

On one of my autumnal visits to "Gad's," after the departure of Mr. and Mrs. Fields, I found the Chief planning fresh alterations to the house with the object of making it more perfect, if possible, than it was already. The principal improvement he contemplated was the enlargement of the dining-room, by the building of a spacious conservatory at one end of it; and this rather expensive scheme was carried out during the London Readings. For convenience during this farewell series, he rented the house belonging to his friends, Mr. and Mrs. Milner Gibson, No. 5, Hyde Park Place, opposite the Marble Arch; and here he moved with his family, early in January of the following year.

The return to hard work, and the confinement consequent on it, brought back the trouble to the foot, and towards the end of the year he was quite unable to take any real walking exercise. With this exception, his health was invariably good; but his animal spirits, although far from flagging, were less gay than of old. I, for my part, noticed a slow but steady change working in him, and had serious doubts whether he would be able to get through the twelve Readings announced, for which I need hardly say there was an extraordinary demand for tickets, long in advance of the dates fixed for their delivery.

My weekly reports on this head always cheered him, and as the time for the Readings drew near, he became very anxious to have the new book as far forward as possible, before he was again called upon to take the platform. He felt that the pressure of the Readings would be great, particularly, of course, at the commencement, when there were to be two a week.

As usual, he went to Gad's Hill to spend the Christmas. Writing to me, he said that this Christmas was one of great pain and misery to him, and contrasted it mournfully with the one we had spent together in America, on our journey from Boston to New York. Then, as he said pathetically, he had the use of his legs, but this Christmas he had been confined to his bed the whole day, only getting up in the evening to join the party in the drawing-room after dinner. It was in this way that he, who had done so much to make the Christmas festival dear to the hearts of his countrymen, spent his last Christmas Day.

The farewell Readings commenced on Tuesday, the 11th January, 1870, and terminated in the middle of March. They were, as I have already said, a series of twelve, of which three were to be given in the morning or afternoon.

These latter were in the place of the course announced for the previous May, which were to have been given specially for the benefit of the theatrical profession, many of whose members had memorialized Mr. Dickens on the subject. Although these entailed on him a vast deal of additional labour and fatigue, he entered into the Readings for the players with greater zest, I think, than into any others of the course. He wanted to show them how much a single performer could do without the aid and stimulus of any of the ordinary adjuncts of the stage; how many effects of a genuinely startling character could be produced without the help of scenery, costume, limelight, or mechanical contrivances.

He succeeded to perfection, in the presence even of so thoroughly critical an audience. They applauded every point, cheering each well-known character as the reader, by mere change of voice, manner, and action, brought forward the people of his tales. The presence of a large number of actors and actresses made these morning Readings very lively and pleasant; but the strain was great upon the reader.

This he admitted himself, and in regard to the past he confessed to me at this time that it was madness ever to have given the "Murder" Reading, under the conditions of a travelling life, and worse than madness to have given it with such frequency.

In the interests of Messrs. Chappell, he had pledged himself to give these Readings, and being, as he fondly supposed, restored to health, these interests far outweighed, in his estimation, any consequences of an unpleasant kind that might accrue to himself.

To be sure, he was fortified by the opinion of Sir Thomas Watson that the Readings could be undertaken with safety, but he himself (no less than his friends), was not without anxiety as to the result. It is only just to add that those most interested in the financial success of the undertaking (I mean Messrs. Chappell), were desirous, even at the last moment, to make any sacrifices rather than that Mr. Dickens's health should suffer by his fulfilment of the engagement.

The journey to Birmingham for the purpose of giving away the prizes to the students of the Midland Institute, a few days before the commencement of the farewell Readings, added to the fatigue of delivering the address (which was one of his longest efforts in public speaking), had shaken him so severely that, on his return to London, he again sought the professional advice of Mr. Carr Beard. Mr. Beard found such a marked change for the worse in the general condition of his patient, that he thought it advisable to be present at the Readings, in order to note carefully their visible effects on his health.

If other proof were wanting as to the immense strain on Mr. Dickens's nervous system during the delivery of the Readings, it would have been sufficient to observe the changes in his pulse.

It was curious to note the different effects of the different Readings. The ordinary state of Mr. Dickens's pulse was 72. "David Copperfield" brought it up to 96; "Doctor Marigold," 99; the first night of the "Murder" (during the last Readings), it was 112; and the second, 118; "Nicholas Nickleby" brought it to 112; and "Dombey" to 114. On one occasion it rose to 124. At the last Reading of all, when he went on the platform for the "Christmas Carol," his pulse marked 108, and at the conclusion of the Reading it had risen to no. He, himself, was astounded at the high state of his pulse after the last "Copperfield" Reading, and explained it by the emotion he felt in parting (for the last time), with the Reading which he liked better almost than any of the others, and which had done so much to popularize the whole series. Although his pulse frequently ran as high during many other Readings, the after effects were not so serious as when he left the platform on the termination of the "Murder" Reading.

On these occasions, he would have to be supported to his retiring-room and laid on a sofa for fully ten minutes, before he could speak a rational or consecutive sentence.

These were painful and anxious moments for all of us, but he allowed himself but this brief interval between each Reading. When time was up he would, however, pull himself together, swallow a wine-glassful of weak brandy-and-water, and rush on to the platform for the final Reading of the evening. This was always a light one, which helped to quiet him after the excitement he had undergone, but was chosen less for this purpose than because he considered it necessary for the audience as a sort of antidote to what had gone before.

Through suffering and anxiety such as this it was that Dickens redeemed his promise of giving these twelve farewell Readings; and as he wiped them out one by one, his feverish excitement and his bodily pain increased.

The final farewell Reading of Tuesday, the 15th March, was one of the hardest struggles he had to face, but he went through it with a manliness and good temper which eclipsed all his previous efforts. The previous Readings of this series had far surpassed, in the matter of receipts, any that had gone before them in England; but this one was the crowning triumph.

The largest audience that had ever assembled in the great St. James's Hall for a Reading was present for this "Farewell." It was a representative gathering, not only in an artistic point of view, but a far wider sense, for all sorts and conditions of men came to bid a public farewell to their great favourite, to the man who, more than any other writer of his generation, had addressed himself to "the people."

Messrs. Chappell's staff had contrived to pack over two thousand persons into the hall, and the receipts amounted to nearly £425. More persons than this have assembled in St. James's Hall, but the conditions under which this crowd was accommodated with seats were not a little remarkable, for it should be remembered that the whole of the platform was screened off by Mr. Dickens's "fit-up," consisting of the back screens and curtains; and further, that the ends of the balconies were partitioned off in conformity with the reading-screens and curtains. This would diminish the ordinary holding capacity of the hall to the extent of nearly four hundred persons.

Long before the doors were opened, an immense crowd had assembled at the Regent Street and Piccadilly entrances, and it was but the work of a few moments to sell sufficient tickets to fill the "shilling" seats. The numbers turned away were far greater than those that were able to be admitted. Had the hall been twice or three times the size, we should have filled it easily. The fact that the highest-priced seat was five shillings and the lowest a shilling makes the receipts all the more astonishing.

The Readings on this memorable occasion were, the "Christmas Carol" and the "Trial from Pickwick," and as eight o'clock, the time for commencing, drew near, the excitement of the people increased. Punctually to the moment, Mr. Dickens walked on to the platform, book in hand, but evidently much agitated. He was thinking, I dare say, that this was to be the very last time he would address an audience in his capacity of reader.

He had taken scarcely less pleasure and delight in his public Readings than in the pursuit of his legitimate calling, and at the thought that he was about to abandon them, there was a struggle in his mind which his fine features reflected. But no feeling of sadness could have been retained in face of the unanimity and splendour of the reception that was accorded him. The immense audience rose to their feet and cheered him to the echo. This

St. James's Hall, London, Where Dickens Gave His Farewell Reading

lasted some minutes. In spontaneity and warmth it was a provincial rather than a metropolitan reception. It had the instant effect of nerving him up to his work, and he never read the "Carol" more earnestly, more fervently, or more effectively than on this occasion. The audience, needless to say, were in supreme sympathy with the reader. Not a word was lost. They seemed to feel that they were hearing him for the last time.

The same may be said of the "Trial from Pickwick," which concluded the evening's entertainment. All the old familiar characters seemed to stand out more deliciously clear than ever; and each was cheered as the reader presented him to the mind's eye of the listener. Sergeant Buzfuz, Mrs. Cluppins, Nathaniel Winkle, Sam Weller, and the little puisne judge ("puny") Mr. Dickens used to say with action, pointing to the late Lord Chief Justice Cockburn when he was present, as he was on this occasion — all of these had their own particular reception.

After this came the saddest, and (so far as Mr. Dickens was concerned), the most dreaded part of all. He had responded several times to the calls for his reappearance, but seemed anxious to defer as long as possible the few words of farewell he had mentally prepared. But it had to be done, and, nerving himself up for this crowning effort, he returned once more to the little table (for the last time and for ever), and, with a voice full of emotion, and amid breathless silence, he spoke as follows: —

"Ladies and Gentlemen, — It would be worse than idle, for it would be hypocritical and unfeeling, if I were to disguise that I close this episode of my life with feelings of very considerable pain. For some fifteen years in this hall, and in many kindred places, I have had the honour of presenting my own cherished ideas before you for your recognition, and in closely observing your reception of them, I have enjoyed an amount of artistic delight and instruction which perhaps it is given to few men to know.

"In this task, and in every other I have ever undertaken as a faithful servant of the public, always imbued with the sense of duty to them, and always striving to do his best, I have been uniformly cheered by the readiest response, the most generous sympathy, and the most stimulating support.

"Nevertheless, I have thought it well in the full flood tide of your favour to retire upon those older associations between us which date much farther back than these, and thenceforth to devote myself exclusively to the art that first brought us together.

"Ladies and Gentlemen, — In two short weeks from this time I hope that you may enter in your own homes on a new series of readings at which my assistance will be indispensable; [1] but from these garish lights I vanish now for evermore, with a heartfelt, grateful, respectful, and affectionate farewell."

During the delivery of this short and impressive speech, notwithstanding his visible emotion, he never paused or made an instant's hesitation, and the strength of his feelings was only slightly observable in the words (and the accent accompanying them), "from these garish lights I vanish now for evermore." These carry with them to this day a sad significance in the remembrance of those still living who, in return for the love and affection he bestowed on them, felt they could never do enough to relieve him, if it were possible, of the sufferings which were only too apparent in their almost daily intercourse with him.

Leaving the platform, amidst acclamations of the most tumultuous kind, he proceeded to his retiring room with quite a mournful gait, and tears rolling down his cheeks. But he had to go forward yet once again, to be stunned by a more surprising outburst than before, and dazzled by the waving of handkerchiefs. Respectfully kissing his hand, Mr. Dickens retired for the last time.

The words he had uttered in his farewell speech in Boston, in 1868: "In this brief life of ours it is sad to do almost anything for the last time," came back to him that night, and he mentioned them to me with a pathetic comment.

In taking leave of Mr. Dickens in this capacity, it may be interesting to set down the total number of public Readings he gave.

Putting aside those given for charitable or friendly purposes between the years 1854 and 1858, in which latter year, at St. Martinis Hall, April 29, 1858, he commenced reading for his own especial benefit, up to the time of his retirement from the platform, at St. James's Hall, March 15, 1870, the full number of Readings was 423.

Of these in were given under the management of Mr. Arthur Smith; 70 under the management of Mr. Headland (who succeeded to the post of manager on the death of Mr. Smith), and 242 under my management. These latter were delivered in England, Ireland, Scotland, and America, between April 10, 1866, and March 15, 1870.

Mr. Dickens kept no particular account of the amount of money he netted from the Readings under the management of Messrs. Arthur Smith and Headland, but he always computed it at about; £12,000. Out of the 242 Readings given under my management (which included the three engagements of Messrs. Chappell and Co.), he cleared nearly £33,000.

Handsome as these results were, and of course highly satisfactory to Mr. Dickens, they were purchased at the dear cost of the sacrifice of his health. But his career as a public reader was his own choice, and setting aside his pecuniary profits, the pleasure he derived from it is not to be told in words. For my part, at this distance of time, I think less of the dark than of the bright side of those never-to-be-forgotten days.

[1] This of course was in reference to "The Mystery of Edwin Drood," which was shortly to be published.

Chapter Fourteen - Hyde Park Place — the Chief's Last Days in Town

WHEN the feeling of pain at parting with the audiences, between whom and himself such kindly relations had always existed, had passed away, Mr. Dickens was relieved by the thought that he would now enjoy uninterrupted leisure for the completion of "Edwin Drood." For at this time only three numbers of the story were in the printer's hands.

The situation of the house he had taken in Hyde Park Place accorded entirely with his fancy. It overlooked the park, where the perpetual movement and gaiety at that season of the year had a great charm for him. He used to say to me that he never minded the noise at night, and in the early morning, the rattling of the heavy waggons passing from the Great Western station at

Paddington to the various markets was a source of satisfaction to him, for if he were awakened by it, he had the gratification of knowing that whilst he had been asleep an important portion of the world was astir. For this reason, too, he enjoyed his nights at the office; and "he had a sense of personal security in living in a street in which, when the last cab had gone 'off,' the first market cart came 'on.'"

With the exceptions of "Edwin Drood," and his editorial duties in connection with "All the Year Round," he had now nothing of importance on his mind. Moreover, as there were many invitations to dinner, &c., which had of necessity to be declined during the Readings, and he had a good many entertainments to give on his own account, he found the situation of the house in Hyde Park Place admirably convenient for the former, and the arrangements of the house itself perfect for the latter.

Amongst the old and intimate friends he welcomed at this time, was Mr. Arthur Helps, whose name I single out because of the little story that follows.

On one occasion when Dickens was entertaining Helps at dinner, he showed him a collection of very interesting photographs, depicting scenes on the battle-fields in the American Civil War. These had been presented to Mr. Dickens in Washington by Mr. Franklin Philp, who at the time held a high official position in that city. These photographs were the means, through Mr. Helps's agency, of bringing about an interview between Mr. Dickens and Her Majesty the Queen. Amongst all his admirers there was none who held him in higher esteem, or had a warmer appreciation of the good and kindly influence of his works, than Her Majesty.

At the time of the sale of Thackeray's effects, the Queen had caused to be bought, regardless of cost, for the private library at Buckingham Palace, a presentation copy of the "Christmas Carol," bearing an appropriate and characteristic inscription on the title page, expressive of the pleasure Dickens had derived from a poem of Thackeray's.

Mr. Helps having casually told the Queen of the interesting character of the photographs, Her Majesty expressed a great desire to see them. This being communicated to Mr. Dickens, he at once sent the book to Mr. Helps for Her Majesty's inspection; and on the Queen expressing a wish to see Mr. Dickens, and thank him in person, he went to Buckingham Palace in obedience to Her Majesty's desires, on an afternoon of March, 1870.

The Queen was in London only for a day or two, and Dickens imagined, not unnaturally, that the innumerable calls on the time and attention of Her Majesty would leave space for an interview of about a quarter of an hour. So, as the time appointed was five in the afternoon, he engaged me to meet him in the Burlington Arcade at half-past, when we were to dine together at the "Blue Posts," in Cork Street. However, the Chief had grievously miscalculated the probable duration of that interview, for instead of lasting ten or fifteen minutes, it was prolonged for an hour and a half. It was half-past six when he put in an appearance at our place of meeting.

When his brougham pulled up at the Piccadilly end of the Arcade, I could see that the interview had been an agreeable one, for he was radiant with smiles. Stepping out of his carriage, he gave hasty instructions to his servant to drive straight home, and to take particular care of a book he had left inside, which was to be given to Miss Dickens the moment he arrived at Hyde Park Place.

Slipping his arm in mine, we passed through the Arcade and proceeded at once to our dining-place, where I had caused his favourite corner to be kept for him. Having settled down to our dinner, I was naturally anxious to hear from his own lips what Her Majesty and the Chief could have found to talk about for an hour and a half.

"Tell me everything," I said, modestly.

"Everything! my dear fellow, everything! I tell you what, it would be difficult to say what we did *not* talk about," was his reply.

"Well, then," I said, "let me have *some* of it, unless they were all State secrets."

He then went on to tell me that Her Majesty had received him most graciously, and that, as Court etiquette requires that no one, in an ordinary interview with the Sovereign, should be seated, Her Majesty had remained the whole time leaning over the head of a sofa. There was a little shyness on both sides at the commencement, but this wore away as the conversation proceeded.

Her Majesty expressed her deep regret at not having heard one of the Readings, and although highly flattered at this, Dickens could only express his sorrow that, as these were now finally done with, and as, moreover, a mixed audience was absolutely necessary for their success, it would be impossible to gratify Her Majesty's wishes in this particular. This, he said, the Queen fully appreciated, quoting to Mr. Dickens his own words in his farewell speech: "From these garish lights I vanish now for evermore," and remarking that even if such a thing were possible, there would be inconsistency in it, which was evidently not one of Mr. Dickens's characteristics. After referring in complimentary terms to the pleasure Her Majesty had derived in witnessing Mr. Dickens's acting in the "Frozen Deep," as far back as the year 1857, the conversation took a general turn. The Queen showed much interest and curiosity in regard to Mr. Dickens's recent American experiences, and some reference was made to a supposed discourtesy that had been shown in America on one occasion to Prince Arthur, This, Dickens was very anxious to explain away, assuring the Queen that no true-hearted Americans were in sympathy with the Fenian body in that country; and that nowhere in the world was there a warmer feeling towards the English Queen than existed throughout the whole of the United States (a sentiment which Her Majesty was pleased to hear from so observant an authority). The Chief told me, with a good deal of unction, that Her Majesty had then graciously asked his opinion on the "servant question." Could he account for the fact "that we have no good servants in England as in the olden times"? Mr. Dickens regretted that

214

he could not account for this fact, except perhaps on the hypothesis that our system of education was a wrong one. On this same subject of national education, he added, he had his own ideas, but saw no likelihood of their being carried into effect. The price of provisions, the cost of butchers' meat, and bread, were next lightly touched upon, and so the conversation rippled on agreeably to an agreeable end. But the interview did not close until the Queen, with gracious modesty, had begged Mr. Dickens's acceptance at her own hands of a copy of the "Journal in the Highlands," in which Her Majesty had placed an autograph inscription, and her own sign manual. This was the book which the coachman had been so particularly enjoined to give into Miss Dickens's own hands.

The Queen, on handing the book to Mr. Dickens, modestly remarked that she felt considerable hesitation in presenting so humble a literary effort to one of the foremost writers of the age. She had. Her Majesty said, requested Mr. Helps to present it for her; but as he had suggested that the gift would be more highly prized by Mr. Dickens if he received it from Her Majesty's own hands, she had resolved herself on this bold act. After asking Mr. Dickens to look kindly on any literary faults of her book, Her Majesty expressed a desire to be the possessor of a complete set of Mr. Dickens's works, and added that, if possible, she would like to receive them that afternoon.

Mr. Dickens, of course, was only too pleased to gratify the wishes of the Queen, but begged to be allowed to defer sending his books until he had had a set specially bound for Her Majesty's acceptance. This was done in due course, and the receipt of the books was acknowledged in the name of the Queen by Mr. Helps, in a letter written from Balmoral, dated and posted on the day of Mr. Dickens's death!

This was the only interview Dickens had with the Queen, but her kindness on the occasion impressed him greatly.

Her Majesty's interest in Dickens did not end here, for a few days after the interview, he received an intimation that it was the Queen's desire he should attend the next Levee, and that Miss Dickens should be presented at the Drawing Room immediately following. Both of these commands, it need not be said, were obeyed, and as some of us were very curious to see what figure he would cut in a costume to which he was quite unaccustomed, myself, and one or two others dropped in upon him at his luncheon time, "just to see how he looked in his cocked hat and sword."

We got a good deal of fun out of the "make-up," in which Dickens heartily joined, but the climax was his utter bewilderment on the subject of the cocked hat. Fancy Dickens in a cocked hat!

"What on earth am I to do with it?" he asked, handing it about in a woebegone manner.

"Why wear it of course," suggested one of the party.

"But how?" cried the Chief.

"Yes, that's exactly what I have been wondering," said another.

"What do you mean, sir?" said Dickens, with mock indignation. "What difference can it make to *you* which way I wear it?"

"Oh! none at all. I was merely wondering whether you intended to wear it 'fore and aft,' or 'th'wart ships;' and I thought I would mention that those I had seen were generally worn 'fore and aft.'"

Mr. Dickens's reception of this lesson on the wearing of a cocked hat was comic in the extreme; for some had said, "it was not intended to be worn, and was a mere appendage any way," others were of opinion that "it was to be carried under the arm," and so on. However, as it was time to start, Dickens tucked the thing under his arm, and, turning to me, said, "Come along, Dolby, drive down to Buckingham Palace with me, and leave me in good society, where at least I shall be free of these ignorant people!"

Court favour did not terminate with his attendance at the Levee, or his daughter's presentation at the Drawing Room, for the Prince of Wales, at about this time, had expressed a wish to meet Mr. Dickens; and as His Royal Highness, accompanied by His Majesty the King of the Belgians, had just then accepted an invitation to dine with Lord Houghton, Dickens, at the special desire of the Prince, was invited to join the party.

This was only a fortnight before his death. On the day of the dinner, Dickens was again suffering from his foot, and up to the last moment it was a matter of doubt whether he would be able to go. But his native pluck came to his aid, and, though in downright bodily agony, he went to the house of his host. He was, however, unable to go upstairs to meet the company in the drawing-room, and proceeded straight to the dining-room, into which he had to be assisted.

In the course of the evening he was relieved of his pain to a great extent, and the charm of his conversation, I was afterwards told, contributed in no small measure to the success of a very pleasant evening. The Prince got a very agreeable impression of Dickens, and Dickens liked the Prince, who expressed at parting a hearty wish for his speedy and complete recovery.

Towards the close of his tenancy of the house in Hyde Park Place, he gave a delightful series of entertainments, the brightest of which was, I think, a concert at which Charles Hallé, Joachim, Edith Wynne, Santley, Cummings, and the Vocal Glee Union lent him their services.

The drawing-rooms were crowded by a company which comprised all the most prominent people in town — literary, artistic, and fashionable. Dickens was suffering very much that evening, and looked jaded and worn, but his exertions for the entertainment of his guests never flagged. He was in good spirits, and moved about amongst his guests, and took ladies up and down to the supper-room, as if he had never known anguish of body in his life.

The supper was sumptuous, there was profusion without ostentation. It is pleasant amongst the many pleasant recollections I have of Mr. Dickens to look back to that evening, when, in spite of pain, he appeared at his very best; but with this memory is joined the sad one, that within two months of that brilliant occasion, he lay dead in his chamber.

At this time it would really seem, in looking back, that all things pointed to the great end.

He had made his last public speech but one at the annual dinner of the "Newsvendors Benevolent and Provident Institution," which was one of his happiest. Delivering it with mock gravity, he told an admirable story, which will bear repeating here.

"I was once present," he said, "at a social discussion, which originated by chance. The subject was 'What was the most-absorbing and longest-lived passion in the human breast? What was the passion so powerful that it would almost induce the generous to be mean, the careless to be cautious, the guileless to be deeply designing, and the dove to emulate the serpent?'

"A daily editor of vast experience and great acuteness who was one of the company considerably surprised us by saying, with the greatest confidence, that the passion in question was the passion of getting orders for the play!

"There had recently been a terrible shipwreck, and very few of the surviving sailors had escaped in an open boat. One of these, on making land, came straight to London, and straight to the newspaper office with the story of how he had seen the ship go down before his eyes. That young man had witnessed the most terrible contention between the powers of fire and water for the destruction of that ship and of every one on board. He had rowed away among the floating, dying, sinking, and dead. He had floated by day, and he had frozen by night, with no shelter and no food, and as he told the dismal tale he rolled his haggard eyes about the room. When he had finished, and the tale had been noted down from his lips, he was cheered, and refreshed, and soothed, and asked if anything could be done for him. Even within him, that master passion was so strong that he immediately replied *he should like an order for the play!*"

The last time Mr. Dickens spoke in public, was at the Royal Academy Dinner on May 2, 1870, when, after responding to the toast of literature, he said a few very earnest and tender words in reference to the loss that he and the art world in general had sustained in the death of Maclise, the painter, who for years had been one of his personal and dear friends.

These were the last words he ever addressed to an audience, and though suffering intensely at the time, he attended this dinner solely that he might render a final public tribute to the memory of an old friend.

He was engaged to be present and to speak at the dinner of the General Theatrical Fund, at which the Prince of Wales was to preside, but a succession of private dinners (the invitations to which had been accepted with much reluctance), had so laid him by the heels, that the time came when he could attend no more, and this one, although for a charity in which he took so deep an interest, had to be given up. At the end of May, he returned to Gad's Hill, in the hope of getting there that rest and peace of mind which he could not obtain in London. Here also he set himself vigorously to work to complete the "Mysteries of Edwin Drood." But the mystery of Edwin Drood was not destined for completion.

Chapter Fifteen - The End

THE last time I saw Charles Dickens, was on Thursday, June 2, 1870, when I made one of my weekly visits to the office. Getting there just in time for luncheon, I found him greatly absorbed in business matters, and although the same old greeting was awaiting me, it was painfully evident that he was suffering greatly both in mind and body.

During luncheon, many plans for the future were talked of between us, amongst others an early visit to Gad's Hill, where we were to make a thorough inspection of the new conservatory, and several other improvements, in which both of us were greatly interested. But he was very busy that afternoon, and I rose to leave earlier than usual. Then came our final parting, though we neither of us thought of it as such. We shook hands across the office-table, and after a hearty grasp of the hand, and the words from him, "next week then," I turned to go, though with a troubled sense that I was leaving my chief in great pain. He rose from the table, and followed me to the door; I noticed the difficulty of his walk, and the pained look on his face, but was unwilling to speak, so without another word on either side, we parted.

An affair of business took me from London immediately afterwards, and I was prevented from calling at the office on the following Thursday, at the usual time. As it was understood between us that whenever I did not do this, a future meeting should be arranged by post, I meant to write him a letter on the following day. But that letter was never written, for I read in the newspapers the next morning that my friend and chief was dead.

I went to Gad's Hill at once, where I was most kindly and gently received by Miss Dickens and Miss Hogarth, who told me the story of his last moments. The body lay in the dining-room, where Mr. Dickens had been seized with the fatal apoplectic fit. They asked me if I would go and see it, but I could not bear to do so. I wanted to think of him as I had seen him last. I went away from the house, and out on to the Rochester road. It was a bright morning in June, one of the days he had loved; on such a day we had trodden that road together many and many a time. But never again, we two, along that white and dusty way, with the flowering hedges over against us, and the sweet bare sky and the sun above us.   We had taken our last walk together.